'Only a Woman'
HENRIETTA BARNETT

Henrietta Barnett

'Only a Woman'
HENRIETTA BARNETT

Social Reformer and Founder
of Hampstead Garden Suburb

Alison Creedon

Phillimore

2006

Published by
PHILLIMORE & CO. LTD
Shopwyke Manor Barn, Chichester, West Sussex, England
www.phillimore.co.uk

© Alison Creedon, 2006

ISBN 1-86077-430-X
ISBN 13 978-1-86077-430-0

Printed and bound in Great Britain by
CROMWELL PRESS LTD
Trowbridge, Wiltshire

For Noel
and
In memory of
Roy and Auriel Beresford

Contents

List of Illustrations

Frontispiece: Henrietta *c.*1885

Acknowledgements

From a tumbling pile of scribbled notes, littered bookshelves, stacks of files and a muddle of domestic debris which would have appalled Henrietta, this book has finally emerged. Obviously, I cannot take all the credit for this. First and foremost, I owe a huge debt of gratitude to Chris and Julia Kellerman. Until recently, Chris was the manager of the Hampstead Garden Suburb Trust and in 2002 he encouraged me to write Henrietta's biography. He and Julia have been perfect hosts, much valued critics and unfailingly supportive. Through Chris and Julia, I met many Suburb residents whose memories and perceptions added spice and texture to Henrietta's life which would otherwise have been missing. In particular, I would like to thank Judy Charlton, Ruth Cass, Jean Dyson and Mollie Tripp for sharing their highly amusing and astute childhood memories of Henrietta. I am also very grateful to Harry Cobb, the Hampstead Garden Suburb archivist who, as well as granting permission to use the photographs in this book, also directed me to innumerable valuable sources during the early stages of research. More recently, Jo Velleman, Richard Wakefield and Jonquil Griffiths have made several helpful suggestions which have been much appreciated. And particular thanks are due to Micky Watkins, who has also recently published a book about Henrietta's earlier years in Whitechapel. It was a real pleasure to meet Micky and share enthusiasm about someone who has spent too long confined to the margins of history. Thanks to the Hampstead Garden Suburb Trust for the frontispiece illustration. I have also much appreciated the patience and advice of Simon Thraves, Sarah Kiddle and Dan Finch at Phillimore, my publishers in Chichester, Sussex.

Librarians and archivists are inevitably the unsung heroes of anything that eventually appears in print. The staff members at the following institutions were unstintingly generous with their time and effort: the York St John library; the Colindale, North London; the British Libraries in London and Boston Spa, Yorkshire; the Brotherton Library at Leeds University; and the Manchester Public Library. John Coulter, archivist at Lewisham Local History Archives, was a fruitful source of information about the Rowland family, for which I am very grateful, and the ever-patient staff at the London Metropolitan Archives spent much time helping me track down sources from the flimsiest of references.

Judy Giles and John McLeod originally shared and sustained my interest in Victorian and Edwardian suburban culture. I will always be indebted to them for their continued support and encouragement. I also value greatly the advice John has given me about the pitfalls and practicalities of writing. Similarly, special thanks are due to Sean Ledwith, who took the trouble to read through, and constructively comment on, several chapters, as well as adding substance to what were initially somewhat pedestrian historical references. However, I have to own up to any oversights or inaccuracies, which remain entirely my own.

Finally, I would like to acknowledge appreciation of the long-suffering band of friends, colleagues and family who have endured my rambling on about Henrietta for the past seven years. So, love and thanks to colleagues at York St John and Leeds College of Technology, Joy and Rosie in Harrogate, Emma, Sue and Chrissie in Saltaire, and last, but never, ever least, Lindsay, Claire, Guy, Jake, Sam, David, Noel and Paula.

Introduction

A Beautiful Green Golden Scheme

Reconstructing Suburbia

In 1932, two 14-year-old schoolgirls giggled and whispered as they sneaked past No 1, South Square, Hampstead Garden Suburb in North London. This was one of the larger houses built in an innovative suburban development over 20 years earlier: a 'beautiful green golden scheme' in which all classes could live in architecturally designed houses with landscaped gardens 'in right conditions of beauty and space'.[1] The 'arts and crafts' design, dotted layout and sweet-briar or wild-rose hedges of these houses were the antithesis of traditional suburban development, typified by the serried ranks of identical terraced houses divided by privet hedges that were derided by many and parodied by George and Weedon Grossmith in their *Diary of a Nobody* (1892).[2] No 1, South Square was the home of a small, stout and elderly – but still formidable – governor of the girls' school. They had been warned by their headmistress that under no circumstances were they to disturb her with their antics. One of these girls, Judy, froze with terror when the front door opened and this imperious figure emerged, shadowed by her timid housekeeper and a curmudgeonly old chauffeur. And as she beckoned the two girls over, Judy – normally an intrepid and high-spirited girl – expected at best a lecture for failing to wear her much-loathed school hat or, at worst, dire punishment for violating her headteacher's instructions. Instead, she and her friend were each given a foil-wrapped bar of Cadbury's chocolate.[3]

Their benefactor was Dame Henrietta Barnett, the founder of Hampstead Garden Suburb and a lifelong social reformer. I came across Henrietta quite by accident when I was researching late Victorian and Edwardian suburban culture for my doctoral thesis. Her intention to build a Garden Suburb for all classes at Hampstead had ignited a splenetic outburst from that most vituperative critic of suburban culture, T.W.H. Crosland. He denounced her intentions as a 'specious, vulgar and undesirable movement' designed to pander to the puny ambitions and pathetic aspirations of the lower middle classes.[4] But as one of my own intentions had been to re-evaluate this much derided socio-economic group, I was fascinated by the spirit of a woman prepared to risk ridicule, disapproval and friction in order to pursue her vision of creating an attractive, healthy and semi-rural environment for all, regardless of class, gender, ability or age. What was to intrigue me even more was Henrietta's virtual absence from social and cultural history. At that point, her most enduring representations were to be found in local histories of Hampstead Garden Suburb and many of these – wittingly or otherwise – tended to underestimate the passion, drive and commitment which fuelled her lifelong commitment to social and housing reform.[5] Even when social historians do mention Henrietta's contributions to welfare reform, these are invariably overshadowed by acerbic evaluations of her 'bulldozing' personality.[6] Meanwhile, the feminist historians who have worked assiduously to rescue countless numbers of women from the margins and footnotes of the past have made only perfunctory acknowledgement of Henrietta's achievements.[7] It is only very recently that the Hampstead Garden Suburb historian, Micky Watkins, has produced an account of Henrietta's work in Whitechapel.[8]

Henrietta has permeated my imagination for the past seven years, not least because of the persistence, wilfulness and irreverence with which she challenged the social expectations of the 19th and 20th centuries in order to pursue her commitment to social reform. Thus, one purpose of this book is to offer insights into the circumstances which variously shaped, repressed and energised the will of a woman determined to circumvent social expectations of femininity whilst maintaining all the outward signifiers of respectability. For these insights to be effective, it will be necessary to recreate the cultural context in which they can be understood. So, this book is as much a cultural history of Henrietta's times as it is a story of her life. Biographers cannot provide a definitive account of a person's life any more than historians can create an absolute portrayal of the past, but what both biographers and cultural historians *can* do is to propose alternative ways of understanding the attitudes, values and motivations of both an individual and the circumstances that produced them. In turn, such re-appraisal can invigorate the tantalising gaps and silences which haunt the texts of the past: what was 'unsayable' in the 19th century can be voiced in the 21st. Conversely, that which could be articulated in the 19th century – such as assumptions about British supremacy or women's inherent frailty – are now considered quite beyond the pale. But no matter how offended or queasy we are made to feel by these old 'certainties', we need to acknowledge the extent to which they informed an individual's sense of identity and place. Such acknowledgement is particularly significant when reconstructing the life of one who has been variously parodied, pilloried or simply misunderstood.

I

The Best of Times, The Worst of Times

Childhood, Education and Class in Victorian London

In 1851, the year of Henrietta's birth, Queen Victoria had been on the throne for 14 years. Depending on one's social class, these years have often been recorded as either the 'best of times' or 'the worst of times'. Perhaps the most prolific chronicler of urban deprivation was Henry Mayhew, whose graphic accounts in *London Labour and London Poor* eventually stretched to four volumes.[1] The novelistic imagination of the 1840s reinforced these perceptions: Benjamin Disraeli's *Sybil, or The Two Nations*, for example, is a powerful evocation of the squalor and misery endured by the urban working classes set against the powers and privileges savoured by an exploitative upper class.[2] Similarly, Elizabeth Gaskell's *Mary Barton* examines the deprivations of the northern working classes during the 1840s.[3] Burgeoning resentment of these iniquities kindled the Chartist riots which inspired Charlotte Brontë's representation of working-class uprising in *Shirley*.[4] Whilst Brontë clearly sympathises with the plight of the individual in this novel, it is underlain by a real fear of collective violence from a proletarian mob brutalised by want and hunger. Such fears also haunted the imagination of social commentators and politicians as well as the entrepreneurs whose wealth was contingent upon on the co-operation of their workers.[5]

As will become clear in later chapters, the urban working classes of Victorian England indeed suffered intense deprivation and exploitation as well as profound condescension from self-righteous philanthropists, who took it upon themselves to inculcate wholesome habits and high moral standards in the lower orders. But the working classes were not, of course, one lumpen mass: they had diverse attitudes, aspirations and beliefs as well as thriving cultural activities ranging from sport, pubs, music halls and street games through to women's groups, political organisations and the less formal but still valued solidarity of the public wash-houses and baths. Equally, not all social reformers were steeped in middle-class piety: some were sensitive to the vibrancy of working-class cultures and the means by which the urban poor maintained a sense of dignity and identity in the direst of circumstances. As George Behlmer discerns, 'just as it would be naive to suppose that these reformers ignored their own class interests when they visited a poor home … so it would be equally naive to assume that they were strangers to compassion'.[6] Similarly, it is a mistake to assume that all middle-class entrepreneurs were avaricious, exploitative and complacent about their wealth and status. Despite dominant images of the successful 'self-made' businessman of the 19th century, many were aware that their social positions were fragile and their fortunes precarious. Indeed, many *arriviste* professionals and entrepreneurs often felt 'isolated and defenceless' in their unfamiliar roles. In consequence, the new middle classes were much more 'vulnerable and unstable' than popularly imagined,[7] as Charles

Dickens demonstrates so vividly in his 1848 novel, *Dombey and Son*. In this, middle-class businessman Paul Dombey's personal and professional status crumble through a combination of sexual subterfuge, duplicitous dealings and his neglect of paternal responsibilities.[8]

Despite these tenuous aspects of middle-class enterprise and the iniquities suffered by the urban and rural poor, the public face mid-Victorian England chose to present was one of optimism and pride in the progress achieved over the past century. Such upbeat enthusiasm was distilled into the stunning display of art, invention and innovation at London's Great Exhibition of 1851 which was housed in the purpose-built Crystal Palace, itself a tribute to the feats of Victorian structural engineering. The exhibits ranged from the ghoulish to the gorgeous and the exotic to the everyday: prosthetic eyes and limbs jostled alongside sumptuous jewellery, artwork and fountains, whilst Eastern artefacts and stuffed elephants brushed against rather more functional items such as condensed milk and preserved foodstuffs. But the greatest source of pride was in British technological advancement: the locomotives, agricultural implements, factory machinery and shipping that had contributed towards Britain's perceptions of itself as a leader amongst the world's nations. People may well have enthused about the opening ceremony of this festival but, more than anything else, the 1851 Exhibition was a celebration and assertion of Britain's industrial supremacy. And, as postcolonial critics have since demonstrated, much of Victorian Britain's wealth and status was predicated upon its colonisation of the natural sources of less developed countries and the concomitant exploitation of their indigenous populations.[9]

It was into this outwardly optimistic Britain and a lifestyle shored up by colonial wealth that Henrietta Octavia Rowland was born on 4 May 1851, just three days after the opening of the Great Exhibition, the eighth child of German-born Henrietta Monica Margaretta (née Ditges) and entrepreneur Alexander William Rowland.[10] Much of Alexander's wealth had been generated by the Macassar oil obtained from the ylang-ylang flower indigenous to Eastern Asian nations. He manufactured and marketed this as Rowland's Macassar Oil, guaranteed as a 'Preserver, Restorer and Strengthener' of hair, along with other applications such as Kalydor cream, held to 'beautif[y] the complexion, produce … soft, fair skin and remove … all disfigurements' and Odonto, a dental preparation intended to 'whiten … the teeth and prevent … decay' without recourse to 'grit or ruinous acid'.[11] Clearly, Alexander was acutely aware of middle-class anxieties surrounding appearance and was sufficiently astute to turn these to entrepreneurial advantage. Nor were these anxieties merely vanity: one's appearance was a signifier of wealth, power and social standing. Whilst well-tailored clothing could conceal some physical imperfections, the condition of a person's hair, complexion and teeth betrayed much more about his or her diet, lifestyle and social origins. Indeed, rumour has it that in order to promote his hair colorant, Alexander Rowland senior, Henrietta's grandfather, appeared in church one Sunday morning with one half of his luxuriant moustache dyed black.[12] Meanwhile, as middle-class femininity was associated with youthfulness and beauty, women were anxious to maintain the smooth, unlined skin and glossy hair that distinguished their features from the rather more weathered ones of working-class women.

Sometimes, however, the apparent comforts and privileges of such a lifestyle were merely 'skin-deep'. Indeed, those in baby Henrietta's home were soon to be disrupted. Her mother was to die only days after her little daughter's arrival and thus responsibility for the care of the newborn infant, as well as the ebullient menagerie of children and pets who romped through the family home in Lewisham, South London, fell upon 28-year-old Sophey Rowland, one of Alexander's unmarried sisters. This responsibility was a considerable one for a woman unused to the clamorous demands of children. To add to Sophey's burdens, Henrietta – known as Yetta to those close to her – was a tiny, delicate baby who was not expected to thrive. Indeed, this frailty persisted throughout her early years and, in consequence, she was sheltered from the rumbustious shenanigans of her robust brothers and sisters and raised instead with her invalid sister, Fanny, for whom a carriage accident in infancy had resulted in irreparable brain damage.[13] Henrietta's loss of her mother was by no means atypical. First and foremost, the leisured lifestyles of middle-class women tended to leave them ill-equipped for the physical demands of multiple pregnancies and the exertions of labour. And haemorrhaging during childbirth or succumbing to puerperal fever a few days later were common fates for all Victorian mothers, regardless of class. Ironically, middle-class women were more likely to be vulnerable to puerperal fever because their husbands were in a position to pay for the fashionable practice of hiring a doctor to supervise labour and delivery. After all, these were the days when a growing faith in a 'rational' and male-dominated sphere of medicine led to a concomitant undermining of 'superstitious', female-centred practices such as midwifery and herbal remedies. But many postpartum women were to die from infections caused by these doctors' inattention to basic hygiene procedures.[14] Sophey was not expected to cope entirely unaided with this motherless troupe of children, however. Soon after the death of her sister-in-law, a nurse, Mary Moore, was hired to help care for baby Henrietta. Mary was to become a lifelong companion of this little baby girl, whom she adored unreservedly.[15]

The first 13 years of Henrietta's childhood were spent in the family homes at Lewisham, a suburb of South East London, and the seaside resort of Brighton in Sussex. Back in the 18th century, Lewisham had been a village incorporating two parishes: St Mary's, Lewisham and St Margaret, Lee. During that period it was primarily an agricultural community with one or two light industries, which were mainly seen in the form of corn mills and breweries dotted along the banks of the River Ravensbourne. Market gardening was a principal money-spinner: luxury fruit and vegetables were much sought after by wealthy Londoners with increasingly sophisticated tastes in wining and dining. By the end of the 18th century, Lewisham had become a desirable retreat for these affluent urban dwellers. As Lewisham's agricultural industry declined, farmhouses were eagerly snapped up and modernised by entrepreneurs weary of the clamour of central London. Meanwhile, villas appeared on former arable land alongside the shops and small businesses starting to flourish on Lewisham's High Street.[16] So, by the mid-19th century, Lewisham had made the transition from village to town, but it retained much of its pastoral charm. The work of Henry Wood, the earliest known photographer of Lewisham, reveals an idyllic landscape: sun-speckled woodland, sparkling rivers, creeper-covered houses and ancient thatched cottages. And the names of the two taverns – *The Two Brewers* and *The Plough and Harrow* – bear witness to Lewisham's former industries, even if they did refresh the spirits of careworn businessmen rather than those of agricultural workers.[17] Meanwhile, the feudal grandeur of Lewisham was preserved by the renovation of its 18th-century mansions. As an 1838 writer enthused:

> A little to the south of the church … a fine panoramic view presents itself. On
> the north, the church tower, through a break in the luxuriant wood, forms the
> chief feature of a beautiful landscape. To the westward is seen the Priory, the
> elegant castellated seat of John Thackeray Esq., with its gothic windows of stained
> glass, and the rich surrounding scenery … Further southward is the mansion of
> Henry Stainton Esq., and beyond it is Rosenthal, the residence of Alexander
> Rowland Esq.[18]

This last was the home of Henrietta's grandfather, the founder of the family business. In the 1851 census, he is listed as a 66-year-old perfumier and employer of seven at his Hatton Garden premises.[19] He shared his home with his widowed sister, Sarah and three unmarried daughters, Elizabeth, Sophia (Sophey) and Rebecca. In addition there were four live-in servants: Anne Shannan, the cook, Elizabeth Nicholson, the nurse, Anne Balls, the housekeeper, and William Elkins, the groom. Given the size of the estate, it seems likely that non-residential servants, too, would have been employed by Alexander senior. Rosenthal House was set back from the main road and surrounded by acres of woodland and landscaped gardens overlooking open fields and farm land. As well as the main house, there were numerous outbuildings, including stables, coach houses and greenhouses. On one of the lawns was a magnificent fountain, around which peacocks would strut.[20]

No doubt Alexander and his contemporaries were very proud of such tangible evidence of their achievements. However, it is not difficult to imagine the sardonic amusement of Lewisham dwellers who had lived there for generations as they watched affluent *arrivistes* emulating the ways of the country squires. Others were probably deeply resentful – particularly those farm workers who were forced to seek employment in the towns as landowners sold out to builders and property developers. Nonetheless, Alexander Rowland's achievements inspired similar aspirations in his eldest son. Sometime in the 1840s, Alexander junior leased the Grange on Honor Oak Road between Sydenham and Lewisham in order to accommodate his growing family.[21] This choice of location was timely: in 1847, Lewisham was still held in high esteem by those eulogising the pedigree of its residents and the beauty of its surroundings; two years later, a correspondent to the *Builder* noted how those who could afford it were moving a short distance away to Sydenham and Penge.[22] No doubt Alexander junior was aware of the social status implicit in living on the Sydenham side of Lewisham. As would befit an ambitious entrepreneur, the Grange was the largest mansion in the road with 12 bedrooms and grounds covering 15 acres. As at his father's house, these featured lawns, gravelled paths, shrubberies, herbaceous borders, rockeries and ornamental water features. The latter greatly appealed to the infant Henrietta who, to the despair of her aunt and nurse, delighted in tormenting the ducks kept on the ponds by throwing stones at them. As the ducks retreated and 'it was no longer any fun to tease them', she continued throwing stones into the pond, fascinated by the ever-widening circles created by the splash of pebbles into water. No doubt Henrietta had demanded to know why, because she recalls that her exasperated nurse snapped that the circles would never stop before attending to the rather more irksome matter of the extent to which Henrietta was 'spoiling her frock'.[23]

Henrietta may well have been regarded as delicate throughout her childhood but her memories of her early years suggest that she was a wilful, wayward and mischievous little girl who took a perverse pleasure in trying the patience of the long-suffering adults around her. Whilst she clearly adored Mary, her nurse, she was by no means deferential towards her. Nurses occupied an ambiguous role in Victorian households. Neither family member nor servants, they were often regarded as objects of pity or ridicule. Even if children were fond of these marginalised members of the household, this affection was often tempered by their intuitive awareness of nurses' subordinate status.[24] So there was often a battle of wills between Henrietta and the 'good and devoted' Mary, who 'did all she could to teach [Henrietta] what was right'. Clearly, that was no easy task. One day, the wilful little Yetta announced that she wanted to take Minnie, her largest and heaviest doll, for a walk. Realising that Henrietta would soon get tired of carrying her, Mary suggested that it would be more sensible to leave her at home. Henrietta retorted that she '*never* got tired of carrying her' whilst silently thinking 'if I do get tired, *you* will carry her'. Mary demurred but gave way and, as she had predicted, Henrietta's arms soon began to ache and she pleaded with Mary to carry Minnie. For once, Mary refused. This enraged Henrietta, who promptly abandoned the doll in a hedgerow. And, despite feeling 'very uncomfortable', the mutinous little girl stalked a resolute path homeward. Mary, although initially equally determined, eventually 'gave way, went back, fetched the doll and carried it herself'.[25]

Henrietta was equally adept at manipulating her father. Rather than conforming to the stereotype of Victorian fiction, the stern paterfamilias, Alexander Rowland was easygoing, affable and indulgent – especially towards his 'special darling baby Yetta', who beguiled him for the rest of his life.[26] Whilst she may have had older brothers and sisters with the potential to curb her wayward streak, Henrietta was no doubt sufficiently astute to take full advantage of her 'delicate' constitution in order to thwart their attempts. Indeed, she bitterly resented the dictatorial manner of her eldest sister, Tessy. When this authoritarian figure returned home from boarding school, Henrietta fumed in her diary that she was '*so* interfering'. Conversely, she adored her sister Alice, four years her senior, and Fitz – the youngest of the Rowland sons and closest in age to Henrietta.[27] As much as anything else, Henrietta revelled in her brother's capacity for mischief. Looking back on her childhood, she gleefully recollected Fritz and herself tormenting her sleeping grandfather by tickling his face with a straw. Duly alarmed, the beleaguered septuagenarian jumped with a start whilst his grandchildren crouched behind his big leather chair convulsed with mirth.[28]

Of all the adults in Henrietta's childhood world, it was Sophey Rowland who inspired the least affection and respect. To some extent, this view could have been shaped by the wider perception of single women as socially inferior to their married counterparts.[29] Rather like nurses and governesses, they were regarded as somewhat pathetic creatures and generated equal measures of pity and derision. So, although Sophey clearly had some sway over the upbringing of her nephews and nieces, this would have been diluted by the children's tacit awareness of her lowly single status. However, it seems that Henrietta harboured a lifelong resentment for the aunt whom she was later to denounce as an 'unsympathetic woman' lacking the imagination to discern what constituted 'intellectual and ethical' value for the children in her care.[30] Clearly, Sophey was irritated by Henrietta's penchant for constant questioning. Once, Henrietta was pondering on whether or not the stars were inhabited, whilst the worldlier Fitz was wondering what they would be having for pudding that day. Sophey declared that the latter was 'better worth wondering about' because Fitz would soon find out whereas Henrietta's questions about the stars would never be resolved.[31] It is hardly surprising, then, that a few years later Henrietta was to identify closely with Elizabeth Barrett Browning's epic poem, 'Aurora Leigh'. In this poem, the eponymous heroine loses her mother at the age of four and is subsequently raised by an austere aunt who, like Aunt Sophey, did not agree with education for girls.[32] But, just as the fictional Aurora had nurtured her poetic imagination by stealing moments with the romantic verse of Keats and Byron, little Henrietta nurtured her fascination with numbers well before she had any formal schooling. It is unclear how this fascination grew into a considerable flair for maths, but it is likely that she contrived to eavesdrop on her brothers' lessons or puzzle over their textbooks after they had sneaked away from the classroom. Whatever the case, she was 'uncannily rapid' with mental arithmetic and paid scrupulous attention to the minutiae of her pocket money account book.[33]

Despite her lack of formal education, Henrietta recalled these early years as 'happy' times. Once again, her experiences were not atypical. The 1851 census indicates that 50,000 middle-class children were educated at home and the quality of this schooling would have been contingent upon the extent to which parents and tutors were aware of the planning, resources and consolidation necessary for successful learning to take place.[34] Much of this home tutoring was the responsibility of governesses, who would have had little training and who often despaired at the unruliness and insolence of their young pupils. Indeed, towards the end of her life, Henrietta confessed that the governesses 'selected' for her by her aunt may well have been 'excellent' but she nonetheless 'despised' them on principle.[35] The frustrations of these reasonably well-educated casualties of middle-class misfortune are perhaps best summarised by an impoverished Charlotte Brontë, forced to earn her living as a governess to the most 'riotous, perverse, unmanageable cubs' imaginable: a 'set of pampered, spoilt, turbulent children' who were 'constantly' baiting her.[36] The extent to which the Rowland children's behaviour resembled that of Brontë's charges can only be conjectured, but Marion Paterson's manuscripts reveal that most of the Rowland children's education began at home before being continued at boarding school.[37]

Over the past three decades, feminist historians have – justifiably – bemoaned the paucity and patchiness of education bestowed on middle-class Victorian girls.[38] Typically, their formal education would comprise the basic 'three Rs', glossed over with a flimsy layer of arts, literature, language and classics. Alongside this formal tuition, middle-class Victorian girls were expected to assimilate all the subtle nuances of correct deportment, etiquette and social protocol, all delicate signifiers of one's social status. To paraphrase the eminent Victorian John Ruskin, it was held that a young woman's intellectual knowledge and social graces should be sufficient to enable her to support her husband but never to outshine or, indeed, disgrace him.[39] Advertisements in contemporary newspapers reveal awareness of these social expectations. For example, a governess offered tuition in 'English, French and music' in return for 'moderate' remuneration whilst a school for young ladies combined a similar curriculum with 'the usual accomplishments'.[40] For many young women, the expectations implicit in such 'accomplishments' were undoubtedly oppressive and undermining. Indeed, tirades of resentment of these social expectations were expressed by fictional heroines of the era – not least in the spirited feminist outburst in Charlotte Brontë's *Jane Eyre* as well as the more desolate musings of Caroline Helstone in Brontë's later novel, *Shirley*.[41] Both books bemoan the subordination of girls to their male counterparts and express the frustrations of possessing an intellect unfulfilled by pastimes deemed appropriate for daughters of the 19th-century middle classes. And, if young girls of Henrietta's generation were allowed – or illicitly managed – to read such fictional diatribes, they would have surely stirred some degree of insurrection against the tender tyranny of their cloistered home environment. That said, it should not be assumed that *all* young girls' experiences of home education were entirely negative. For example, the diaries of one of Henrietta's contemporaries reveal that governesses could be feisty, independent women who inspired their pupils with radical politics, classic European literature and moral philosophy.[42]

Even without such erudite input, Henrietta may well have indirectly benefited from her haphazard learning. To begin with, institutionalised education in the 1850s was hardly inspiring: much of it consisted of the learning by rote parodied by Dickens in his 1854 novel *Hard Times*. In this, working-class children 'had imperial gallons of facts poured into them' by an unyielding Mr M'Choakumchild, while any creativity in their middle-class counterparts, Louisa and Tom Gradgrind, was stifled by the mind-numbing collection, classification and organisation of quantifiable data.[43] Of course, Dickens exaggerates the joyless grind of Victorian education for comic effect, but many historians have drawn our attention to the Utilitarian philosophy underpinning such educational methods and its adverse effects on teachers and pupils alike.[44] Nor were contemporary HMIs impressed by the instruction received by student teachers:

> [Teacher training] tends to *impart information* rather than to *develop the faculties* and to *discipline the mind*. Vast demands are made on the memory, little is done for the improvement of the judgement or reasoning powers … In such subjects as Old Testament history, Church History, outlines of English history, there is necessarily an immense preponderance of names, dates, and facts, which have to be *remembered* but not *digested*.[45]

Of course, education was class, as well as gender, specific. Once again, advertisements in contemporary newspapers confirm the extent to which education was perceived as a means to a vocational end. Just as working-class children were moulded into factory fodder or domestic servants, their middle-class male counterparts were primed for the 'military' and 'civil' services via their indoctrination with the 'Greek', 'Latin' and 'mathematical and physical sciences' deemed necessary for success in such careers.[46] Henrietta's older brothers would have received such an education, in which the acquisition of classical knowledge was on a par with the gaining of a network of acquaintances necessary to maintain and further one's social status. However, her older sister Alice's aspirations to study at medical school suggest that she had benefited from the values of one of the more progressive girls' schools, which were beginning to recognise that young women's penchant for frivolity was the inevitable outcome of a patchy and superficial education.[47] But such schools tended to follow a very similar curriculum to that taught in boys' public schools – by teachers who had left college 'with *full* but comparatively *languid* and *unbraced* minds': people overflowing with 'knowledge' but lacking both pedagogical commitment and the inherent spark needed to inspire their pupils.[48]

Conversely, much of Henrietta's home education would at least have been imparted by someone with a passion for their subject. Sunday evenings in the Rowland household were not spent reading the Bible or other improving tracts. Rather, Alexander Rowland would gather his children around him and foster their appreciation of art by looking at paintings with them and encouraging them to engage with their diversity of style, themes and techniques. One outcome of this was the kindling of Henrietta's fascination with colour, texture and light. From an early age, she was captivated by both urban and rural sunsets as well as 'colour in any form'.[49] Some twenty or thirty years later, she attempted to inspire the disaffected poor of London using similar methods in the art gallery she opened in Whitechapel. Henrietta's grandfather, too, used the 'learning by doing' approach to teaching the Rowland children about botany and gardening. Not only did this impart practical knowledge about the growth of flowers, fruit and vegetables, but it also ignited Henrietta's lifelong passion for gardening and her enduring belief in its re-creative properties. Meanwhile, religious instruction was provided by governesses or her nurse, Mary.[50] As Mary doted on her little Yetta, it is likely that this would have incorporated the more benign Biblical teachings.[51] As for more formal aspects of her education, it is doubtful that Henrietta followed much in the way of a systematic approach to learning, but her later writings suggest that she picked up sufficient snippets of philosophy, classics, poetry and literature to inform, but not over-determine, her attitudes, values and beliefs. In other words, Henrietta's home education may have been jumbled and perfunctory but from it she was able to piece together a patchwork of information, ideas and influences which lent these writings plausibility while preserving their quirky irreverence. If she struggled over any subject, she was quick to take remedial action. On 24 January 1863, the 11-year-old Henrietta's diary entries proudly assert that she had 'burnt' her French book after yet another frustrating – and futile – attempt to grapple with foreign languages.[52] A year or two earlier, she had fumed: 'Why should everybody not talk alike, and then I need not learn French?'. The adult Henrietta conceded the short-sightedness of this question but still vindicated the 'educational value of wondering':

> I remember when I was seven or eight years old being assailed with torments of painful, irreverent doubt because no one would reply seriously to my questions … In those days … 'it is rude to ask questions' was a constant method of reply to requests for information – a method the young ones were quick to suspect as being a cloak for ignorance.[53]

Henrietta's home education may well have inadvertently taught her a shrewd indifference towards adult prevarication in addition to the learned proclamations of the great and the good. But what she had not experienced were the socialisation processes endured by her school-educated counterparts. Most Victorian schools, whether lower-, middle- or upper-class, had a distinct pecking order, in which children learned 'the role of pupil' and its concomitant 'deference and compliance' to teachers and older students.[54] As well as learning conformity from the disciplined and highly structured nature of the school day, schoolchildren would rub one another's rough edges off as they negotiated the squabbles and rivalries of the playground. So for Henrietta childhood was by no means the oppressive and austere environment conjured up by the children's literature of the period and some historians' accounts of growing up in middle-class Victorian England. The former's unequivocal moral content, which equated disobedience with, at best, punishment and, at worst, death and eternal damnation,[55] suggest that little boys and girls were terrorised into submission – or intended to be. However, Walvin also argues that Romantic belief in the innate goodness and innocence of children meant that Victorian parenting was 'generally less harsh' than that of earlier generations.[56] Certainly, Henrietta's lifelong capacity for waywardness and mischief suggests that her childhood ebullience and disobedience often remained unchecked. Perhaps most significantly, the lack of a mother figure, although a fact that may well have been deeply regretted by Henrietta, meant that she had the space to forge a personality unfettered by maternal expectations of feminine decorum, modesty and deference. Similarly, she never experienced at first hand the deference married women were often obliged to show to their husbands.

During the winter months, the Rowland family moved away from London in order to escape the fog and smog which frequently enshrouded London from November to March. Their winter home was No 18, Brunswick Terrace, Brighton: a tall, white-stuccoed construction which overlooked the often mesmeric, but occasionally menacing, brown-grey surge and sway of the English Channel. Initially 'terrified of' but later 'delighted' by this chaotic seascape, Henrietta conquered her terrors by forcing herself to walk first near, then along the shoreline as the waves rumbled and rolled towards the beach.[57] All the Rowland children – along with their assortment of dogs – adored romping across the sands with their hoops and chasing each other in the 'strong sea-winds which made the waves leap and dance', activities that left the brothers and sisters exhilarated and rosy-cheeked.[58] In her more pensive moments, Henrietta was equally enchanted by the gentle contours of the South Downs, and she 'revelled in the light and shade playing on them'. For Henrietta, already attuned to the nuances of colour, this kaleidoscopic melding of light, hue and texture was the 'very touch of heaven' and one for which she was always to hold a deep affection. As Marion Paterson observed, 'to the end of her life, she eagerly looked for the first glimpse of them'.[59] In contrast to the gentle terrain of the South Downs was the 13-year-old Henrietta's visit to the rather more ravaged and bruised charms of the Peak District in Derbyshire. This occasion was recorded in her diary under the heading 'My Tour to Buxton in Derbyshire' and was no doubt special to her because it was her 'first trip away with Papa and Auntey'.[60] Buxton was a spa resort fashionable amongst the Victorian mercantile classes; its stone cottages, taverns and hotels nestled amid the melancholy beauty of the surrounding crags, streams, woodlands and moors. It was also renowned for spectacular sunsets, especially on June evenings. Henrietta was particularly mesmerised by the 'uncultivated' appeal of the woodlands, which she explored with her father. There she drank in meticulous details of the plethora of wild flowers which proliferated and tumbled through sun-dappled clearings: yellow pimpernels, periwinkles, late primroses, and the ferns which unfurled in the denser and damper corners of the Derbyshire woodlands. During this trip, she 'noticed all and everything', but the botanist in her was particularly intrigued by the seed formations on the back of the fern leaves.[61] Although Henrietta was energised by this trip – not least because it was one of the few occasions on which she had her father's undivided attention – it was also tinged with regret. A few days after their return to London, they were due to move from the Grange to a much grander mansion in Sydenham. No doubt Henrietta had taken for granted the comforts of this home as much as any middle-class child would have done, but the idea of leaving behind the house with so many affectionate associations seems to have been particularly unsettling for a young girl just approaching adolescence.[62]

So, for the first 13 years of her life, Henrietta grew up in apparently sheltered, prosperous and comfortable surroundings in both rural and urban environs. During the

19th century, many people subscribed to notions of environmental determinism: the belief that one's identity is inevitably shaped by one's immediate physical and cultural environment. Indeed, such beliefs were instrumental in shaping the adult Henrietta's approaches to social and housing reform.[63] However, if that had been wholly the case, then it is doubtful that she would have ultimately resisted what she was later to define as the 'lavish' lifestyle of her childhood and adolescence.[64] The use of the term 'lavish' is significant because as well as carrying connotations of generosity and abundance, it can also signify profligacy, extravagance and even dissolution. No doubt the sharp-eyed and shrewd little Henrietta was all too aware of the disparity between the material comforts of the Rowland households and the wretchedness endured by the street children living in the seamier districts of London and Brighton. Equally, she cannot have failed to suspect the more decadent luxuries savoured by her father and his friends, particularly in Brighton. As John Walton has noted, affluent entrepreneurs may well have ostensibly chosen a winter home in such a setting for its health-giving properties but nonetheless, Brighton's respectability was tenuous to say the least. Indeed, it retained its 'raffish' reputation throughout the 19th century.[65] Increasing prosperity allowed Alexander Rowland to move his family from the Grange to the even more opulent surroundings of Champion Hall, a newly built mansion in nearby Lower Sydenham. It was part of the canny – if somewhat unscrupulous – property dealer William Woodgate's speculative development of an estate previously known as the Lawns.[66] By 1860, the advent of the Mid-Kent railway line had encouraged most speculative developers to construct cheaper housing aimed at the lower-middle and working classes, who were keen to distance themselves from an increasingly crowded and polluted central London. However, sharp-witted and opportunistic developers like Woodgate realised that there was still a building market for the wealthier buyers seeking homes in verdant and more spacious suburbs such as Sydenham, Norwood or Dulwich, which at that time were unsullied by the despised and derided suburban homes designed for the lower-middle classes.[67]

Indeed Sydenham, deemed 'firmly upper-middle-class' in the mid-19th century, would have been particularly desirable to ambitious entrepreneurs like Alexander Rowland.[68] The horse-riding lessons offered in the surrounding Surrey countryside, for example, certainly indicate the disposable wealth in Sydenham, but they also hint at the extent to which the *nouveau riche* mercantile classes were eager to emulate the pursuits of the leisured aristocracy.[69] Certainly, Alexander Rowland had already emboldened his children by ensuring that they had learned to trot, gallop and canter their horses – '*not* ponies', as the 10-year-old Henrietta asserted – over the Sussex Downs and the fields and woodland of Surrey. Initially, Henrietta was daunted by the speed and potency of Peggy, Paris, Charger and Buffer as they bounded over springy turf, along with craggier terrain, but she soon became addicted to the exhilarating charge inherent in such pursuits.[70] Suburban homes were also expected to fulfil emotional needs: John Tosh, for example, points out that the activity of gardening was perceived as contributing to these needs by 'refresh[ing] the soul and delight[ing] the eye'.[71] Certainly, Henrietta's early affection for sowing, planting, watering and nurturing her own little patches amongst the family gardens was to convince *her* of the wholesome and regenerative properties of gardening, but it would be simplistic to assume that everyone derived the same pleasures from such a pastime. For a start, it is doubtful whether Alexander Rowland and his peers would have had the time or the inclination to do much more than take an occasional stroll around the grounds surrounding their homes. Rather, they would have employed gardeners to clip, mow, prune and lop their gardens into miniaturised versions of the country parks encircling aristocratic estates. Thus, these gardens – or more accurately – landscaped grounds were not so much the results of their owners' labours as they were an expression of their aspirations towards the sophistication and *savoir-faire* emanating from the old wealth of the nobility.

Despite the enduring stereotype of the respectable Victorian paterfamilias, many middle-class Victorian men were all too eager to shed the mantle of patriarchal responsibility as often as possible. In part, this sprang from a desire to escape the stifling boredom of suburban life in general and domesticity in particular. For many of these men, while the suburbs may have provided the security, landscape and elegance which befitted their families and status, they lacked the vibrancy and dynamism so abundant in urban life. Only tantalising allusions are made towards Alexander Rowland's libertine lifestyle during the family's years at Lewisham, Sydenham and Brighton: clearly, the adult Henrietta chose to enshroud its more 'reprehensible' qualities in a veil of discretion. Demonstrating habitual candour, however, she does acknowledge that her father and 'his worldly art-loving friends' took their 'pleasures with a careless generosity'.[72] The specifics of these 'pleasures' are left to her readers' imaginations but nonetheless do much to destabilise the notions of propriety implicit in the Victorian middle-class men's uniform of frock coat and trousers, which lent its wearers an air of funereal respectability. Looking back at her childhood, the elderly Henrietta underplayed any sense of frustration or dissatisfaction with her home background. Indeed, many of the experiences of her early years emboldened her physically, socially and intellectually, and it is clear that her subsequent efforts to alleviate the mental, physical and spiritual poverty of London's underclass were influenced by her positive recollections of her suburban childhood, including picturesque surroundings, physical comforts and cultural pursuits. But she had plenty of fun too: on rainy and cold days she would create imaginary worlds with her dolls, crayons and boxes of bricks.[73] As she grew a little older she would sew clothes for her dolls or lose herself in books that she would 'read … again and again': *The Swiss Family Robinson, The Daisy Chain, Robinson Crusoe* and that obligatory text for Victorian children, *The Pilgrim's Progress*.[74]

At the same time, the remaining fragments of her youthful diaries leave no doubt about Henrietta's profound indignation at her classification with her 'feeble-minded' sister, Fanny.[75] This is not to imply that Henrietta harboured her sibling any personal grudges: indeed, she was very protective towards her sister and cared for her until this 'frail', 'sweet-tempered' and 'generous' child-woman died in 1926.[76] But it would seem that the young and spirited Henrietta was determined to resist both the contrasting moulds cast for her by the contradictory desires of an 'ice-cold' aunt and an over-indulgent father.[77] Sophey wanted her wilful little niece to grow into a sombre, deferential young woman whilst Alexander – who must have revelled in his daughter's defiance, irreverence and waywardness – would have done his utmost to transform her into a highly desirable debutante: a dazzling ebony-haired and pewter-eyed beauty who, gowned, coiffured, jewelled and furred, would rank highly in the marriage market. However, the 16-year-old Henrietta had other ideas. Quite how she finally managed to cajole her doting father and austere aunt into allowing her to attend boarding school can only be speculated. Perhaps their resolve was eroded by Henrietta's characteristic persistence, or possibly both hoped that a degree of formal education might temper her recalcitrance and rebelliousness, qualities which, no matter how endearing to her father, would not have been perceived as attractive by potential middle-class suitors. Nonetheless, the three terms she was subsequently to spend at the Haddon sisters' school in Dover ensured that she circumvented both of the destinies envisioned by her aunt and her father.

II

An Awakening Conscience

Education and Social Work in Dover

By 1867, the major port and seafaring town of Dover was also home to a number of industries. Along its snickleways and streets the leather workers who supplied boots and belts to the Navy and Army jostled alongside the watchmakers who specialised in making ships' chronometers and dress watches for Army and Naval officers. Nearer to the port, industries more traditionally associated with coastal towns thrived: all manner of shipbuilders, boat repairers, rope and sail makers were clustered around Dover's harbour. Meanwhile, the banks of the River Dour abounded with corn, paper, timber and oil mills, as well as numerous breweries. These industries thrived by providing the ships' and garrisons' personnel with flour, bread and ale, and raw materials for ship-building and maintenance. The advent of the London, Chatham and Dover Railway in 1841 facilitated the transportation of these goods even further afield.[1]

For the 16-year-old Henrietta, the clutter and hustle of this dynamic and diverse community would have been something of a culture shock. Unlike the seaside resort of Brighton, which was hastily constructing a veneer of respectability over its reputation for licentiousness, Dover was primarily a hub of industry and commerce. In common with most coastal towns, it had its salacious elements: incidents of brawling, drunkenness, prostitution, robbery and violence frequently spilt over into its alleys, courts and backstreets. The local press lingered over lurid details of 'ill-favoured' miscreants who had variously murdered, smuggled, embezzled, fought or drunk their way into the dock at the East Kent Quarter Sessions, and positively revelled in the minutiae of cases involving disreputable women such as the 'drunk and disorderly' Fanny Stringer, who was fined and jailed for vehemently resisting officers' attempts to restrain her. Even 'respectable-looking' women were somewhat vulnerable: the same paper also reported an incident where such a woman, allegedly mistaken for a prostitute, was subjected to vicious physical and verbal abuse by a mob of drunken naval cadets. No doubt painfully aware of these seamier aspects of the town, the local police were more assiduous than most in their efforts to control the drunkenness which precipitated such crime. A number of pub landlords fined for exceeding legal opening hours grumbled that the police were 'much stricter' in Dover than any inland town. Meanwhile, a group known as the 'Midnight Mission Movement' had taken it upon themselves to steer 'fallen women' away from the 'disgraceful course' onto which they had strayed.[2] Of course, Henrietta would not have had the opportunity to explore these more sordid aspects of Dover: as she recalled in later life, the 1860s were the days when it was considered ' "fast" for a woman to ride in a hansom' and completely out of the question to wander unchaperoned through respectable

streets, let alone their shadowy counterparts.[3] But although she would have been
sheltered from direct contact with the underworld of Dover, the innocent victims
of such chaotic lifestyles – the children abandoned by the parents in this underworld
– were to fuel Henrietta's lifelong sense of social responsibility. Unlike the majority of
schools for young ladies, the establishment she attended was not so much concerned
with instilling the ornamental knowledge deemed appropriate for girls as it was to
realise individual potential. And in marked contrast to the utilitarian approaches
that characterised much Victorian education, the girls were encouraged to think for
themselves rather than have their memories crammed full of facts.[4] The school was
run by the Haddon sisters, Carrie and Margaret, whose commitment to enhancing
the quality of Dover's abandoned children's lives was to have a profound impact on
their new pupil. In addition to the study of traditional subjects, the Haddon sisters
were keen to raise their middle-class pupils' consciousness of those less fortunate
than themselves. To this end, they opened an orphanage for the neglected children
of Dover and involved girls of Henrietta's age in the teaching of this ramshackle
bunch. This would have been by no means an easy undertaking. These children may
well have been puny and malnourished but they were also wily, quick-witted and
most likely to be well seasoned in the arts of street crime and survival.[5] This did
not deter Henrietta, however, who more than anything else 'was intensely interested
in Ragged Schools … education and culture'.[6]

Henrietta's diaries reveal another intense passion fermenting beneath her newly-
kindled fervour for education and social reform. In short, she had quickly become
besotted with Carrie Haddon who, as her 'teacher and friend', had a 'dynamic effect'
on her character. Perhaps for the first time in her life, Henrietta had met a woman
who enabled her to envision a feminine role beyond those deemed appropriate by her
father or her aunt. At the end of her first term, she eulogised her 'inspiring teacher'
and 'beloved friend' thus:

> This half year I have been as happy as I could possibly be. Indeed, the more I
> learn, and the older I grow, the happier I seem to become. I heartily thank you,
> dearest Miss Carrie, for all your boundless goodness to me which has been the
> foundation of my happiness.[7]

Henrietta's exalting of Carrie could of course be read as a schoolgirl 'crush': an
infatuation that embodied the desire to emulate the virtues of an older and more
assured role model.[8] Her memories of Carrie are often garlanded with heady imagery
that spills over with the exuberance and vitality of spring. On 6 May 1868, Henrietta
was delirious with the 'joy, joy in everything' as they celebrated Miss Haddon's birthday
amongst the wild hyacinths of Ewell as the Dover ragamuffins sang under 'a dear [sic]
bright sky'.[9] However, any romantic yearnings awakened by Carrie were tempered by
the awe she evoked in her young pupil. In her memoirs, the adult Henrietta recalls:

> On Sunday, after supper, the girls assembled, and having lowered the gas, started
> a hymn, during which Miss Carrie entered. She spoke for 20 minutes on some
> great thought of life and duty, sometimes illustrating what she said from various
> school events she had noticed through the past week. We often felt rebuked for
> *little* deeds we thought no-one had noticed or encouraged when we felt our feeble
> efforts towards goodness were recognised.[10]

This somewhat stage-managed entrance, with its quasi-spiritual undertones, gives some indication of how Carrie Haddon enslaved the hearts, minds and souls of her pupils. Clearly, she was a charismatic figure and, to a group of impressionable young girls, she must have seemed both omniscient and omnipresent. Yet she was by no means an austere or formidable figure; rather, she would use the gentle persuasion of her 'soft tones' to 'draw out' the girls' potential, which had until then laid dormant.[11] Perhaps this awakening of their inner potential alongside their consciences had much to do with her belief that social work was a pleasurable vocation rather than one prompted by a sense of duty or self-sacrifice. For Carrie had been influenced in her turn – notably by Sir James Hinton, the aural surgeon and moral philosopher who was later to marry her sister, Margaret. He was deeply committed to social reform and, in particular, took it upon himself to frequent music halls in order to save young girls from prostitution. However, Hinton was by no means a dour figure. Rather, he held the 'passionate belief that personal service to humanity was necessarily linked to pleasure not asceticism'.[12]

After his death, it was Carrie who took the trouble to edit and annotate his vast collection of essays and articles.[13] However, it would appear that Hinton's idea of 'personal service to humanity' was not confined to work amongst the poor and promiscuous. As Martha Vicinus notes, he maintained that he had a 'God-given task to relieve single women of their sexual frustrations'.[14] Hinton was also renowned for his radical views on women's capacity for sexual desire and, moreover, was a 'prophet of [the] polygamous free unions' which respectable Victorians perceived as destabilising the fundamental structure of 19th-century society. Indeed, as Judith Walkowitz notes, the 'sexual scandals unfolding' after his death left many worthy Victorians 'horrified' at the thought of their being tainted by any association with 'Hintonianism'.[15] Not surprisingly, then, the adult Henrietta makes only oblique references to this spellbinding but rather controversial character. However, as Seth Koven observes, she 'must have been aware of the extremely close ties of marriage and intellectual disciplineship binding her beloved teachers' to Hinton.[16] Equally, she cannot have failed to assimilate – consciously or otherwise – his commingling of sensual and intellectual pleasures in vocational work. After all, Henrietta's diary entries reveal how any confusing emotions sparked by Carrie Haddon's influence were swiftly sublimated into the passions and pleasures of her commitment to her own education and teaching the Dover orphans.

The orphanage school founded by the Haddon sisters was run on the lines of the Ragged School movement that began in London in the 1840s. As the name indicates, these schools specifically targeted 'raggedly-clothed' street urchins who marauded through the East End of the city. Ambivalence has been shown by 20th-century historians regarding the motives underlying the establishment of such institutions. Thomas E. Jordan concedes that inasmuch as 'Ragged Schools addressed a class below the poor … they were an inspired example of voluntarianism'. However, he also condemns the 'shallowness and self-serving nature' of certain establishments – notably, church-run schools whose relentless programmes of religious instruction did little to edify street children's hearts or minds.[17] These schools also had their contemporary critics. Many social commentators – notably Charles Dickens – recognised the inappropriateness of texts used to educate these children. Much scorn was poured on the 'ludicrous pretence' that childhood was a time of 'innocence and fun': a pretence that would, at best, bewilder and, at worst, infuriate children for whom life was anything but.

Equally, others argued that the moral content embedded in the elaborate language used in more earnest texts would be lost on children who communicated through a vibrant street language of their own.[18]

The earliest Ragged Schools were usually located in the seediest and most run-down areas, which were often saturated with crime, violence and prostitution. They had little in the way of teaching materials and were chronically under-financed. According to Dickens, who modelled his fictional waifs and strays on the wretched inmates of Ragged Schools, their teachers were both 'narrow-minded and odd' and not properly trained.[19] The schools' original purpose was to stem the tide of crimes perpetrated by children who rampaged through the urban streets in a fashion that the middle-class Victorian imagination associated with a licentious freedom.[20] Gradually, the moral panics relating to childhood disorder and disobedience subsided, and by the time the Haddon sisters opened their orphanage school teaching methods had become more enlightened. One reason for this was that the shift towards more sympathetic representations of these children in both fiction and social commentary of the period had encouraged 'good-hearted men and women' to volunteer to teach a variety of subjects. Dickens' sentimentalist portrayals of street ragamuffins in novels such as *Oliver Twist* had helped in part to reshape public perceptions of these children. However, as Steedman notes, 'the veritable explosion of information' about childhood psychological, emotional and physical development from the mid-19th century onwards prompted more professional efforts to address the issues underlying juvenile crime.[21]

As Ragged Schools gradually became more professionally recognised, it was acknowledged that qualified teachers, improved premises and a wider range of curricula materials were needed. Thus, instead of – or, at least, in addition to – what Dickens called the 'viciousness' and 'irrelevance' of 'catechisms' and 'creeds', children began to receive instruction in reading, handwriting and arithmetic. Having grasped these skills, older children would be taught industrial and domestic skills in order that they might 'earn an honest living'. As well as having access to this widening range of activities, regular attenders were rewarded with food, clothing and shelter.[22] Such a curriculum betrays much about what middle-class philanthropists deemed appropriate for children of the urban underclass and, as will be discussed later, the recipients of such assistance were by no means uniformly grateful for such interventions. There is no doubt, however, that the motivations underpinning the foundation of the Haddon sisters' orphanage school were well intentioned. As in London, Dover's poorer quarters were overrun with grubby, disruptive and neglected children whose survival was contingent upon foraging and scuffling through its streets and derelict buildings. Rather than contain the children in one of these decrepit hovels, the Haddons located their orphanage school in Ewell, a semi-rural district on the outskirts of Dover. Here, they reasoned, the children would be distanced from the sordid and bawdy distractions of the town centre at the same time as benefiting from the fresh sea breezes and country surroundings. It is likely that their approach to social reform inspired Henrietta's passionate belief that 'love and friendship', rather than stern moral upbraiding, was the key to the awakening of 'the better self of a wrong doer'.[23]

Quite how the Dover orphans responded to the 'love', 'friendship' and ambient surroundings offered by the Haddon sisters and their protégées can only be conjectured. But for Henrietta, her first visit to the Dover Workhouse evermore alerted her 'ignorant mind to revolt against the social injustices made evident by boys, odorous of institutionalism, dulled to inanity'.[24] In turn, this suggests that the Haddon sisters' methods of teaching orphans via the animation, rather than the enervation, of their senses had a profound effect on Henrietta's subsequent approaches to education. Indeed, as a Whitechapel student was to comment several years later, Henrietta's own teaching was 'provocative rather than informative' and thus, 'whatever the theme, she was instructing us in life in all its aspects'.[25] However, 'provoking' rather than 'informing' the boisterous and streetwise senses of the Dover orphans would have been no mean feat – particularly for a 16-year-old girl whose former pampered and privileged existence had suspended her own mind in 'ignorance'. But perhaps there was something about the irreverence and vitality of these buoyant, if deeply unprepossessing, children with which the inherently rebellious Henrietta could identify. After all, they had resisted the prison of the workhouse and its repressive regime just as she was defying the stultifying traps of middle-class femininity set by her father and her aunt. It is also likely that the vibrancy of their language, the guile of their survival strategies and their means of dodging authority strongly appealed to Henrietta's own subversive streak. Finally, it is conceivable that her irrepressible sense of humour meant that she felt less threatened by the children's rowdiness and insubordination than most girls her age.

This is not to say that Henrietta could admit to the frisson of excitement generated by her vicarious involvement with the street life of the underclass – least of all to herself. Rather, her fervour was sublimated into further eulogising of her teachers' virtues into a copy book specially reserved for the purpose:

> I am going to write all my remembrances of pleasant things and pleasant thoughts – Miss Carrie's Bible Classes, Miss Haddon's little talks, Mr Ward's sermons, in fact anything and everything that I like and have thought about.[26]

Henrietta's emphasis on the 'pleasant' here suggests she was trying a little too hard: her express intention in writing this book was to gain the attention, affection and respect of Miss Carrie, who always gave encouragement when 'real thoughtfulness' was shown.[27] In Carrie Haddon, Henrietta may well have discerned ideals to which she would have *liked* to aspire but, in much the same way as the fiery and spirited heroine of Charlotte Brontë's *Jane Eyre*, she was often to fall short of these ideals. In Brontë's novel, Jane is enchanted by her schoolteacher, the 'very good' and 'very clever' Miss Temple, and tries hard to emulate her.[28] Indeed, it is this woman's capacity for a 'serenity … which precluded deviation into the ardent, the excited [and] the eager' which – to an extent – helps Jane to curb her own wilful streak.[29] However, once Miss Temple has left the school, Jane feels 'the stirring of old emotions', which urge her forward into a 'real world' in which 'a varied field of hopes and fears, of sensations and excitements, awaited those who had courage to go forth … amidst its perils'[30]. It is likely that Henrietta harboured similar yearnings for adventure, which she realised were not entirely compatible with the qualities of grace and goodness that radiated from Carrie Haddon. Thus, it is hardly surprising that Henrietta declared that she was 'haunted … ever since' by Carrie's farewell address to pupils leaving her school: 'Whatsoever things are pure, whatsoever things are lovely, whatsoever things are of good report, think on these things.' [31] At first glance, 'haunted' seems an odd way of recalling one who had such a profound impact on her adolescent self but perhaps, even at 17, Henrietta was sufficiently shrewd to discern that grace and goodness alone would not be enough to fuel her own burgeoning commitment to social reform.

Whilst at the Haddon sisters' school, Henrietta also learned to value the company of her peers. Indeed, the sisters were keen to promote friendship between the girls and always 'encouraged and respected' these relationships.[32] This was Henrietta's first opportunity to mix with girls of her own age and it appears to have sown the seeds of what became her lifelong respect for the attributes and achievements of women. As she was much later to elucidate, 'I like the female nature far better than the male nature and think women much more influential in the world than men'.[33] Once again, her experiences at school have their literary precedents in *Jane Eyre*. During Jane's eight years at Lowood School, she learns how to temper feistiness with self-discipline from the various female friendships she forged. The intensely spiritual Helen Burns suffused Jane with 'a controlling awe' whilst the 'witty and original' Mary Ann Wilson entertained her with 'racy and pungent gossip' at the same time as satisfying her 'curiosity' about worldlier matters.[34] Henrietta's own blend of intensity and youthful ebullience is suggested by her school friends, who recalled her as being a 'very clever girl, not at all interested in games but with a good sense of fun'.[35] In his discussion of 19th-century female friendship, Rod Edmond highlights the intensity of many of these relationships and argues that they were one of the very few 'emotional and behavioural' outlets for women and girls cloistered within a narrow domestic sphere:

> Women lived in a world inhabited by children and other women. It was a world of 'mutual validation' in which sharing was paramount and hostility and criticism discouraged. In such a world relations between women were close, devoted and long-lasting.[36]

In this context, Edmond is defending fictional friendships between women against the more prurient suppositions of certain critics who grope through Victorian literature in the hope of finding – or imagining – a homoerotic, or even pornographic, subtext. This is not, of course, to deny the deeply encoded sexual content to be found in some literature and poetry of the era. The point Edmond is making is simply that such emotional and – in certain cases – physical closeness between women was very much a 19th-century norm. This may well have been the case, but Edmond's arguments are underpinned by the assumption that *all* women and girls were confined within a domestic sphere. From this, he suggests that bonds between women were forged through shared experiences of puberty, menstruation, pregnancy, childbirth and menopause. No doubt women did confide in and support each other over such concerns: for example, it is implied in *Jane Eyre* that the 'shrewd and observant' Mary Ann elucidates the mysteries of menstruation and hormonal mood changes to the regularly hot-headed and impulsive Jane.[37] There is no doubt either that Henrietta and her friends would have exchanged similar information: indeed, in an era when such topics were rarely acknowledged, such intimacies were vital to coming to terms with young womanhood.

However, friendship between women and girls extends beyond the sharing and comparing of female biological experiences; the intellectual pleasures of such relationships tend to be subordinated in Edmond's account – intellectual pleasures that may have encouraged young girls to question the roles forged for them in middle-class Victorian society and seek a more fulfilling alternative. Indeed, Martha Vicinus notes how the 'new education' for young women was intended to cultivate a 'modern individuality' through which young girls were 'encouraged to take responsibility for [their] actions' as well as develop personal intimacy through intense friendships.[38] Having observed the self-seeking and competitive undercurrents of business and social relationships between men, perhaps the Haddon sisters wanted to promote an alternative spirit of co-operation among their young charges before they ventured into the public sphere of work for which they were being prepared. Equally, it is easy to underestimate the petty quarrels and rivalries which would have festered alongside the cloying intimacies forged within narrow social and domestic circles. Apart from her simmering resentment of her eldest sister's authoritarian streak, Henrietta's girlhood diaries give little indication of such rivalries within her own home. However, by the age of 24, she was violently castigating the profligate lifestyles of the 'heartless rich' and their trivial preoccupations.[39] And, later in life, she spat out her contempt for the shallow pleasures enjoyed by the rich upper classes and *arrivistes* alike: she raged against their 'racing, hunting, shooting, fishing, yachting, card-playing, sun-seeking, play-going, dancing and eating', along with their penchant for displaying wealth through ostentatious clothing or possessions.[40] This enduring disdain for profligate and sensational pastimes surely reveals much about Henrietta's uncomfortable recognition that she herself had spent the first 16 years of her life influenced by many of these same idle pleasures. Not surprisingly, there are only veiled references to the privileges of this existence, but it is not difficult to imagine the extravagances and indulgences which enlivened the social lives of upper-middle-class Victorians. Dinner parties would have been sumptuous occasions with bountiful supplies of exotic foodstuffs served with the finest burgundies or clarets and jewel-coloured liqueurs, all set amidst a dazzling array of silver, crystal and bone china arranged on crisp white linen. The mingled hues and aromas of such dishes as the piquant *Crevettes à l'Indienne* and the pungent *Salmis de Canards Sauvages* alongside glistening *Gelée Dorées* and the dark succulence of *Compote de Cerises* would – at the very least – have appealed to the young Henrietta's fascination with colour, light and texture. Similarly, the female guests' gowns and jewellery would have provided a spectacle of vibrant colour: shades of crimson, flame and gold dominated fashion in the 1850s and '60s as did the crinoline-style dresses inspired by the feats of engineering displayed in the Great Exhibition of 1851.[41]

As a child, however, Henrietta was largely a spectator rather than a participant in these splendid affairs and, no matter how beguiling the sense of occasion, it is likely that she was sufficiently astute to pick up nuances of the insecurities, spite and jealousies that underlay these glittering soirées. It is also likely, of course, that the sheer futility of social climbing and competitiveness was anathema to the puritan streak she had absorbed – however unconsciously – from her Aunt Sophey. These puritan leanings may have been reinforced by the fiction of the period. In *Dombey and Son*, Dickens' magnificent, if grotesque, creation, the aristocratic and impoverished Mrs Skewton shamelessly inveigles her way into nouveau riche circles in order to secure her proud and insouciant daughter a place in the marriage market. Meanwhile, Brontë's principled young heroine, Jane, is aghast at the brazen strategies employed by the scheming Blanche Ingram as she attempts to ensnare the enigmatic Mr Rochester at one of his more lavish house parties. Similarly, the novels of authors such as George Eliot, Elizabeth Gaskell and William Makepeace Thackeray all bristle with acutely observed instances of the hypocrisy, backbiting and duplicity simmering beneath the veneer of polite Victorian society. No doubt there were some squabbles and rivalries amongst the girls at the Haddons' school too, particularly between pupils vying for Carrie Haddon's approval, but it did at least provide a space away from the claustrophobic, if privileged, homes of middle-class daughters. Within this space, girls were encouraged to forge identities and aspirations in an atmosphere where they were valued not so much for their looks and feminine charms as they were for independence of thought, commitment to justice and loftiness of ideals. Above all, the Haddon sisters wanted their pupils to leave the school with a real sense of social purpose, combined with the self-confidence to believe that they could help to address the issues which divided Victorian England into 'two nations'. Thus, fired up with a fervent sense of purpose, Henrietta was to inscribe her school-leaver's copybook with Thomas Carlyle's declaration that 'Blessed is he who has found his work; let him ask no other blessedness'.[42] So, in just one year, she had made the transition from a pretty, pampered and somewhat petulant child to an earnest young woman brimming over with the urgent desire to address the social inequities to which she had been exposed during her time in Dover.

In comparison to the curriculum taught in typical Victorian girls' schools, the Haddon sisters' approach to education was indeed radical. It is worth remembering that even in the 1860s the alleged inferiority of the female sex was constantly reinforced from a number of viewpoints to justify women's subordinate status in the family and society,. One of the most enduringly persuasive of these arguments was rooted in biological determinism. One mid-19th-century proponent of this view, for example, reasoned that as women's head and brain sizes were smaller than those of men, it 'followed' that women's reasoning abilities would be limited, to say the least:

> It is evident that the man, possessing reasoning faculties, muscular power, and courage to employ it, is qualified for being a protector: the woman, being little capable of reasoning, feeble and timid, requires protection. Under such circumstances, the man naturally governs: the woman as naturally obeys.[43]

Needless to say, arguments such as these were deployed to oppose women's participation in higher education. Indeed, June Purvis' research reveals that, in 1871, the right-wing *Saturday Review* went so far as to suggest that competing with men in universities would 'further unsex' women, who were already allegedly prone to emotional and physical fragility by dint of their biological differences from men.[44] The writer is here drawing on the premises held by Herbert Spencer in his *Principles of Biology*. According to Spencer, 'overtaxing a woman's brain with intellectual work might unfit her for maternity and make her less fertile'.[45] Others made much of how participation in intellectually challenging areas of study could provoke mental instability and hysteria in women pushed beyond their 'natural' limitations.[46] The fact that so many middle-class women succumbed to mental illness precisely because their personal lives were so mind-numbingly tedious was conveniently overlooked.[47] As later chapters will show, Henrietta Barnett herself often succumbed to bouts of melancholy that were no doubt triggered by her frustration at society's limitations, which constantly curbed her efforts at social reform.

These proclamations about women's inferiority to men and their 'natural' place in the home also preoccupied Victorian novelists, artists and poets – hence the proliferation of variously sweet-natured, submissive or self-sacrificing angels in literature and art. Emblematic of the latter is George Elgar Hicks's 1863 'Woman's Mission' series of paintings in which women are shown to nurture their children, support their husbands and dispense comfort to the aged and infirm. A stern warning for women who deviated from this worthy existence was embodied in Augustus Leopold Egg's 1858 triptych, 'Past and Present', which tracks an adulterous woman's rapid descent from the decorum of a middle-class drawing room to the fetid depths of a seedy railway arch. Others, too, turned their attention to the 'threats' posed by educated women and male representations of these range from the ambivalent to the downright hostile.[48] Tennyson's 'The Princess' (1847) is a lengthy deliberation on the controversial idea of an exclusively female university. Tennyson is sympathetic to the feminist aspirations of Ida, the heroine of the poem, but these ideals are ultimately subsumed as Ida re-channels her 'womanly' energies into the care of the sick and wounded after her university is converted into a hospital.[49] Equally, Wilkie Collins is sympathetic in his depiction of Marion, the intelligent and level-headed older sister in his sensationalist novel, *The Woman in White* (1860). However, she is constructed as more 'masculine' than 'feminine'. In contrast to the ethereal beauty of fair-haired and delicate Lucy, her highly-wrought sister, Marion has a 'large, firm, masculine mouth and jaw; prominent, piercing, resolute brown eyes and thick, coal-black hair. Moreover, she is 'altogether wanting in those feminine attractions of gentleness and pliability'.[50] And of course, female novelists were all too aware of the suspicion and derision generated by intellectual women. For example, George Eliot is renowned for her sensitive, intelligent *and* attractive heroines but they are frequently 'punished' for these attributes. For predictably, the London literati sniggered at the dazzlingly intellectual George Eliot's own physical shortcomings: rumour had it that Eliot's 40-year-old bridegroom, John Cross, attempted to commit suicide rather than consummate his marriage to the 60-year-old Eliot.[51] Still later in the 19th century when, despite this opposition, more and more women were becoming educated, male representation became even more hostile. George Gissing's portrayals of intelligent women are perhaps the most vitriolic. They are shown as pretentious and physically repulsive viragos who channel their unfulfilled sexual desires into cultural pursuits funded by their fathers. Nor are they above stooping to the most duplicitous and cunning of means when thwarted in love by their more demure and attractive counterparts.[52]

Given such a cultural climate, the Haddon sisters' efforts to encourage their pupils' independence and resourcefulness went very much against the grain of popular opinion. Yet they could also be seen as deeply conservative. After all, their girls may have been given the opportunity to supplement their academic studies with 'real' work beyond the confines of the schoolroom, but they were still expected to show the traditional middle-class feminine virtues of self-denial, patience, tolerance and understanding. And, above all, they were expected to be 'ladylike'. Clues to the ethos underpinning the Haddon sisters' curriculum can be gleaned from Henrietta's first published work, written when she was 23 years old. In this somewhat self-righteous tome, she declares that 'every young girl will know the kind of thoughts she ought to drive away, and the sort of ideas on which her mind should dwell' and she is extremely censorious about 'the foolish, silly ways' in which 'thoughtless girls "carry on" with boys'. Elsewhere, she berates the 'selfishness' of young women guilty of 'staying out late' and the vulgarity of 'eating in the street' or 'making a noise'.[53] Rather — and here she draws heavily on John Ruskin's *Of Queens' Gardens* (1865) — she asserts that 'the good and the happiness of the family, and through the family, that of the nation' is contingent upon women's 'fairy-like' power to 'turn the house into a home'.[54] Later, she further proclaims that such alchemy demands 'much patience, bravery, foresight, and endurance' combined with 'hopefulness, tenderness and above all, unselfishness'. Such sanctimonious exhortations would undoubtedly have irritated her feminist contemporaries who would have seen this as her collusion with the patriarchal principles on which Victorian society was founded. From a Marxist perspective, it reads like the worst possible type of condescending philanthropy, which attempted to impose middle-class values on working-class people struggling to survive in the direst of circumstances. No matter how queasily we may respond to Henrietta's model of femininity, however, it is worth remembering that it was formed from the same teachings that had caused Henrietta to reflect upon – and reject – the fripperies of middle-class life. Perhaps, too, she acknowledged how perilously close she had veered towards selfishness and impatience and was all the more censorious for that. When she wrote this particular book, Henrietta had certainly witnessed some harrowing examples of poverty, but she clearly lacked the insight to see any causes beyond negligent parenting and promiscuity. Moreover, as the following chapters will show, Henrietta found it almost impossible to measure up to this blueprint of femininity herself. Rather, she was to spend the rest of her life circumventing social expectations of women whilst appearing respectable in the eyes of others. Finally, whatever the shortcomings of the education she received, Henrietta was at least enabled to build up the inner resources necessary to live a life very different from that envisioned by her father or Aunt Sophey.

III

⊸•⊱

London Calling

Philanthropy and Social Work in Marylebone

5 September 1869. So much has happened since I last wrote in this little book and I hardly like to write again. Our Daddy has left us (28 June 1869) after his long and weary illness. At first this seemed very, very dreadful, but now, thank God it has allowed us to see in part the reason for it. I dread the future so dull, dreary and weary. Moreover, the money seems to diminish. £30,000 gone already and our legacies not realised.[1]

In keeping with the financial conventions of the times, Alexander Rowland had left his business interests to his eldest son and another £45,000 to be divided amongst his other seven children, Sophey and another unmarried sister, Elizabeth. However, there would have been debts and duties to be settled from this sum which would have diminished the £5,000 each which these beneficiaries expected to receive.[2] Remaining amongst the opulence at Champion Hall was not an option either. In September 1869 – about the time that Henrietta poured these despairing entries in her diary – she, along with Alice, Fanny, Sophey and Mary Moore moved into what she called a 'very modest house' in Westbourne Terrace, Bayswater, London.[3] As Micky Watkins notes, this property seems, from a 21st-century perspective, to be an 'elegant white stucco bow-fronted terrace house, but by comparison with Champion Hall, it was a sad comedown'.[4] As much as anything else, the suburb of Bayswater was somewhat down on its luck. Until the middle of the 19th century, it had been a prosperous district featuring 'detached family residences, stately gentlemen's residences and villas with large gardens', which appealed to the 'upper and middle-classes'.[5] It also had a certain metropolitan charm, conveyed by the 'long array of magnificent and well-stocked shops' opposite Kensington Gardens; the 'most favoured residential' location was characterised by 'shrubbed flower borders and the open views of forest scenery'.[6] Yet by 1863 Bayswater was beginning to provoke the disdain of suburban critics:

> We cannot omit to remark the lamentable want of taste displayed in the outskirting suburbs of London. We only have to name Bayswater, Norwood [...] and some other suburbs in proof. Instead of detached or semi-detached villas [...] between which glimpses of country, light and air could have been obtained, we have barbarously-stuccoed streets and terraces, of most contemptible architecture, stereotyped *ad infinitum.*[7]

Henrietta's profound desolation at the loss of her father and the concomitant change to her lifestyle was to linger until the following January. On the 7th of that month, she made a languid diary entry recording that she was 'very, very miserable and sadly tired'.[8] Clearly, she was still grieving for her much-loved father, but she was also probably bored rigid. After all, it was only a short time since her passion for involvement in social reform had been fired by her brief experience of education and, instead of finding an outlet for all these energies, she was cooped up in a mediocre suburb with Fanny, Sophey and Mary. There is no record of this forlorn autumn and winter, but it was to trigger the first of many serious bouts of melancholy that were to descend on Henrietta throughout her life. According to Victorian codes of behaviour they would have been in deep mourning for at least one year after the loss of such a close relative. This involved dressing in black garments unrelieved by any ornamentation, save for the jet jewellery that, for the Victorians, was redolent with images of death and grieving. In addition, the windows of their (comparatively) poky terraced home would have been shrouded in heavy black drapes. This would have made the rooms almost unbearably gloomy and claustrophobic for a young girl whose very spirit depended upon the air, light, colour and space which had sustained her throughout her childhood and adolescence. Indeed, a few years later Henrietta was to rail against Victorian preoccupation with mourning: its 'dramatic displays of grief', 'undue thoughts about coffins, hearses and horses' and the 'fussy preparations' about 'black' and 'crape'.[9] Finally, to make matters worse, her sister Alice was away studying for much of the time. But the very next day after Henrietta had wearily confided her misery to her diary, Alice returned. Instantly, her younger sister felt ' gooder [*sic*] and happier'. And after a couple of days, she wrote that the scales had fallen from her eyes and she 'saw God in part, how he worked with [her]'.[10] This declaration has all the markings of a religious conversion and Henrietta was certainly drawing on her Christian upbringing to make some sense of her life.

It is also likely, however, that Alice, troubled by the lethargic despair of one who had formerly bubbled over with ebullience, sought the advice of her friend and soon-to-be husband, Ernest Hart, the Jewish surgeon and editor of the *British Medical Journal*. In addition to these commitments, Hart was also involved in a number of social reform initiatives. More enlightened than most male doctors of the era, who would have attributed Henrietta's condition to inherent feminine frailty, Hart must have recognised that this listless young woman desperately needed an outlet for all her energies. Hart was acquainted with Octavia Hill, a co-founder of the Charity Organisation Society based in Marylebone, North West London. So, within the week, Henrietta was to begin voluntary missionary work with Octavia, who she soon declared to be the 'heroine of [her] life'.[11] As Ellen Ross has observed, such work had the potential to add 'zest and romance' to the otherwise 'staid' lives of young middle-class women trapped in the chains of Victorian gentility.[12]

The Charity Organisation Society (COS) had evolved as a response to what were seen as the 'seven curses of London': neglected children, thieves, beggars, fallen women, drunkenness, gambling and, above all, waste of charity:[13]

> The COS was born in an atmosphere of panic, which was exacerbated by the frequent abuses and corruption within the vestries and the disorder of private almsgiving. It operated from a standpoint of defensiveness, and from a deep fear that pauperism would get wildly out of control. The COS may have shared Christian concern and involved a number of churchmen, but it had little in common with Christian Socialism or the clergy in general, who were largely unpersuaded by COS claims.[14]

Its main objective was to be a *referral* rather than a *distributive* association. District Visitors – usually middle-class women of all ages – were appointed to visit homes and obtain details about the individual circumstances of those applying for financial relief. They would then decide who was entitled to benefits.[15] Not surprisingly, it was considered by many to be over-rigid, judgmental and deeply moralistic. Clues to the underlying ethos of the COS can be gathered from its full and former title, the Society for Organizing Charitable Relief and Repressing Mendicity.[16] Octavia was staunchly opposed to the indiscriminate distribution of money to the poor, arguing that it was 'injurious to their characters'.[17] Rather, she argued that they should be given the opportunity to elevate themselves from pauperism by gaining regular employment, even if the jobs had to be artificially created. That way, she reasoned, the 'deserving' poor would benefit whilst their workshy counterparts would be left to languish in their alcohol-soaked squalor. Nor was this work distributed indiscriminately: Octavia would only be willing to provide employment – carpentering, decorating and portering for men; washing, tailoring and upholstery for women – if they could justify their need for it.[18] This had been her preferred method of charity work for some years. When a District Worker herself, Octavia had little patience with conventional philanthropic acts of largesse, such as distributing parcels of food, sums of money or bundles of fuel; rather, she advocated self-help as the only viable means of gaining self-respect and self-sufficiency. It hardly needs stating that such inflexible views generated a great deal of resentment and rancour from her clients as well as sustained denunciation from her broader-minded colleagues. Octavia was not totally devoid of human feeling, however. Early on in her career, she had been immensely touched by the actions of a 'bright, quick child of 11' and her valiant efforts to clean the 'dirty faces' of the four younger brothers and sisters left in her care.[19] Perhaps observations such as this epitomised for her the determination of some to transcend the wretchedness of their circumstances. Nor was she entirely devoid of sympathy from others: several illustrious Victorians – amongst them John Ruskin and George Eliot – gave both moral blessing and financial support to her unconventional approach to social reform.[20]

On 19 January 1869, Octavia's newest volunteer turned up at St Mary's Relief Committee in Marylebone. Instantly, she was struck by Henrietta whom she perceived as brimming over with 'high aspirations … child-like reverence and energy'.[21] In turn, Henrietta worshipped the woman who gave her the opportunity to apply her fervent commitment to social reform. So, for a while at least, Octavia was fundamental in the reshaping of her young protégée's attitudes towards the poor and ways in which they could be assisted. And she could be highly persuasive; in an address to the Social Science Association in 1869, she had proclaimed that:

> Alleviation of distress may be systematically arranged by a society; but I am satisfied that, without strong personal influence, no radical cure of those who have fallen low can be effected … if we are to place our people in permanently self-supporting positions, it will depend on the various courses of action suitable to various people and circumstances, the ground of which can be perceived only by sweet subtle human sympathy, and the power of human love … By knowledge of character more is meant than whether a man is a drunkard or a woman is dishonest; it means knowledge of the passions, hopes and history of people; where temptation will touch them, what is the little scheme they have made of their own lives, or would make, if they had encouragement; what training long-

past phases of their lives may have afforded; how to move, touch, teach them. Our memories and our hopes are more truly factors of our lives than we often remember.[22]

Such sentiments – especially that powerful entreaty to engage closely with the minutiae of the 'passions, hopes and history' of Marylebone's underclass – would have been heady and inspiring stuff to a young woman already fired by her experiences of working with the Dover orphans. This new role as District Worker would have given her involvement well beyond a mere dalliance with social reform, as well as some detachment from the pseudo-philanthropy dispensed by others to salve their consciences, epitomised for Henrietta by those who 'flung coppers to beggars and complained that their presence spoiled the pleasure of their walks'.[23] It must also have given her the sense of belonging she had lacked since the death of her father.

Quite how the poor of Marylebone – 'deserving' or otherwise – responded to the sympathy of young, idealistic and inexperienced workers like Henrietta is not recorded in detail. However, the observations of journalists and social commentators of the period – some more scrupulous than others – give some insight into the ways in which these interventions were received. James Greenwood, for instance, a journalist whose main objective was to amuse the middle classes with tales of 'low-life' London, revealed spirited resistance in a young working-class woman – possibly a prostitute – who refused the opportunity to work as a servant in a 'respectable' family. With proud defiance she asserted that she was 'above that poor scum that mustn't wear a feather or a ribbon' and further declared that she valued 'liberty' over 'respectability'.[24] More recently, social historians have explored 'the well-worn path leading from the well-off West End and suburban districts *toward* the slums': one trodden first by church lay workers spreading Christian hope and salvation and later by middle- and upper-class women dispensing fuel, food and clothes. By the 1870s, this procession of worthies had been supplanted by more organised interventions from schoolteachers, school-based social workers, employment trainers and of course, District Visitors from the COS.[25] Such figures earned the greatest contempt from Marxist historians such as E.P. Thompson, who – with some justification – regarded their efforts as a blatant form of social control.[26] Others are more measured: Thomas Jordan acknowledges the judgmental and moralistic basis of organised philanthropy but argues that 'however condescending their approaches' they did at least attempt to address social problems that were largely ignored by the government.[27] Ellen Ross discovered similar ambivalence in both dispensers and recipients of these charitable endeavours:

> The visitors had trouble penetrating the mothers' cautious reserve, their 'provoking diffidence' … But the ladies were just as guilty of such reserve. They seldom told their own stories; when they spoke it was to ask questions, offer advice, give instructions, provide sympathy or deliver threats. Maud Pember Reeves, describing the early work of her Fabian Women's Group with a number of mothers in Kennington … recalled the stiff courtesy of the working-class women, who readied themselves to wait out the lectures they expected.[28]

Not all these exchanges were stiffened by such awkwardness, however. Ellen Chase, a rent-collector in South East London, built up warm relationships with the women she met and learned much about the threads of 'quarrels, romance and violence' woven into their everyday experiences. Other charity workers were humbled by the 'uncomplaining acceptance' of 'neglect and abuse' endured by the women of 'outcast London': an acceptance which made them feel 'ashamed' at their 'own dissatisfaction with their 'far easier' lives. A few, of course, were less than compassionate. Some griped that they were shown insufficient deference by their clients and one 'uniquely uncharitable' worker came to the 'harsh' conclusion that working-class poverty 'was not a result of low wages but of the workers' failings in thrift, foresight and planning'[29].

Clearly, these middle-class responses to working-class attitudes and values overlooked the sheer tenacity which characterised much of life in the slums. To the middle-class missionary workers, the women they sought to help were either 'feckless' or 'pathetic' figures: raucous slatterns or careworn, downtrodden drudges who lacked the most basic skills in household economy, cookery and parenting. No doubt some women did fall into these categories: there were as many violent, abusive and hard-drinking women as there were wives terrorised by brutal husbands. But these missionaries' inability to see beneath the surface grime and squalor of slum life meant that they remained oblivious to the resourcefulness with which countless other women fed and disciplined their families and maintained their homes. As well as pestering charities for furniture, cooking utensils, food and cash, they would find odd jobs for their older children, cajole drunken and workshy husbands out of their idleness, share with or scrounge from one another, rehash leftovers into new dishes and, towards the end of the week, make frequent trips to the pawnshop. And, of course, there was always the tallyman, from whom goods could be purchased 'on tick'. The idealistic young Henrietta was horrified by what she saw as the 'nasty and indelicate' practice of pawning, which meant subjecting 'a family's clothing' to the 'ugly company of dirt and disease' that she saw as infecting the very essence of pawnshops.[30] And it must be said that there was medical evidence to implicate the role of body lice in the spread of virulent infections such as typhoid and typhus.[31] The tallyman didn't meet with her approval either. She regarded the 'fault of improvidence' in such dealings as being further compounded by 'the sin of deceit' involved in keeping these transactions secret from husbands.[32] Nor was she impressed with working-class diets. This became abundantly clear in her first publication based on her observations during her first few years working with Octavia Hill. What she probably didn't fully comprehend at that time was the extent of the pride and independence that fuelled these working-class practices. Working-class women knew perfectly well that it would be cheaper to feed their families on meals based on oatmeal, macaroni, gruel and pease pudding, but all these dishes signified dependence and degradation.[33] In addition, many of the so-called cheap and nutritious dishes recommended by middle-class charity workers would have required baking, stewing or roasting, processes that demanded much more fuel than boiling, frying or grilling. In consequence, working-class pantries in the 19th century were stocked with kippers, chops, saveloys, pickles, pot herbs, suet, potatoes, bread and sugar rather than dairy produce, vegetables, cereals and pulses. Of these, meat was most prized by working-class mothers. Without it, they believed their children would fail to thrive. They also tried to make staple foods like bread more appetising by spreading it with the jam, margarine and golden syrup made available by the industrial food processing that evolved during the 1870s.

Henrietta would have noticed the slum children gorging on these sweet and sticky delights which were washed down with sugary tea – another commodity which became much cheaper during the 1860s and '70s. As Ellen Ross points out, products from colonised nations were making it possible for families on the most meagre of budgets to feel well-nourished.[34] Henrietta would also have witnessed the popularity of food stalls offering piping-hot ready-cooked fare: the Victorian equivalent of our 'food to go'. On these, aromatic smoked and cured fish, spicy sausages and rich meat pies oozing gravy would be hawked alongside famed Cockney delicacies such as jellied eels, brawn, sheep's head, pickled trotters and tripe. For the middle-class and thrifty Henrietta, this working-class extravagance was reprehensible. In *The Making of the Home* – and, no doubt, during her visits to the homes of the London poor – she extolled the virtues of 'plain but wholesome food' such as tripe stew and stewed cow heel. Even 'bones which seem only fit for the dog', she opined, contained 'meaty nutriments for soup' and she positively glowed with admiration for one cook who allegedly used 'every scrap of bone … bacon parings and egg shells' to make soups and stock. And she included recipes for such culinary delights as 'rice pie' – a gluey compound of rice, oatmeal, bacon bits and onions – or (for those teetering over the poverty line) 'bread pudding', an unprepossessing amalgam of stale crusts, herbs and onions.[35] As well as appearing oblivious to the blandness of such a diet for those craving piquancy and diversity of texture in their food, the sheer practicalities of preparing the suggested food did not occur to the earnest young social worker. For a start, working-class kitchens were frequently unusable: gas supplies – for those who had access to that comparative luxury – were erratic and coal ranges were notoriously troublesome. Kitchens were also dark, cramped and hazardous: pans of boiling stock would have posed a particular danger to small children clamouring for their mothers' attention during cooking. To compound the problems, the kitchens in tenement houses were often shared and on a different floor to a family's living quarters. This meant negotiating steep, dark and rickety staircases: tricky at the best of times, but downright lethal for women hampered by overbrimming utensils and toddlers scrambling at their ankles. If they could afford it, it's hardly surprising that these women stole a few moments' peace by placating their children with apples, sweets, cakes and biscuits – yet another practice that ignited Henrietta's disapproval.[36]

Also of concern to COS workers were the standards of personal and domestic hygiene in slum homes. To some extent, this concern was rooted in the scientific links made between dirt, disease and poverty during the 19th century.[37] As much as anything else, however, working-class dirt and disease were seen as 'moral' issues which middle-class lady visitors regarded as their mission to address. As a result, working-class mothers were variously cajoled and coerced into cleansing their homes by what must have seemed like philanthropic terrorists. Not only did they go butting into slum homes in order to issue their instructions, but they also returned to ensure that they had been carried out. To drive their point home, these lady visitors barraged slum-dwellers with health publications containing advice which ranged from the 'accusatory' to the 'downright unrealistic'.[38] Predictably, Henrietta saw fit to devote a whole chapter of her first book to matters of cleanliness within the home. Working-class women were berated for their slatternly ways and browbeaten into scrubbing, scouring and polishing their houses as well as boiling, rinsing, blueing and mangling their family's clothing.[39] In fact, grubby clothing seemed even more repugnant to Henrietta than the malodorous and grime-infested houses. As she put it, 'every girl with right and delicate feeling will shrink from the idea of the clothes she has worn next to her body' being contaminated by dirt and germs, especially if these garments have been 'seen and handled by strangers' in pawnshops.[40] Clearly, one of her concerns here was the spreading of diseases and skin infections, but she also seems to invest this sort of contamination with connotations of sexual impropriety from which the 'right and delicate' would (or should) recoil in horror. This betrays the middle-class notion linking not only disease, dirt and poverty but also promiscuity to outcast Londoners. Indeed, middle-class sensibilities were deeply troubled by the dishevelled appearance of the young girls who loitered around the streets of London. 'Brashness', it seems, was acceptable in boys but not in girls. Their lengths of 'foul matted hair, which looked as if [they] would defy sponge, brush or comb to purify it' seemed to evoke connotations of their wantonness as much as their 'broken and filthy boots' and ripped clothing.[41]

Such views were certainly shared by Octavia Hill. Henrietta embarked on her career as volunteer District Visitor steeped in piety, but she was soon to rebel against the inflexibility of her mentor's attitudes. Whilst still an inexperienced and 'inefficient rent-collector' she confronted Octavia with her tendency to compel their clients 'to attain *her* standards for them, instead of instead of *their* standards for themselves'. To illustrate her point, she cited the case of one of their tenants, whose 'standard [was] only getting drunk once a week instead of every day' and suggested that they build on that rather than forbid alcohol entirely. Needless to say, Octavia was not in the slightest impressed by Henrietta's logic and immediately 'scorned' such a notion. Not that this bothered her young trainee very much. Whilst she still held the upmost respect for Octavia's 'deep heart, steadfast mind and dauntless spirit' – perhaps qualities which she narcissistically recognised in herself – she had a shrewd awareness of the older woman's personal shortcomings.[42] According to Henrietta, Octavia had no sense of humour, was affronted by the mildest of jokes, and was addicted to a degree of self-denial that bordered on masochism:

> Somehow, personal poverty is a help to me. It keeps me more simple and energetic, and somewhat low and humble and hardy in the midst of a somewhat intoxicating power. It pleases me too, to have considerable difficulty and effort in my life, when what I do seems hard to the people – though they never know it.[43]

Unsurprisingly for one so charged, Octavia had no interest in her personal appearance whatsoever. Henrietta dismisses her taste in clothes as 'unnecessarily unbecoming' for one already disadvantaged by being 'small in stature with a long body and short legs'. She did have 'soft and abundant hair' but the beauty of this was diminished by twisting it into a severe bun at the back of her head. And only when she 'was made passionate by her earnestness' did her 'brown and very luminous eyes' sparkle with light and vitality.[44] In contrast, Henrietta was stunningly pretty: indeed, the defiant 'brown curls' which tumbled down her back, her sweetly rounded face and pewter-bright eyes attracted many admirers. She also had a sharp, witty and irreverent sense of humour.[45] But no amount of flirting or flattery would distract Henrietta from her commitment to the COS: 'Bother the men,' she grumbled in her diary in July 1870, 'why can't they let me do my work?'[46] Henrietta's heady mix of exuberance and earnestness must have been irresistible to men who shared her high ideals and aspirations. One, Walter Webb, was clearly enchanted by 'dear Yetta', whom he first met in 1866. He writes that, after this initial meeting, he frequently visited her, first in Sydenham and later in Bayswater. They also spent some time together in Guernsey where they were fellow

guests of mutual friends. During these ten brief days in the summer of 1871, they
went on 'many excursions' together during which they shared their enthusiasm for
ideas sparked by 19th-century writers. Walter was particularly struck by the quality of
literature which inspired the young and idealistic Henrietta:

> She gave me Carlyle's S & R [*Sartor Resartus* (1833-4)] to read … These were the
> high-class books she enjoyed – her character and demeanour were of the highest
> order and much impressed me. When she joined Octavia Hill, the early promise
> of her life was justified.[47]

Henrietta herself, however, remained impervious to Walter's admirations: at least,
there is no mention of him in her diaries. What these do reveal at this time is the
extent of passion and energy which she channelled firmly into her work. Reflecting
on all that happened during 1870, she mused on the 'overwhelming sense of awe
and responsibility' which suffused her 12 months' experience of charity work. Made
older and wiser by what seemed to her like a 'lifetime' of these events, she grew more
appreciative of the love and warmth radiating from those close to her. Sophey remained
'as cold as ice', but the 'love' of Mary Moore continued to 'grow and grow', and this
was much valued by Henrietta. She was also flattered by the friendship of Octavia,
whom she clearly idolised. In turn, Octavia had introduced Henrietta to a wide range
of influential Victorian figures including George Lewes, husband of George Eliot.[48]
No doubt these new friendships contributed to her development of a wider, and
more political, awareness. Deeply disturbed by the carnage of the Franco-Prussian
war, Henrietta decided to sell her rings to help the Prussian cause.[49] Above all this,
Henrietta's Christian faith remained steadfast:

> I begin this year with … rejoicing in all God's great goodness and love to me
> during the past year. He has taught me so much and led me so gently and tenderly,
> opened my heart, enlarged my capacities. What will be his will for me this year?
> Success in my work, health, travel, ideas – may – might I add love? God please
> grant Yetta these, if good for her.[50]

The rather wistful question that concludes this diary entry suggests that Henrietta was
not entirely oblivious to notions of romantic, as well as Christian, love. Interestingly, it
was written a month *after* she had met Samuel Barnett, the man who would eventually
become her husband. However, he doesn't feature in her diary until February 1872.
As her words suggest, Henrietta still yearned for the worldly adventure and intellectual
stimulation which she no doubt sensed would be snuffed out by romantic entanglement.
At the same time, she recognised her capacity for 'temptations many and strong' and
'begged God to keep her pure and good'.[51]

Throughout 1871, Henrietta continued her work in Marylebone. In April of that
year, she was entrusted with the responsibility for the relief district of Circus Street
in St Mary's parish. Thus, her 'work went on as usual – full of life and pleasure'.[52]
There were lighter moments, too. Henrietta, her entourage of sisters, nurse and Aunt
Sophey spent a 'delightful month' in Guernsey at a coastal retreat far from the grime,
squalor and responsibility of the COS. The delights of this vacation must have included
Henrietta's meetings with Walter, but these must remain enshrouded in mystery. What
she does record is that Sophey, now middle-aged, became ill during the holiday and,

in consequence, became 'more loveable'. Of course, this also suggests that Henrietta herself was becoming a little more tolerant of her aunt's foibles. It was also whilst the women were in Guernsey that Alice decided to become a doctor. Rather surprisingly – given her wholesale adoration of her older sister – Henrietta was somewhat dismissive of this decision. Not only was she 'disappointed' that such a career move would necessitate Alice giving up her painting but she was also concerned by the latter's 'lack of steadfastness'. As Henrietta puzzled to herself, 'Why should she change her work in life so often?'[53] But it was not long before she was to become afflicted with a similar restlessness herself. It was also in 1871 that Henrietta began to work more closely with a young curate, Samuel Barnett. They had first met at a party held at No 14, Nottingham Place, Marylebone to celebrate Octavia Hill's birthday on the 3 December 1870. The guests were a 'motley group' of Octavia's family, fellow philanthropists and 'artistic souls' who mingled with 'low, and often coarse' tenants. Henrietta had arrived early in order to fashion Octavia's 'beautiful' hair into a more flattering style than usual. After a year working for the COS, she still held Octavia in high esteem but was beginning to pick up on the older woman's social awkwardness. Octavia was frequently crippled by an aching shyness which she attempted to conceal by either an 'unattractively brusque manner' or the 'exaggerated cordiality' with which she greeted her guest tenants as they arrived at her party.[54] Even though she was more than twelve years younger than her hostess, Henrietta's recollections of this party suggest that she was perfectly at ease amongst this eclectic social and intellectual mix. And, what's more, she was singularly underwhelmed by 'the Curate' who was to be her companion at dinner: his lowly status caused her to dismiss him 'half contemptuously' as a mere 'member of that fraternity'. But Samuel Barnett's memories of their first meeting suggest that he was instantly smitten by the astute, witty and utterly beguiling 'child with brown curls down her back, handsome furs and a Tyrolese hat'. He also recalled Henrietta's frank admission that she privately considered the tenants to be 'painfully ugly, not in their clothes but their faces and figures'. Looking back over four decades later, Henrietta affects not to have any memories of making such damning observations but does concede that Samuel's company – despite his tendencies towards 'sententiousness' – must have enlivened their first evening together.[55]

Samuel Barnett had first become acquainted with Octavia Hill through his work with the COS following his appointment as curate of St Mary's, Bryanston Square in December 1867. He had just returned from a trip to America, which had been funded by the two years he spent teaching following his graduation from Wadham College, Oxford in 1865. In America, he was intensely moved by the aftershock of the recently ended Civil War, and this was to revolutionise his political attitudes. As he put it, 'born and nurtured in an atmosphere of Toryism, what I saw and heard there knocked all the Toryism out of me'.[56] And his first-hand observations of the social injustices and unrest which still divided America were to ignite a compassion for suffering along with a contempt for greed and self-indulgence that stayed with him throughout his life. Aged only 23 when he was appointed as curate, Samuel was a diffident and unassuming young man who struggled to articulate his values and beliefs in his sermons. Even his most diplomatic supporters conceded that there was 'a little want of art, on his part, of throwing himself into [his parishioners'] thoughts and translating them into his'. But more forthright were his future wife's comments on his delivery of sermons:

I was amongst those who found his sermons out of touch with life and 'difficult to follow', and I remember – long before our engagement – making a vigorous protest to him against wasting his opportunities of speaking to the people whose lives he knew so well, and of whose need for spiritual food he was aware.

According to Henrietta, Samuel accepted this criticism with a 'patient meekness' and a fumbling attempt to justify his 'line of thought'. This provoked an even more vehement retort from an indignant Henrietta, who left him in no doubt that the congregation would benefit much more from a minister who was prepared to engage with 'the line of thought which *they* were then considering and bring it to the test of Christ's standard'.[57] Such earnestness from this pretty, principled and petulant young COS worker probably made Samuel fall even more hopelessly in love with her, but for a while, at least, he kept his feelings under wraps and confined his communications with her to parochial matters. Gradually, however, his personal fascination with Henrietta began to seep into letters ostensibly relating to his professional concerns. In August 1871, he demonstrated his respect for her by expressing his 'perfect confidence' in her powers of diplomacy. He himself was clearly influenced by her opinion: he wrote that he was following her 'advice by making friends' outside his immediate circle.[58] But, by 31 December 1871, he was beginning to admit how much he looked forward to seeing her:

> I know that you are always at home on a Thursday and the knowledge does not add to the pleasure I usually find on those nights in Walmer Street … I hope that I shall see you on Friday; it seems an age since we met, long enough to make one fancy that you really did 'take the veil' as you threatened when I dropped you at that mysterious door. Thank you for your good wishes; I can use no words so fitting as yours. You have your own hopes for your future work, and I have my own hopes about that future which I wish to be realised … How the last hours of the year stir up one's memories and one's hopes![59]

Samuel may well have been daring to dream about a future with Henrietta, but the idea of Samuel as a suitor had certainly not occurred to Henrietta. Thus, she was 'surprised very much' to receive a written marriage proposal from the besotted young curate on 4 February 1872. This is perhaps an understatement written with the benefit of hindsight. Her diary entry of 22 February 1872 – just over two weeks *after* Samuel's proposal – merely mentions that during 1871, she 'got to know Mr Barnett' who was always willing to 'do [her] work' when she 'was ill'[61]. But in her biography of her late husband, Henrietta is much more vociferous about her initial reactions to Samuel's proposal. First, she had assumed that his interest in her was a purely professional commitment to the supervision of a young and inexperienced COS worker. Second, she makes it quite clear that Samuel was 'far removed from a girlish idea of a lover'. For a start, his 'bald head and shaggy beard' made him seem much older than his 27 years and his dress sense was, to say the least, questionable:

> He dressed very badly, generally obtaining his clothes by employing out-of-work tailors in the district. He always wore a tall silk hat which, as he had purchased by post, never fitted, and so was usually tilted over his forehead or rammed on at the back of his head. His umbrella was a byword, and he always bought his black cotton gloves two or three sizes too large. He approved of wearing a flannel shirt and united it to a white collar with a black silk ready-made tie.

The shortcomings in Samuel's appearance were further compounded by the uneasiness and diffidence of his manner which rendered him simultaneously 'shy and aggressive'. But what really rattled Henrietta was the 'frequent nervous laugh' – one of his many 'irritating mannerisms' – which he used to compensate for these defects. Nor was she impressed by his lack of chivalry: she had been speechless with indignation after one of Octavia Hill's tenants' parties when Samuel and a fellow curate bundled a drunken man into a carriage already occupied by Henrietta and other women. As far as she was concerned, this demonstrated an utter 'absence of the instinct of sex protection'.[62] In short, for the 20-year-old Henrietta, this bumbling, bashful and awkward young man was 'entirely different from any of the men [she] had known'. And more to the point, he was the antithesis of Henrietta's 'beau ideal of a man': the much-loved father for whom she was still grieving. Where the urbane, pleasure-seeking and witty Alexander Rowland had epitomised carefree generosity and extravagance, the self-denying and earnest Samuel was 'punctilious', 'servile' and, in the words of one of his acquaintances, 'plain and insignificant'. Also, quite apart from all Samuel's shortcomings, Henrietta had already made up her mind that 'marriage, with its obedience and ties' had no place in her life. However, she was sufficiently astute to realise that if she were to turn down Samuel outright, this would seriously compromise their work with Octavia Hill. So, in reply to his letter, she suggested that he give her six months in which to consider his offer of marriage.[63]

Henrietta 'said nothing to anybody' about Samuel's feelings towards her, but they clearly dominated her thoughts over the next few months. For his part, while Samuel complied with her request 'not to refer to the matter [of marriage] during that period', his ensuing letters to her were suffused with a poignant tenderness that leaves no doubt about the extent to which he adored her.[64] Reaching beyond her outward reserve, Samuel declared that she was the only person with whom he could talk freely and that he 'love[d]' her 'so much he would help her at any price'.[65] Yet these letters were not simply outpourings of affection: they also provide one side of the intense intellectual, emotional and spiritual dialogue developing between the two. Henrietta's letters from this period no longer exist – it is likely that she asked Samuel to burn them – but the content of his letters shows how much she was beginning to treat him as a confidant. Samuel's responses to her correspondence offer glimpses into the turbulent state of Henrietta's mind as she struggled to reconcile the myriad doubts, contradictions and anxieties besetting this period of her life, and he was probably one of the few allowed insights into the vulnerability usually masked by Henrietta's veneer of toughness and irreverence:

> I won't say that I was sorry not to see you this morning, I am more glad that you should take care of yourself than give me the chance of meeting you. You see, I want you to live even though you dislike the body and its requirements so much, and though I know that life cannot die with the body, I do not think my wish is wrong; after all, it is only through our bodies that we are able to be ourselves and know others.[66]

Quite why Henrietta 'disliked' the body and its needs so much can only be speculated. But the fact that Samuel saw the life-threatening potential of this distaste for all things corporeal suggests that she may have wilfully neglected herself by working too hard, having insufficient sleep and not eating properly. Such conduct smacks of religious fervour, self-abnegation and even self-flagellation, but it could also amount to a ferocious denial of bodily pleasures and desires. Equally, she may have been frustrated by the messiness and inconvenience of menstruation: it would have been indelicate for a woman of Henrietta's times and circumstances to make direct references to such an occurrence but her allusion to frequent bouts of nerve failure suggest a cyclical rhythm to these periods of uncertain health. Of course, these spells of sickness could be turned to her advantage – she certainly wouldn't have been the first Victorian woman to use illness as a means of resistance to unwelcome duties.[67] But, rather than dismiss Henrietta's bouts of doubt, melancholia and perplexity as womanly hysteria, Samuel took the time and trouble to empathise with her complexities and cares:

> I burnt your letter last night and today I feel as one who has had a troubled dream. I think of you in a great passion of sorrow, tried and worn by the forms of hopes and fears. The fancies of the night stand on the same level as the facts in the letter. Imagination is my master and surrounds you with sorrow just as it will. I see you so. Some voice says, 'Go and find her,' but another says, 'You are one more cause of sorrow, keep away.' I remain alone and the loneliness of unhelpfulness is worse than the loneliness of helpfulness. I do though believe in your future, for God will help you and make you happy and sure.[68]

The perceptive and sensitive Samuel recognised that unresolved grief for her father underpinned many of Henrietta's dilemmas: a grief she attempted to avoid by throwing herself headlong into her work Whilst he undoubtedly admired her commitment to social reform, he also discerned a certain martyrdom fuelling her energies – especially in her taking the responsibility for the violent, rough and abusive teenage attenders of a night school held in an 'underground cellar' sited in a 'terrible court'. These young people were almost impossible for a young and inexperienced woman to teach. In consequence, most lessons were disrupted by quarrels and fights which 'resulted in all the girls tearing out to watch or join in'. As far as Samuel was concerned, it was not 'useful' for Henrietta to 'devote [herself] so much to the night schools because [her] martyrdom [did] less for the cause of education than [her] life'.[69] Thus, for all his diffidence, he was probably one of the few who had the courage to alert Henrietta to her own shortcomings. Samuel was also aware that Henrietta's overdeveloped sense of responsibility in her professional life frequently spilled over into her personal life. The strain of these conflicting personal circumstances was the catalyst for Henrietta's decision to take a sabbatical from her work in London. At this particular point, she was beset with a 'sad heart and a puzzled mind'.[70] Not only was she desperately confused about her feelings for Samuel, she was also deeply troubled by the actions of a relative who appeared bent on 'wrecking her life by a mistaken judgement'.[71] Alice was in a similar turmoil. She had recently received a proposal of marriage from Ernest Hart, which she had rejected. The sisters' initial impulse was to submerge themselves in even more demanding charity work – this time, offering their services as nurses in the Franco-Prussian battlefields. By this time, Alice had already passed part of her medical examinations,[72] but in the event both were turned down on account of their youth. Instead, Sophey, Alice and Henrietta set off for an extended stay in Europe. It was Henrietta's intention to travel and study alone in Germany. This, she reasoned, would give her the mental space and physical distance necessary to reflect on the prioritising of 'life's duties in their true relation'.[73] Samuel was devastated and, for once, he gave real vent to the depth of his feelings:

I can't conceive how there can be another woman in the world who will so meet my wants and stimulate my powers. To bear the loss of you will strain my faith in God as no other loss has ever strained it … I suppose on Saturday we shall have one more quiet talk and then you will be out of sight for a time. I wonder if you ever guess what a storm of passionate words and acts a man has to hold back as he talks calmly to the one he loves?[74]

This was the closest Samuel ever came to declaring his sexual attraction to Henrietta. As she was later to comment, he would always shrink away 'from any talk, however pure or necessary, on sex questions'.[75]

At this point, Samuel was tortured by the thought of losing touch with Henrietta. Three days later, he plunged into an even greater despair:

I am driven to write to you, simply to write to you, for I do not know what to say. I can't tell you how wretched you made me. To plead with you is what I won't do; to argue with you is I know of no use. Just see how theories fly at the touch of truth. I tried to teach you that we make our own troubles, and here is a trouble which I dare not face. Let me, however, as I have all along, trust you. If you do think it best, think it in your own heart best, to decide against me before going away, do so.[76]

This impassioned outburst leaves little doubt about the extent of Henrietta's stubbornness and independence. She had obviously grown much closer to Samuel over the months since his proposal and was able to see beyond his outward servility and awkwardness. What continued to trouble her, however, was the idea that marriage would stifle her aspirations and ambitions for social reform. After all, the positive female role models she had met so far were all single, self-supporting and fulfilled in their chosen careers. Issues involved in 'The Woman Question' fuelled much debate in the 19th century and women's rights and responsibilities were frequently mooted by Henrietta and Samuel in their correspondence. Samuel must have made some ill-considered remark that 'men [were] only props for women to lean on' which provoked a 'richly deserved' tirade from Henrietta.[77] And to underscore her points, she reminded him of the following passage from *Aurora Leigh*:

You misconceive the question like a man,
Who sees a woman as the complement
Of his sex merely. You forget too much
That every creature, female as the male,
Stands single in responsible act and thought,
As also in birth and death. Whoever says
To a loyal woman, 'Love and work with me,'
Will get fair answers, if the work and love,
Being good themselves, are good for her – the best
She was born for.[78]

Henrietta would have identified closely with the dilemmas experienced by the fictional Aurora. Like Henrietta, Aurora was also torn between romantic attachment to her cousin, Romney, and her passionate commitment to art. Even more pertinently, Romney was, like Samuel, deeply committed to social reform. Whilst Aurora respected Romney's 'noble' vocation, it made her uneasy on two counts. First, she suspected that he 'wanted a helpmate, not … a wife to help [his] ends' and, second, she sensed more than a whiff of sanctimoniousness about this earnest young man.[79] In other words, Romney held about as much appeal for Aurora as the cold and ascetic St John Rivers generated for the heroine of another of Henrietta's favourite novels, *Jane Eyre*. Implicit in these fictional rejections is the notion that spirited and intelligent Victorian women wanted married relationships to be fulfilling intellectually, emotionally *and* sexually. Not for nothing did Charlotte Brontë associate the moody and sexy Rochester with fire, storms and energy, whilst St John Rivers was frozen into a landscape of stone, marble and snow.[80]

Of course, Henrietta could not admit to yearning for such frissons of desire, but she clearly wanted a relationship in which her needs would not be overshadowed by those of her partner. Samuel was quick to reassure her on this point. Spelling out how he depended upon herself and Octavia Hill for the 'inspiration to enable him to do his work', he went on to make clear the extent to which he disputed the notion that women were 'either playmates or despots':

> Have you ever noticed how much women's influence has been wanting in history? It is hard to mark the mighty work it doubtless has done because it works secretly, but in many great characters we may see the want. How many have been Lydgates, making women the companions of their holidays, how many have sought in them a 'semi-servile and feebly intelligent solicitude,' how many, like Voltaire, have looked to find in them the friendship they might have found in men?[81]

This was persuasive stuff from Samuel which appears quite radical for its time, but it also has shades of John Ruskin's contention that men and women were equal but different. In some respects, Ruskin's arguments did pose a significant challenge to dominant Victorian notions that women were inherently inferior to men. He maintained that women had special powers to bestow a benign influence on their partners and children: an influence which could usefully be applied to moral reform beyond the home. However, Ruskin still differentiated between power – a 'masculine' attribute – and its 'feminine' counterpart, influence.[82] And here, Samuel certainly appeared more concerned with women's influences on men rather than the former's independent achievements. Outwardly, Henrietta was pro-Ruskin herself, but her intense identification with the dilemmas explored in *Aurora Leigh* suggests that she would have resented forfeiting her active role as a single woman for the more passive 'influential' role deemed appropriate for married women. Samuel, however, was perceptive enough to realise this. Not for nothing did he conclude this letter by implying that above all, he valued Henrietta for her intelligence and friendship. Nevertheless, it was still another three months before Henrietta would make a decision regarding Samuel's proposal.

IV

The Personal and the Passionate

Women, Work and Companionate Relationships

The correspondence between Henrietta and Samuel continued as she travelled first through France with her aunt and Alice and, later, through Germany, where she spent a few weeks alone in Boppart, an ancient town nestling in German woodland overlooking the Rhine. Inspired by these 'quiet valleys' and the sublime beauty of the Rhine, Henrietta struggled 'to fight the devil and try to see what was right'.[1] Meanwhile, Samuel was aching with love, loss and uncertainty:

> Somehow I never do like talking to other people about myself, perhaps it is because I don't think the subject would interest them. I know I do talk about myself to my mother because I know she is interested in the smallest thing that concerns me. I can't think it is the same with you. Sometimes indeed I feel that your life is part of mine and that the love that binds me to you can never perish, but then your words of refusal come in, and to them feelings have to give place.[2]

But that didn't stop him from sharing all his musings with the young woman who had utterly bewitched him. It is these letters which reveal the extent to which Henrietta, despite her youth and inexperience, was causing Samuel to defend or re-evaluate his fundamental attitudes, values and beliefs. During her travels through France, Henrietta had been intensely moved by the evidence of carnage on the Franco-Prussian battlefields and described examples in graphic detail to Samuel. His response to this was that as he 'hated war' he would not 'study its details', let alone 'try to find interest in them'.[3] This would have irritated Henrietta. She was by no means pro-war herself but did at least have the courage to witness the atrocities suffered by the French soldiers at first hand. These experiences must also have made her even more frustrated that her youth and gender prevented her from nursing the casualties of war.

Henrietta and Alice also visited Paris for the first time. It was in this romantic city that Alice's 'heart went out' to Ernest Hart and she decided to return to England.[4] Henrietta stayed on in Paris and was enchanted by its architecture and art. Although she wouldn't have admitted it, it is likely that she was fascinated by the life, vibrancy and hedonism of Parisian society, too: its glittering department stores, chic cafés and ubiquitous casinos. Her accounts of these must have betrayed some of this fascination because Samuel made his disapproval of such decadence quite clear. He opined that Parisians, with their endless pursuit of 'pleasure', their rowdy habits and 'loudness' of taste 'wearied and disgusted him'. Moreover, he remained unmoved by Henrietta's enthusing over the wealth of art to be seen in Paris. Reminding her that he had 'no real taste for art', he justified this by arguing that men and women affected to 'understand and worship art' merely because middle-class society expected it of them. As for

French churches, these were 'tawdry' buildings adulterated by what Samuel saw as the ostentation of 'paint and gilt ornamentation'. These responses would have added to Henrietta's confusion. Quite apart from the admonitory tone of Samuel's words, they clearly implied that he would have thoroughly disapproved of her father's penchant for luxuries, worldly pleasures and art.[5] Whilst Henrietta had rejected most of the privileges and comforts of her childhood home, she would still have felt a profound loyalty towards her much-loved reprobate of a father.

But Samuel's disparaging comments about art and architecture also betray his insecurities about his class and background. Until the age of 16, Samuel and his younger brother, Francis, had been educated by a series of home tutors. As discussed in Chapter 1, this was highly unusual for Victorian boys, not least because it was assumed that a home education was emasculating and enervating. It also implied an unwholesome maternal influence: young boys were expected to learn self-reliance and stoicism from a very early age and, for these lessons to be learned effectively, the less contact with feminising influences the better. Mary Barnett and her boys, however, clearly adored one another. As Henrietta was later to put it:

> That [Samuel and his brother] were 'spoilt', as the word is used, there can be no doubt, if to have every desire lovingly gratified is to spoil human character. The extraordinary prominence given by both parents to nice food and fruit could not have been a wholesome influence, but this was of less importance than their yielding to 'the boys'' childish dislike of going to school.[6]

This suggests that Mary was all too willing to acquiesce to her sons' whims. Moreover, in Henrietta's eyes, matters were made even worse by their father's apparent indifference to the importance of public education. Dismissing Francis Barnett senior as 'mentally indolent', she held him mainly responsible for the 'nervousness' and 'hypochondriacal' tendencies which dogged Samuel throughout his life: 'feminine' weaknesses which she would have expected to be countered by a single-sex education.[7] For all her father's penchant for excessive pleasures, he had at least spent some time ensuring his children developed a love of art and literature. Underlying Henrietta's contempt for Samuel's parents' attitudes to education, however, was a kind of snobbery: only the *lower* middle classes would have been parsimonious enough to skimp on such a vital part of the maturing process. Conversely, those from Henrietta's social background, the affluent upper middle classes, regarded education as paramount – especially for their sons.

In the event, Samuel did eventually go to school. At the age of 16, he went to a weekly boarding school or 'crammer', as they were known. However, the cruelty of his fellow pupils – a dissolute bunch 'who had either been expelled from school or failed in one way or another' – left him deeply traumatised and, of course, the gentleness of his lower-middle-class upbringing had made him incapable of retaliation. Not only was he appalled by the attitudes of these boys to their tutors but he was also singled out for systematic abuse and bullying. Henrietta did not make explicit the details of this abuse but she does hint that his experiences there left him with numerous sexual anxieties.[8] As for Samuel, his observations and experiences of the school appear to have ignited within him a deep loathing of the privileged and profligate classes, to which most of his fellow pupils had belonged. As far as he was concerned, they could only be redeemed by 'hard words and cruel cuttings'.[9] Yet it is likely that he also felt threatened by the languid nonchalance with which they could discuss the arts and literature – despite their affectations and flimsy understanding of these topics. Thus, not for nothing did he confess to Henrietta that he was somewhat apprehensive about the extent to which she was immersing herself in books during her stay in Boppart. As he put it, 'I shall be afraid of you when you get back; I am almost tempted to go to some quiet spot and read myself'. For all Samuel may have felt intimidated by Henrietta's social confidence and urge for self-knowledge, he was still sensitive to her underlying vulnerability. He was missing her dreadfully, but with customary gentleness he wrote:

> Do you really think it good for you to be away from home? I hope it is. What you say of its loneliness and quiet makes me think it may be, but then I know how you long to be with your sister and the people.[10]

Henrietta must have been moved by his concerns, for when she replied she reiterated the reasons for her need to study and also hoped that she was not making him ill with worry.[11]

Samuel's desire to answer her letter 'bit by bit' indicates that Henrietta went on to explore topics as diverse as the 'solid strength' of the Germans, Christian values, the ethics of dinner parties and the books she was currently discovering. We cannot know her exact musings on these issues but, as always, Samuel gave each of her reflections careful and measured consideration. But his romantic feelings were never far from the surface. He concluded this letter with one of the most poignant and frank declarations of his love for her:

> It is five weeks since we parted, and I am sure your absence has not decreased my love. It is a treasure laid up in heaven which moths cannot corrupt and sometimes I think that not even words from you could destroy it. If you say 'No', still shall I feel that you cannot tear yourself from me, and I shall look on to a more distant future. Please write soon, for your letters are so good to me. I grant I read them through hoping to find grounds for a better hope, but if I find none then I can and do rejoice in the present. Now goodbye. You know without my saying how dear you are to me, and you told me once I had no right to call you 'mine'. Believe then that I have not learnt to care the least bit less am now and always, your
>
> SAMUEL BARNETT.[12]

This was the last of the letters exchanged by Samuel and Henrietta during her stay in Germany. How much these proclamations helped to sway Henrietta can never be known but, just over two weeks later, she had returned to England and accepted Samuel's proposal because, as she put it, 'his gift of love was too holy to refuse'.[13] In her diary, she recalled that 'one fine day on the Rhine, God spake and bade me love him and my heart obeyed'.[14] These may well have been two of the reasons, but there were other, more worldly motivations underlying her decision to marry this shy and sensitive curate. For a start, her sister Alice had just announced her engagement to Ernest Hart and wanted Henrietta to return to England as their marriage was to take place very shortly. Perhaps Henrietta didn't want to be 'left on the shelf', but it is much more likely that she was horrified at the thought of having to move back in with Aunt Sophey without Alice to act as a buffer between them. Certainly, relations between Sophey and Henrietta had become less strained but Henrietta still became profoundly irritated by her aunt's tendencies towards snobbery and narrow-mindedness.

The memory of one such instance stayed with Henrietta for many years. During the first year of her work with Octavia Hill, Henrietta had encountered a young girl called Katie who had fallen into 'bad hands'. Henrietta was very fond of this spirited and irreverent miscreant and decided the only way of saving her from an otherwise inevitable decline into crime and prostitution was to take her home with her and give her employment as a parlourmaid. Sophey was apoplectic with indignation: 'What, a girl with no training and a bad character, out of a low court, handling our cut glass and Spode?'.[15] Over four decades later, this outburst amused Henrietta, but for a socially committed 19 year old, it would have been infuriating.

Personal circumstances aside, there would have been other reasons why Henrietta decided to forfeit her single status. Most research into Victorian middle-class marriage, particularly that of feminist historians, dwells on its repression of women and their incarceration in the domestic sphere of hearth and home. That this was the case for many women cannot be disputed; historians have recently, however, begun to re-evaluate this somewhat deterministic account. Alison Light, for example, has argued that the 20th-century conception of Victorian marriage as a wholly repressive institution for women is only a 'half-truth'. She points out that, for some, marriage offered a release from the 'twilight world' of young, single womanhood: a world in which however earnest their intentions, they were rarely taken seriously.[16] Moreover, it is likely that Henrietta, for all her vitality and commitment, would have been all too aware of the extent to which single Victorian women were seen as a 'threat to the conventional bases of society' as well as the lowly esteem in which they were held.[17] Such condescension was to be a continual source of irritation to her and, even after marriage, she denounced the notion that 'a woman is a nonentity unless joined to a man' as 'blasphemous'.[18] Finally, no matter how much she valued her single status, Henrietta would have no doubt realised that marriage to the mild and ineffectual Samuel would be a means of furthering her aspirations for social and educational reform without forfeiting too much of her independence.[19] After all, as M. Jeanne Peterson acknowledges, Victorian clergymen's wives exerted 'a wide influence' on their husbands' 'career decisions'. That said, she goes on to speculate that most clergy wives were content to work in the shadow of their husbands;[20] as co-social worker Beatrice Webb – a close friend of the Barnetts – observed, such acquiescence was not Henrietta's style. According to Beatrice, not only was Henrietta a high-profile partner in her husband's missionary work right from the start of their marriage, she also inspired, initiated and implemented many of their projects.[21]

Henrietta's decision to marry Samuel provoked mixed reactions. His mother was greatly relieved – not least because she had privately feared that her son would end up in the clutches of the austere and intense Octavia Hill. Above all, Mary Barnett was delighted to discover that Henrietta was Samuel's junior by seven years. In her view, 'men should marry women younger than themselves, and not older ladies whose views were all settled, and who liked the work they had given themselves better than taking care of their husbands and their homes'.[22] Little then did she suspect the spirit and independence burning under Henrietta's youthful prettiness and apparent ingenuousness. As for Octavia Hill, she was touchingly gladdened by the news of their engagement. In a letter to Samuel, she wrote effusively:

> What it did most for me ... was to make me feel your kindness in letting me
> share in a little of your joy; it is very good of you both ... What your help has

been to me, no one will ever know. I believe it will be even more in the years to come, for whatever makes you both better – as your love must – will make me richer. So, you see, my joy in the evening's news becomes real selfish joy after all.[23]

At that point, Octavia was beginning to nurture secret romantic plans for herself. She had been emotionally dependent on Samuel for several years but was becoming more and more attached to Edward Bond, a wealthy barrister and fellow COS worker. Young, exceptionally handsome and highly intelligent, he was perhaps the one man who ever broke through Octavia's reserve. As she put it, 'one easily gets on subjects with him, and he seems to have much to say; there is a pleasant sense of friction and stimulus, though none of peace'.[24] The two did become engaged very briefly in 1877 but their relationship ended abruptly. Some argued that Bond's elderly widowed mother disapproved of her son's entanglement with an older woman and that he acceded to her objections. According to Beatrice Webb, however, Octavia misinterpreted Bond's intentions: 'Alas for us poor women! Even our strong minds do not save us from our tender feelings. Companionship, which to him meant intellectual and moral enlightenment, meant to her "love". This, one fatal day, she told him'.[25] This was perhaps rather patronising. After all, Beatrice must have known from her relationship with Sidney Webb, her husband and partner in social reform, that love and intellectual enlightenment were not mutually exclusive. She was equally outspoken in her appraisal of Henrietta and Samuel's engagement. To put it simply, she was astounded by the liaison and was blunt in her contrasting of the 'pretty, witty' Henrietta with the 'plain and insignificant' Samuel. She did acknowledge his 'fathomless sympathy' and 'utter absence of human vanity' but diluted these qualities by emphasising his 'muddle-headed' lines of argument and complete lack of 'personal magnetism'.[27] On the other hand, she notes Henrietta's 'keener and more practical intellect' and her 'directness and intention of speech' as well as her capacity for 'self-assertion – sometimes to the point of bad manners':

1   *Henrietta at the time of her marriage, 1873.*

> Lavishly admiring, loving and loyal to her friends and comrades, her attitude towards those she condemned – for instance the heartless rich, the sweating employer, or the rack-renting landlord – was that they required 'spanking', and that she was herself prepared to carry out this chastisement.[27]

Beatrice may well have been astute in her observations of Henrietta and Samuel, but her unspoken expectation that the male should be the stronger partner in a relationship betrays a conventional streak. After all, Henrietta and Samuel announced their engagement three years after the publication of John Stuart Mill's powerful and provocative essay, 'On the Subjection of Women' (1869). In a challenge to John Ruskin's assertions that men and women were 'equal but different', Mill demonstrated how such a premise enabled women's influence to be undermined by male power. In turn, he argued that conventional middle-class marriage was a mere veneer of civilisation and cultivation which allowed men to indulge their baser instincts at the same time as causing women to become devious and manipulative. Thus, Mill argued the case for companionate marriages: ones founded on friendship, intellectual companionship and mutual respect. However, Mill also recognised that the forming and maintenance of such relationships were hampered by the existing frameworks of financial and legal inequality between married men and women.[28] That, however, was soon to change. In 1870, the year after 'On the Subjection of Women' was published, the first of the Married Women's Property Acts was passed. Prior to this, upon marriage, all a woman's personal belongings and savings automatically became the property of her husband. Effectively then, married women were reduced – legally and financially – to a state of infantile dependence upon their husbands. Following the 1870 Act, women were allowed to keep their own earnings and were entitled to the ownership of property acquired *after* marriage. They were also deemed sufficiently responsible to hold a separate savings account. However, it was not until the passing of the 1882 Married Women's Property Act that they were entitled to keep property acquired before marriage. Yet whilst the 1870 Act only secured a modicum of independence for married women, it was at least a partial acknowledgment of the injustices of the past. And more was to follow. For example, in 1873, the year of Henrietta and Samuel's marriage, 'innocent' divorced or separated mothers were allowed custody of children aged up to 16 years. Until 1839, divorced and separated fathers were automatically granted custody of their children and, even after that, 'innocent' mothers were only granted custody of children aged up to seven years. That proviso of 'innocent' reveals much about the hypocrisy of Victorian moral double standards. No such condition was attached to fathers' rights to custody.[29] It was as much informal resistance as public legislation that was gradually eroding the patriarchal structures on which Victorian marriages were founded. As early as 1844, Ann Lamb was ridiculing 'the one rule of "Wives, obey your husbands", no matter how silly the … command may be'. By 1870, women of Mary Barnett's generation may still have been content to subscribe to Sarah Ellis's 1838 proclamation that it was a woman's duty to 'suffer and be still', but Henrietta and her contemporaries clearly had other ideas.[30] Henrietta was as appalled by Francis Barnett's 'assumption of his right to the best of everything' as she was by Mary Barnett's meek acceptance of this status quo.[31] So, whatever reasons motivated Henrietta to marry Samuel, the desire to become an acquiescent and self-effacing wife was certainly not among them.

On the day of their engagement, 25 June 1872, Henrietta and Samuel spent a long sunny afternoon on the river at Cookham in Kent. This sounds idyllic but it's not difficult to imagine the lingering doubts which would have been drifting in and out of Henrietta's consciousness as they meandered along the riverbank making plans for their future together. She carefully avoids any mention of such inner conflict in her diary, where she merely comments that, following her engagement to Samuel, her 'life seemed to have found its use and [its] whole'.[32] Samuel, on the other hand, must have been delirious with joy: his patience, understanding and tenacity had finally paid off. As he put it, every single detail of their engagement day was 'printed on his soul'.[33]

No matter how hopelessly in love he was, however, Samuel still had the capacity to unsettle his young fiancée. No doubt she had been expecting him to want to spend every single moment with her after the turbulence of their five-week separation, but Samuel had other plans. Prior to Henrietta's acceptance, he had arranged a three-week holiday in Europe with his brother, the fun-loving and irreverent Frank, who was the perfect foil for the somewhat reserved and diffident Samuel. They were due to depart the following day. Even looking back more than 40 years later, Henrietta's appraisal of Samuel's reluctance to alter these arrangements remains somewhat acerbic:

> An incident in his own life – even so great a one as betrothal – was not to be allowed to interfere with carefully-made plans, so he punctually departed by the very train which had been arranged weeks before. Whether he was right or wrong I do not know, for during all our glad years together this reverence for punctuality was a frequent small trial to me, and the complete mastery of his thoughts a cause of envious bewilderment.[34]

Perhaps it was also a subduing experience for Henrietta who, after all, was used to having her own way – especially from the men in her life. In any case, their relationship was to be continued by letter for a few more weeks whilst Samuel and Frank toured Switzerland and Italy. This disturbed Henrietta, not least because her 'troubles and perplexities' were exacerbated by his absence.[35] Characteristically, she does not elaborate on these 'troubles and perplexities' but it can be surmised that, on the one hand, she feared that her commitment to Samuel was still too fragile to survive such a separation and, on the other, she may have been deeply affronted that he should have the nerve to go ahead with his arrangements after all his declarations of love and longing. She was also preoccupied with private misgivings concerning Alice's imminent marriage to Ernest Hart.

Whatever the causes of this inner turbulence, they were to manifest themselves in physical illness; and she also – subconsciously or otherwise – 'punished' Samuel for his absence by writing much less frequently than before. Predictably, he was mortified and plunged into an abyss of self-doubt:

> ZURICH, *29 June 1872* – I hope to find a letter at Coire tomorrow just to feel and know that you are well. Do you know I shrink more from losing you through death than any other cause? I always have felt this, I don't know why, so please take care of yourself, take extra care, foolish care …
> COIRE, *30 June 1872* – Here I am writing to you, and I think I want to hear from you much more than you want to hear from me. I have been to the post-office in vain, your letter for me has not arrived, and there is no other comfort but to write to you …
> PONTRESINA, *3 July 1872* – If letters are not at the *poste restante* I don't know what I shall do. It will be a week since I have heard. When I think what a pleasure I found and then gave away again, I am inclined to complain …[36]

Henrietta must have thought Samuel had suffered enough, because she had finally contacted him by 4 July 1872. He clearly drew little comfort from her letters, which were brimming with details of the trials and tribulations besetting her troubled mind. And yet for all that Samuel sympathised with her cares and concerns, he was sufficiently shrewd to let her know that he didn't see himself as her protector:

I am not going to spoil you. I once promised that you should have room for self-sacrifice. You will see life as it is, find out its real beauties through its real uglinesses. Oh! It is horrible how men shut women up in a false, glittering, smiling world, and how women love to have it so. Better far that they should know how ugly, how terrible life is, and yet find, as they alone can find, how good is human nature.[37]

Samuel was well aware that giving Henrietta the space to resolve her difficulties for herself would make her stronger and even more self-reliant. He also realised that paternalistic interventions from himself would not have been welcomed by this defiant and spirited young woman. Above all, Samuel is to be admired for his refusal to protect his adored fiancée by incarcerating her in a gilded cage of domesticity. Clearly, he sensed that such a fur-lined trap would crush her spirit far more than the social and emotional complexities she was in the process of unravelling. But some would have seen him as spineless and self-centred; certainly he berated himself for these shortcomings. In his final letter from Lucerne – which coincided with the ending of Henrietta's 'troubles' – he declared that he had been 'selfish, very selfish to leave Yetta alone in her trials' as well as extremely 'unfair' to her.[38]

The remainder of their engagement was rather less traumatic. Octavia Hill went away for an extended summer break, leaving Henrietta and Samuel in charge at St Mary's. There were few distractions in July and August: most of their fellow workers had left London for the coast or countryside, seeking refuge from the clamour and clatter of the East End. Thus, once work was over, Henrietta and Samuel had the time and space for shared leisure. Both loved wandering alongside the rivers in London's surrounding countryside, but they also visited numerous art galleries and museums. In these, Henrietta was able to help Samuel overcome his deeply ingrained prejudices against art and artists. Throughout their married life, Samuel remained insistent that Henrietta was his 'teacher in art',[39] but she was equally beguiled by his freshness and quirkiness of perception, and his sensitivity to hitherto undetected nuances in these paintings. So, in many ways, it was these shared visits that cemented the mutual respect between the two and, perhaps more importantly, a tacit acknowledgement that each could learn from the other. Other decisions were made too: they both agreed that, despite their affection for the countryside and small market towns, they would always live and work in a city – preferably London – where social needs were greatest. They also shared a love of books: George Eliot's *Middlemarch* (1872) was a particular favourite, although Samuel was at pains to point out that he was no Mr Casaubon, the ageing and pedantic husband of the novel's heroine, the young and idealistic Dorothea Brooke.[40] Gillian Darley has speculated that George Eliot based the character of Dorothea on Octavia Hill, but it seems even more likely that she was modelled on Henrietta. Like Henrietta, Dorothea was earnest, principled and highly disapproving of anything remotely frivolous. This prompted her decision to marry Mr Casaubon in order that she may be 'useful' to him. Predictably, the relationship was intensely unhappy and this must have given Henrietta much to ponder upon during her eight-week separation from Samuel. Fortunately for her, although Samuel may have lacked the irreverent wit and physical charms of Will Ladislaw, who was to become Dorothea's lover, he was infinitely more sympathetic – and much more amusing – than the austere and egocentric Casaubon.[41]

In the autumn of 1872 Samuel was offered a job in Oxford. This was very tempting as he was frequently exhausted by his work in London, and Henrietta's health was a

cause of some concern to both him and
Octavia Hill. Alice and Ernest Hart were
likewise troubled by Henrietta's fragility and
urged the young couple to accept this offer
of an easier life in a pastoral setting; never
ones to settle for the easy option, however,
they declined the offer. Henrietta's family
and friends were strongly opposed to this
decision, maintaining that the East End
was unhealthy and unwholesome. Octavia
Hill, on the other hand, understood and
respected their decision. In a letter to
Samuel, she sent her 'warm congratulations
on [their] refusal':

> I feel so proudly thankful of and for
> you both for your decision. It seems to
> me so wholly right. Many would be
> quite right to take the easier course;
> but for one to whom the greater work
> had become once distinctly visible the
> choice of the lesser would be, to my
> mind, simply fatal … I am so very

2   *Samuel at the time of his marriage, 1873.*

thankful you both stood firm. Of course I knew it would be so with both of you;
still, it seems to have given your purpose such a groundwork to stand on.[42]

Octavia, in fact, was more astute than most about Henrietta's 'health and strength'.
She recognised that the responsibility for this largely lay in the younger woman's hands.
Perhaps she had discerned a pattern in Henrietta's bouts of illness: one which coincided
with the fluctuation of fulfilment and frustration in her life. She also recognised
Henrietta's dangerous penchant for seeking 'passion and pain': Octavia may well have
sympathised with this but she also realised that only 'self-control' could temper the
emotions generated by such extremes.[43] In short, Octavia saw the psychological causes
underlying Henrietta's fragile physical health and she must have communicated this to
Samuel. According to Henrietta, during the first years of their marriage, he was less
than sympathetic when colds or 'feminine fatigue' prevented her from carrying out
their plans.[44] Even when she professed to have been at death's door whilst suffering
from a particularly virulent chest infection, Samuel ignited her wrath by immersing
himself in a copy of *Ivanhoe*.[45]

Once Octavia had determined that Henrietta and Samuel were firmly committed
to working in the East End, she intervened on their behalf. She contacted Edmund
Holland, who had close connections with the Bishop of London, and asked him to
keep her informed of vacancies arising in that area. They didn't have to wait long. In
November of that year, a position at St Jude's Church, Whitechapel fell vacant. The
Bishop contacted Samuel as promised, but was at pains to point out the enormity of
the task facing this young and relatively inexperienced couple:

> Do not hurry in your decision. It is the worst parish in my diocese, inhabited by
> mainly a criminal population, and one which has, I fear, been much corrupted by
> doles [undeserving recipients of charitable handouts].[46]

This was no exaggeration. Whitechapel had a population of just over 6,000, most of whom were men. These men tended to live in the many lodging houses littered along the main street, whilst families lived in the squalid labyrinth of 'courts and alleys' riddled with 'poverty, brutality' and 'countless vermin'.[47] Indeed Caroline Dutton, an early volunteer at Whitechapel, was scandalised by her first sight of the interiors of these tenement houses. She gave a graphic account of the 'dark and broken staircases' and the 'faulty front doors' which could not be locked, thus encouraging the homeless to 'wander in' and doss down amongst the squalor and filth of the stairwells.[48] Even St Jude's Church was a mean and flimsy construction: the brickwork was crumbling and soot-smeared, and its coping stones were gradually falling to the ground. Its interior was equally steeped in gloom, being dark, dreary, oppressive and freezing cold. Similarly, St Jude's Vicarage – which was to be the young couple's home – was singularly unprepossessing, especially to those accustomed to the comforts and privileges of middle-class life. It was poky, cramped, dilapidated and had neither a pantry nor a bathroom. It did have a kitchen, but this was located in a dark and dingy cellar. Henrietta was never to forget even the finest details of their first impressions of this lawless, chaotic and ramshackle neighbourhood:

> When we went to see our proposed home, it was one of those warm winter days when drizzle seems to magnify the noise and make sunshine a distant memory. It was market day, and the main street was filled with hay-carts, entangled among which were droves of frightened cattle being driven to the slaughter-houses … The people were dirty and bedraggled, the children neglected, the streets littered and ill-kept, the beer shops full and the schools shut up. I can recall the realisation of the immensity of our task [and] the fear of failure to reach or help these crowds of people.[49]

What Henrietta didn't linger over were the smells of these streets: the reek of rotting vegetation, burning carcasses, untreated sewage, animal droppings, human sweat and stale beer would all have intermingled with the miasma of acrid smoke and steam spewing from the interminable chimneys and railway lines surrounding the district. That cloying and murky winter drizzle would only have amplified this malodorous cacophony of sights and sounds. But none of this squalor and misery was to deter the idealistic young couple, who vowed to persist with their efforts to address the blighted lives of the Whitechapel residents.

Before embarking on married life and missionary work in Whitechapel, Henrietta and Samuel spent Christmas with his family in Clifton. For a week, they revelled in games of charades, feasting, dancing and – weather permitting – horse rides through the surrounding countryside. Here, they discovered yet more common ground as Samuel, himself a keen and confident horseman, introduced Henrietta to the haunts of his childhood; he had revelled in the scenery whilst his brother sought mischief and amusement. So, together, they explored the soft beauty of the West Country: the Mendips, Brockley Coombe, Portishead and Weston. This extended stay also gave Henrietta the opportunity to become better acquainted with her in-laws-to-be. Samuel's father, Francis Augustus Barnett, had founded an iron company which specialised in the manufacture of bedsteads and provided the family with a comfortable lifestyle. When Samuel was eight they had moved from their townhouse in Portland Square, Bristol to a larger house with a rambling garden in Clifton; the family was sufficiently affluent to keep a number of servants who, largely due to Mary Barnett's sweet nature, only left her service if they were going to be married. Up to a point, Henrietta became very fond of Samuel's mother, describing her as radiating 'love, kindliness, generosity and hopefulness'. She also appreciated her ability to be a 'patient and sympathetic listener' and admired her optimism and sense of humour. She was less impressed, however, with her unquestioning devotion to her sons, which meant that she was completely incapable of chastising them. When they were children, one of Frank's shenanigans had resulted in the decimation of her Worcester and Crown Derby dinner service; while their father was incandescent with fury, Mary was more concerned that the boys may have hurt themselves. For Henrietta, this 'enwrapping and absorbing love' was perceived as rather too indulgent.[51] She was irritated, too, by Mary's relentless deference to her husband. Henrietta had little time for Francis Barnett senior. She did describe him as 'more than usually good-looking, with large and beautifully-shaped eyes and regular features' but that was where his charms began and ended. According to Henrietta, he was also selfish, over-cautious, indolent and given to prolonged periods of sulkiness if others failed to comply with his wishes.[52] Moreover, as far as she was concerned, many of his shortcomings were Mary's responsibility. Henrietta reasoned that if Francis Barnett's brusqueness and selfishness had been challenged more often, then he would have been much less likely to rule his family using these unattractive traits. Samuel probably agreed with her: subverting all the Victorian notions of female deference to the male, he asserted that 'It is a wife's first duty to make her husband *uncomfortable*' – that is, to shake him out of any patriarchal arrogance and complacency that would ultimately be to the detriment of his character.[53]

Henrietta and Samuel were married on Tuesday 28 January 1873 in St Mary's Church. The service was conducted by the rector and Henrietta's brother, Fritz. It was bitingly cold, but the sun shone throughout from a sapphire-blue sky. Henrietta was in a buoyant mood: in her diary that morning she enthused, 'My wedding day – a great, good day. God has been very good to me to give me my Samuel'.[54] Such an upbeat declaration suggests that any lingering doubts over her compatibility with, and commitment to, Samuel had been assuaged by the leisure time they had spent together over Christmas and New Year. However, she was not completely dazzled by the romance of the occasion. Like her fictional heroine, Jane Eyre, Henrietta had no intention of being bejewelled and 'dressed like a doll by Mr Rochester, or sitting like a second Danae with the golden shower falling around me'.[55] Indeed, her wedding ceremony immediately signalled her perception of marriage as 'a serious partnership rather than a romantic pageant'. Out of deference to Christian symbolism and morality, Henrietta agreed to wear a traditional white dress and veil. Despite the strident protests of her sisters and aunt, however, she rejected what she perceived as the frivolous extravagances of bridesmaids, diamonds and formal bouquets.[56] Yet other guests' accounts of the wedding suggest that it was not as low-key as Henrietta would have liked. Miranda Hill, Octavia's sister, was touched by the crowds packed into St Mary's: as well as families and friends, the galleries were overflowing with 'poor people' from the district who wanted to share in the celebrations. The Hill sisters' mother was also moved by the presence of the Barnetts' clients from Samuel's Walmer Street district and Henrietta's Circus Street. Even the incorrigible young girls from Henrietta's night school turned up and were, for once, subdued into silence by the awe of the occasion.[57]

The wedding breakfast was held at the home of Alice and Ernest Hart. Showing customary Rowland-style largesse, it was a 'magnificent' affair in which no expense was spared. Indeed, Henrietta looked bewitching in her 'rich but simple' white satin dress and delicate lace veil as she and Samuel drank and toasted each other from the 'immense gilt loving-cup'. According to Mrs Hill, the bride remained in the best of spirits all day, her normally pale skin flushed with pleasure throughout.

The couple were showered with gifts, which were on display in the drawing-room: these would have included books, china, crystal, household implements, paintings and ornaments. It was a measure of the popularity of the newly married couple that these gifts had all been thoughtfully chosen and showed 'genuine feeling'. Octavia's gift to the Barnetts was a modest picture of primroses in a bare spring wood, but the sentiments of this clearly moved the couple. For Octavia, this little picture symbolised 'life and loveliness, sense of growth … sunlight from above, and all the mystery of the future life hidden in the folded buds of the present' – in short, all that she hoped for in the Barnetts' life and work together.[58] Another simple gift particularly touched Henrietta. It arrived on the morning of her wedding and comprised a spray of myrtle, lovingly packaged and sent through the post by Henrietta's co-worker, Caroline Dutton.[59] A sprig of this symbol of patience, enduring love and fidelity was also carefully added to the simple bouquet of wedding flowers given to Henrietta by the tiny children from the Walmer Street School. Henrietta and Samuel had also given Octavia a present to mark the occasion of their marriage. It was a diamond ring which Henrietta had inherited and, for her, at least, was 'rich with associations'.[60] As Henrietta later observed, this generous, if somewhat opulent, gesture was rather ill-judged considering the older woman's austerity. Octavia neither wore the ring nor showed it to any of her family. But not even Octavia's sombre wedding outfit – a black silk dress and a half-mourning bonnet – could disguise her joy at her friends' wedding celebrations. According to Mrs Hill, her eldest daughter was uncharacteristically bright all day long and even sparkled with wit as she regaled her table companions with a string of amusing anecdotes relating to her work amongst the poor of St Mary's Parish.[61]

Henrietta and Samuel left the wedding party at 4.30 that afternoon and travelled to Winchester en route to the Isle of Wight. They spent five weeks touring the south of England and visited numerous cathedral cities including Winchester, Salisbury and Exeter. The freezing weather persisted throughout their honeymoon, though the couple still managed to explore some of the countryside on horseback. Many more hours were spent in the hotels, where Samuel would grapple with dense tomes such as Lecky's *History of Rationalism* or 'stiff treatises' on theories of political economy which, as will be shown in the next chapter, were gradually displacing the gloom-laden Malthusian economics which had dominated political thought between 1820 and 1870. Henrietta regarded this as the intellectual 'gymnastic effort' of self-imposed discipline rather than recognising that it was a necessary engagement with the principles underlying Samuel's practices. This would have had as much to do with her strong pragmatic streak as it did the understandable resentment of a newly married 21 year old having to listen as her husband read these works aloud to her. She was no doubt less than overjoyed that they spent the final week of their honeymoon with Samuel's parents in Clifton. Indeed, Henrietta's comment that they came away 'carrying a hundred reminders of his mother's love' suggests that she found her intimacy somewhat cloying and that it left her yearning for the first part of their married life to begin in earnest.[62]

V

Roughs, Rags and Repulsive Courts

Social Reform in Whitechapel

Henrietta and Samuel moved to Whitechapel on 6 March 1873. St Jude's Vicarage was not yet vacant as the previous vicar was suffering from a chronic illness which had left him too debilitated to move out. So, prior to March 1873, when they moved into St Jude's Vicarage, they first lived together in 'small and frugal' lodgings in Eldon Street, Finsbury, a few miles from their parish. Not only were these rooms dingy, they were also 'dominated by the unceasing noise of the Goods station of the Great Eastern Railway'. Samuel suffered the privations of their accommodation in silence but Henrietta was appalled by their grim landlady's slovenly attitude to housekeeping. One Sunday evening, Samuel's trek home had been lightened by the prospect of his favourite dish awaiting him on his return: a warm and wholesome rice pudding. He was to be denied this small pleasure, however. On settling down at the table, he was informed that 'a mouse had drowned itself' in his pudding and, to make matters worse, the landlady had not bothered to prepare an alternative dish. Samuel merely expressed pity for the wretched little creature's ignominious end, but Henrietta was furious with this 'incompetent woman who had neglected to set traps or put a cover on her lodger's pudding'.[1] Henrietta's frequent outbursts about such inefficiency were not uncharacteristic, but they must have also have served as a displacement for her forebodings about the enormity of the responsibilities confronting them in Whitechapel, long regarded as a 'suspicious, unhealthy locality'.[2] Both Samuel and Henrietta had witnessed the effects of extreme poverty in Marylebone, but nothing was to prepare them for the hostility, bitterness and racial tensions pervading the streets of Whitechapel. As well as its London-born population, Whitechapel was home to a large number of Irish and Jewish immigrants. According to Henrietta, the Jewish population lived in 'fairly decent cottages' in the more respectable streets running off Whitechapel High Street and most had regular employment in the local warehouses, factories and shops.[3] Despite these relative material comforts, the Jewish residents of Whitechapel often encountered hostility from the London-born population. As Gareth Stedman Jones points out, Jewish immigrants' willingness to work for minimal wages in the clothing and cabinet-making industries resulted in their receiving the blame for 'forcing' English workers into casual labour at the docks. On the subject of dock labour, one contemporary commentator grumbled that:

> These foreigners will not come to that work. It is too hard for them; but they go into shoe-making, tailoring and cabinet-making. That is more easy and cleaner for them; and should a foreigner go in to do that to all intents and purposes an Englishman will have to step out.[4]

3   *St Jude's Church and Vicarage, Whitechapel*

Such a comment is steeped in the anti-Semitism which was all too rife amongst the xenophobic middle-classes in Victorian Britain. On one level, Brien was insinuating that the Jewish workers in the East End were weak and lazy and, on another, opportunistic and selfish.

Despite her affection for her Jewish brother-in-law, Henrietta herself betrayed certain prejudices against the Jewish immigrant population. She perceived them as variously 'uncouth', 'ribald' and 'irreverent': all too ready to think that they could 'clear up their troubles quicker if they all talked at once and in loud voices'. She was also less than complimentary about their appearances, mocking 'ugly' young Polish Jewesses with their 'false fronts' (wigs worn by orthodox married Jewish women) and the 'unkempt heads and shaggy beards' of their male counterparts.[5] But if these German, Russian and Polish Jewish immigrants were volatile and vociferous, then they had plenty of good reason. They were frequently exploited by unscrupulous landlords and persecuted in the law courts, and, far from having 'more easy and cleaner' employment, some had to endure unimaginably rank conditions in the sweatshops of the East End:

> Workshop conditions were … socially and medically hazardous. Hands slept on the floor or on benches in the workrooms, particularly the new arrivals with no fixed abode, and breathed in an atmosphere already foetid with the sweat of congested day-labourers and the steam of the press irons.[6]

In Henrietta's defence, she did recognise that the Jewish immigrants were justifiably 'angry and afraid' about all the iniquities dealt out to them, but her somewhat condescending acknowledgement of this reveals much about how anti-Semitism pervaded the literature, journals and consciousness of the indigenous middle classes.[7] Perhaps the most infamous and enduring stereotype of Jewishness is Charles Dickens' portrayal of Fagin in *Oliver Twist*.[8] As Anne McClintock observes, this anti-Semitism was also persistently reinforced by other representations of Jews, such as Rider Haggard's in *King Solomon's Mines* and cartoons in the popular press that undermined Jewish people by portraying them with grossly distorted simian features.[9] Nor was it simply the middle classes who snubbed and derided Jewish immigrants: they also provoked vehement hostility from indigenous and Irish Cockneys who suffered at first hand from being squeezed out of the clothing industries into the precarious casual labour of the East End docklands.[10] Even those most vociferous critics of bourgeois exploitation of the working classes, Karl Marx (himself Jewish by birth) and Frederick Engels, couldn't resist 'scurrilous anti-Semitic gibes' in their private correspondence.[11] Of course, what all these critics of Jewish immigrants and their perceived colonisation of the labour market conveniently ignored was the extent to which competition from provincial and European industries was affecting London-based manufacturers.[12]

Jewish immigrants may well have provoked derision and contempt from their English neighbours, but they also earned a grudging respect for their self-sufficiency and – for the most part – their subscription to a work ethic. However, their Irish counterparts commanded no respect whatsoever – they were subjected to relentless castigation from the moment they set foot in England. The first immigrants arrived in the 1830s and their alleged penchant for 'mischievous luxuries' provoked outrage from such worthies as Poor Law Commissioner George Cornewell Lewis, who opined that charitable handouts would have deleterious effects on their already 'vicious appetites'.[13] Despite this wholesale contempt, the number of Irish immigrants moving to England increased considerably, particularly after the Irish Famine of 1845-7. Some sought work in rural areas, especially during the spring and summer months, but many more were drawn to the cities. Those who ended up in London initially settled in the centre, but, as an 1872 COS survey shows, civic improvements in the City meant that Irish workers were evicted from their homes and forced to seek accommodation in the already overcrowded East End.[14] Whitechapel and its surrounding districts seemed especially attractive because of the possibility of casual labour in the docklands, but in reality many were forced to resort to begging, thieving or crossing sweeping in order to eke out a living. As one splenetic middle-class observer fumed:

> At every crossing, an impudent urchin trails a dirty broom before us, and would fain lay upon us a tax … in the short intervals we encounter the whining interruptions of the sturdy Irishman who is always starving, or that odious girl who is forever taking God's name in vain.[15]

Without doubt, the beggars, thieves and casual workers of the East End streets did gain much pleasure from harassing the 'toffs' who invaded their turf. Those who refused to pay crossing sweepers a copper or two for clearing the street of the detritus of London life gained retribution in the form of a brushful of mud and grime splattered all over their clothes. In an effort to tug at affluent heartstrings, they did sometimes exaggerate the magnitude of their sorrows: many would lay claim to imminent starvation, ailing children, gin-sodden partners or sick parents – any circumstances, in fact, sufficiently wretched to ignite middle-class sympathies.

That said, their material lives were frequently dire. Irish immigrants tended to live in the most crumbling, vermin-ridden and filthy three-storey buildings which festered in the networks of courts and alleys which proliferated throughout the East End. Unlike the poor of Marylebone, who were often enervated and made apathetic by their circumstances, the Irish residents of Whitechapel were spirited, rebellious and vociferous. It hardly needs stating that such insurrection provoked outrage tinged with fear in middle-class observers visiting the district. Already horrified by the dilapidated conditions in which the immigrants were housed, an estate agent was even more alarmed by the 'den of wild Irish' carousing inside these buildings and their propensity for violence towards rent collectors. More than once, these hapless collectors were subjected to an 'Irish attack of poker and broom' which deterred future visits. Henrietta's friend and colleague from her Marylebone days, Beatrice Potter, was none too impressed either. According to her, the Irishman was 'the worst scoundrel' of all those who slouched, begged and bullied through the streets of Whitechapel. She was particularly censorious about their addictions to strong tea and tobacco, and what she saw as their readiness to exploit each other. Here, she was referring to some homeless dossers frisking one of their sleeping companions in the hope of tracking down a stray halfpenny or two.[16] As far as Henrietta was concerned, these feckless reprobates deserved little sympathy:

> If the men worked at all it was as casual dock labourers, enjoying the sense of gambling which the uncertainty of obtaining work gave. But usually they did not work; they stole or received stolen goods, they hawked, begged, cadged, lived on each other with generous indiscrimination, drank, gambled, fought, and when they became too well known to the police, moved on to another neighbourhood.[17]

To young, middle-class women like Henrietta and Beatrice Potter used to more deferential attitudes from their charges, these men must also have appeared extremely threatening. But merely dismissing them as lazy, workshy and feckless obscures the grinding insecurity of their everyday lives. Contrary to Henrietta's contention that the precariousness of casual dock work appealed to their gambling streak, these men fought – literally and metaphorically – to catch the eye of the docks foremen as they hand-picked their daily gangs. Inevitably, this would result in stronger men jostling to the front of queues, tearing out clumps of hair and chunks of flesh in the process. Older, very young and weaker would-be labourers would be trampled or pushed aside by kicking, thumping, spitting and swearing hordes desperate to secure the most tenuous of employment. Inevitably, there were many who were thwarted and, after half-hearted exchanges of blows and curses, these men would skulk off to the gin-shops and beer houses surrounding the docks. As many were already drooping from spent adrenalin, hunger and fatigue, it would only have taken a few nips of gin to lull them into an alcoholic stupor. And it was cheap: 'blue ruin' or 'jacky', the blends of gin popular with the most strapped of drinkers, cost only a halfpenny or two – much less than the price of a meal.[18] Nor were all Victorians unsympathetic. By the 1880s, Charles Booth was propounding the view that people became over-reliant on alcohol *because* they were poor, rather than vice versa. His contemporary, William Booth, was even more emotive on this subject:

> Let us never forget that the temptation to drink is strongest when want is sharpest and misery the most acute. A well-fed man is not driven to drink by the craving that torments the hungry; and the comfortable do not crave for the boon of forgetfulness. Gin is the only Lethe of the miserable.[19]

Meanwhile, for those sufficiently 'fortunate' to secure some casual labour at the docks, working conditions were at best, precarious and at worst, downright lethal. For a start, earnings were notoriously erratic. A dock labourer could make more than £1 in one week – and then nothing for the following fortnight. This had two major consequences: first, a lack of regular income meant that it was difficult to budget for the cost of accommodation; second, men who had not worked for two weeks or more were unlikely to have had much in the way of food. Secondly, this made them progressively weaker and their wasted frames and grey complexions would in turn make them less appealing to the gimlet-eyed docklands foremen, who always chose the brawniest of labourers. Given these circumstances, it is hardly surprising that they resorted to other means of procuring food and money – legitimately or otherwise. However, their predicaments raised little sympathy from the COS, who argued that they should learn to save a proportion of their wages against leaner times. But that was easier said than done. These labourers would have had numerous debts hanging over them, which would be paid off as and when cash was available. And even if they could have stashed away some of their earnings, the money would probably have been stolen: official savings accounts were not part of East End working-class culture. Erratic earnings aside, the physical conditions endured by the dock labourers were dire – especially during winter. Most of these men were employed to load and unload cargo from the hulks which lumbered up the Thames from all over the world. Freezing conditions and the thick yellow fog which hovered over industrial London combined to create icy walkways on which the clutter of obstacles such as chains, ropes and crates was rendered invisible. At the same time, fingers bitten by frost became clumsy – particularly when grappling with heavy and cumbersome wooden crates or palettes. As a result, many dockers were crushed to death by either their own load or one wielded by a half-frozen workmate. Others slipped off the treacherous walkways and plunged sideways into the steely turbulence of the Thames. Frantic yells for help were of little avail: even if they could be discerned above the ever-present rattling, clanging and clatter resonating around the docks, the miasma of fog, smog and smoke would inevitably obscure their whereabouts. Health and safety issues may well be at the forefront on

4 *Interior of St Jude's Church, Whitechapel*

the agenda of modern industries, but no such legislation – or much interest for that matter – troubled 19th-century shipping entrepreneurs. Contemporary medical journals such as the *Lancet* deplored such 'callous indifference to human life', and cited the 'commercial greed' which had dominated the 19th century as entirely responsible. Their protests, however, had little impact. As this ironic and frequently echoed refrain demonstrates, the dockers were all too aware that they were utterly expendable:

> Rattle his bones over the stones
> He's only a docky whom nobody owns.[20]

Not only does this imply employers' disdain for the welfare of their workers, it also suggests that the deaths of these men – followed by burial in the anonymity of a pauper's grave – would have had little impact on family or friends. There may well have been some truth in this, for the circumstances in which these people eked out an existence were hardly conducive to stable relationships and secure family units. Of course, marital disharmony and domestic violence occurred in all strata of society, but amongst the poorest of East Enders, these matters often spilled out from the home into public streets, making them much more visible – and here 'home' is merely a euphemism for the cramped, foetid and verminous lodgings in which many of these dockworkers and their families were incarcerated. The observations of Henrietta and her co-workers may well evoke the physical privations of these leprous dwellings but the day-to-day psychological and emotional implications of existing in such squalor have received less attention. For these casual labourers and their families, home would sometimes be no more than a doss-house: a murky and dilapidated two- or three-storeyed hovel carved up into makeshift dormitories. These were jam-packed with small iron bedsteads (often bearing the name of their manufacturer, Henrietta's father-in-law, Francis Barnett). If they had mattresses, they would be thin, worn and stained with the sweat of countless previous occupants. The only other 'comfort' provided would be coarse grey blankets, as likely as not to be threadbare and crawling with bed bugs – perhaps the only creatures to thrive in such conditions. Sleep in these foul surroundings would have been fitful at best. Not only would the nights be rent by the thin wailing of hungry children, the stertorous breathing of the drunk and insensible or the carnal passions of prostitutes and their clients, but there was also the ever-present danger of thieves spiriting away any meagre possessions if their owners dozed off too deeply. It's hardly surprising, then, that violent altercations frequently erupted between these residents – especially in the communal kitchens, where men and women would congregate around the cooking ranges, stewing the various bits of meat, bone, bread and potatoes they had cadged or pinched earlier. There was no question of sharing these resources: the grinding poverty in which they lived was not conducive to acts of altruism. These unprepossessing dishes were thus jealously guarded and if so much as a scrap went missing vicious kicks, curses and blows would soon ensue. Meanwhile, ravenous children, whining and scrapping amongst themselves, would be cuffed and sworn at by tetchy, exhausted parents.

Other families were incarcerated in the rookeries (one-storey houses) or teetering tenements which mushroomed in Whitechapel's maze of courts and alleyways. Though self-contained, they were cramped and gloomy dwellings with nothing to redeem them. As Henrietta put it:

> In some [of these courts], the houses were three storeys high and hardly six feet apart, the sanitary accommodation being pits in the cellar; in others courts the houses were lower, wooden and dilapidated, a standpipe at the end providing the only water. Each chamber was the home of a family who sometimes owned their indescribable furniture, but in some cases, the rooms were let out furnished for eightpence a night … In many instances broken windows had been repaired with paper and rags, the banisters had been used for firewood, and the paper hung from the walls which were the residence of countless vermin.[21]

Whilst recognising – and sympathising with – the abject squalor in which these residents were enmeshed, the 22-year-old Henrietta regarded these conditions as worsened by what she perceived as wanton vandalism. She was also deeply disturbed by the blatant acts of prostitution facilitated by the renting out of furnished accommodation: 'a bad system which lent itself to every form of evil'. More than anything else, she was appalled by the culture of violence which pervaded every nook, cranny and corner of this neighbourhood. As Ellen Ross observes, domestic violence was commonplace amongst the angry, thwarted and often desperate residents of the East End. Vicious arguments would flare up over the slightest trifle but more often than not, money – or rather the lack of it – would be the underlying cause. Meanwhile, the stress triggered by the costs involved with a newborn child would frequently result in frayed tempers. In one instance, a Whitechapel woman told her COS visitor that her 'husband was awful angry because [she'd] had another baby … He swore at her something shockin' [and] 'e took isself to a public house because there was no dinner for him'. Another unfortunate woman in the late stages of labour was subjected to a savage battering from a husband infuriated that she had not cooked his dinner.[22] Given such violent beginnings, it's not difficult to imagine the brutalities subsequently endured by these children at the hands of such immature and ill-equipped parents. Newspapers of the day abounded with lurid details of unimaginable acts of cruelty meted out by mothers and fathers to their wretched, half-starved offspring. Not surprisingly, these children soon became embroiled into this culture of violence themselves. The streets of Whitechapel were vibrant, noisy and bawdy places: newspaper sellers would bawl out the minutiae of gruesome murders and sex scandals, whilst irreverent and inebriated pedestrians would corrupt Salvation Army tunes with crude – if not downright obscene – lyrics. As Henrietta and Samuel soon realised, the street violence was endemic throughout the neighbourhood. Soon after they arrived in Whitechapel, they were frequently besieged by volatile, stone-throwing mobs outraged by the COS policy of giving payment in exchange for services rather than charitable handouts.[23] Four decades on, Henrietta made light of incidents, but it must have been an intimidating experience for a young couple bent on social reform in a seemingly hopeless environment.

As well as being on the receiving end of hostility and menacing threats from a volatile population, Henrietta and Samuel constantly witnessed vicious confrontations between men, women and children scuffling and scrapping in the courts and alleys of Whitechapel. These tended to take place late at night when tipsy humour transmuted into venomous exchanges. Men and women would end up sprawled in gutters, bleeding profusely from blows or stab wounds. Others would slump in drunken disarray, easy targets for pickpockets and those with a penchant for gratuitous violence. Unsurprisingly, fights between prostitutes – often scantily-clad – provided their very own street theatre for the children of Whitechapel. As Henrietta noted, such altercations never failed to provoke enthusiastic responses from their young audiences.[24] Such episodes of street violence, however, were only a small part of a much greater whole: the barbarism which pervaded the whole of the Whitechapel environment. Recent TV adaptations of Victorian novels have tended to sanitise – or at the very least dilute – the menace lurking within the cultural and concrete environment of Victorian London. These adaptations foreground the vibrancy of crowd-cluttered working-class streets: apothecaries aglow with jewel-coloured bottles and potions, the myriad hues of torn and fluttering theatre posters pasted on shop corners, the gaudy pleasures of gas-lit gin palaces, the shimmer and glitter of play-houses and music halls and the glowing braziers of roast chestnut vendors are typical backdrops, whilst organ grinders with their impudent little monkeys, and sassy flower girls chatting up toffs sneaking the forbidden delights of lowlife London, are common characters. But, that is only part of the picture. As historians have demonstrated, these streets were also imbued with brutality.

Bloody meat was speared on prongs outside butchers' shops in a manner redolent of executed convicts. Dogs and cats – tortured by children made ruthless by boredom and neglect – lay dying in the gutters, their death-throes providing additional sadistic pleasure for their juvenile tormentors.[25] And as Thomas Jordan reminds us:

> Abuse of spavined horses was a common sight, and it led to organised, voluntary effort to prevent cruelty to animals. Blood sports ranging from fox-hunting to cock-fighting were common events, and bare-knuckle boxing and the mass violence of some festival days were the milieux of growing children.[27]

Perhaps the most repugnant sights and sounds of all – for middle-class observers at least – were those of terrified animals as they were herded through the streets to the slaughterhouses. Not content with jeering at these hapless creatures, some residents of Whitechapel would scramble up and over the slaughterhouse walls in order to witness the stunning of bullocks or the slitting of a calf's throat.[27] Such lurid fascinations were particularly repellent to Henrietta, who never ceased to be appalled by those

5 *New Court, Whitechapel*

who stood 'eager for fresh sights of blood, excited by the horror and the danger of [these] scenes':

> It was a horrible sight to see the herds of cattle … followed by troops of cruel boys who goaded the frightened beasts with pin-pointed sticks and hideous cries. Sometimes the poor creatures would entangle their great horns in the spokes of moving wheels, and the cries of inarticulate pain from dumb fellow-creatures are not easily forgotten.[28]

Indeed, observations like these were to ignite her lifelong belief in environmental determinism, the notion that social identity, attitudes and values are inevitably forged by one's physical surroundings. For Henrietta, this macabre revelling in gruesome street theatre was indicative of an assimilation into and an acceptance of a culture of cruelty and vice. Moreover, she quickly came to believe that the 'gloomy' buildings and filthy streets splattered with blood seeping from the surrounding slaughterhouses served to further brutalise the Whitechapel inhabitants.[29]

So where were this idealistic and utterly bewildered couple to start unravelling the complexities, injustices and brutalities of an environment which had long been notorious for its vice, violence and poverty, in addition to racial tensions and a simmering resentment of both middle-class privilege and interference? Samuel began by targeting the souls of these people in order to alleviate the sin he perceived as tainting Whitechapel life. As he put it after his first few years at St Jude's:

> If one sentence could explain the principle of our work, it is that we aim at decreasing, not suffering, but sin. Too often has the East End been described as if its inhabitants were pressed down by poverty, and every spiritual effort for its reformation has been supported by means which aim only at reducing suffering. In my eyes the pain which belongs to the winter's cold is not so terrible as the drunkenness with which the summer heat seems to fill our streets, and the want of clothes does not so loudly call for remedy as the want of interest and culture. It is sin, therefore, in its widest sense against which we are here to fight … Sin must be recognised as manifold, and anything which mars the grandeur of human life must be brought under a converting influence.[30]

Taken out of context, such a declaration verges on the sanctimonious. Samuel may well have had his faith to keep him warm, but those hard-bitten by the winter cold and other privations were hardly likely to be convinced by such an argument. Samuel and Henrietta were much more pragmatic than the above sentiments imply, however. Indeed, the very first service that Samuel held at St Jude's made them both realise the limitations of institutionalised Christianity. Only a handful of elderly women made the effort to attend this service and this was not so much for spiritual replenishment as much as the anticipation of a financial reward for their presence. They were no doubt bewildered by Samuel's sermon: he was still struggling to translate his thoughts into language and concepts accessible to a lay congregation. As Henrietta put it, his sermons may well have been 'thoughtful' and 'unhackneyed' but they were so convoluted that 'only a philosopher' could follow their lines of reasoning. So, Henrietta took it upon herself to address these shortcomings and supervised all the stages of Samuel's writing. Often, a week's work would be thrown into the fire if she deemed that it was beyond the comprehension of a coster. It's not difficult to imagine the acerbic edge to Henrietta's appraisal of Samuel's efforts, but he apparently responded to her criticism with 'awe-inspiring humility'.[31] Clearly, these revisions must have had some effect because by the end of Samuel's first year at St Jude's, the Sunday congregation had risen to around thirty at the morning service and to between fifty and one hundred in the evening. Further progress, too, was taking place: a choir had been formed and special services were run for the children of Whitechapel. Also, refurbishment of the church itself had begun. Within a couple of years, its unsightly galleries had been removed, heating had been installed and the chancel had been re-painted.

Whilst her husband was engaged with his parishioners' spiritual welfare, Henrietta was in pursuit of their hearts and minds. Within the first year of his office, she had initiated the following: classes in a variety of subjects for children and adults, flower shows, concerts, lending libraries and a penny bank. In addition, she had secured the services of a nurse, a mission-woman and a host of lady visitors who she hoped would help to dispel the all-too-tangible antipathy between the middle and working classes.[32] By now, Henrietta was developing the drive and determination which would enable her to navigate the seemingly impossible throughout her life. To accomplish such feats in the first year of her married life must have demanded considerable charm, cajolery and coercion on her part. No doubt she also drew liberally on the expertise and wisdom of those she had met whilst working with Octavia Hill. Henrietta was not content with a merely administrative role, however. Right from her earliest days in Whitechapel, she plunged herself into the lives of its inhabitants. Her streak of audacity would have prompted her entry into these deeply mistrustful homes but for Samuel, still diffident and much less confident than his wife, these visits must have been agonising. Nonetheless, Henrietta insisted that he must meet his parishioners on their own ground if he were to have any credibility amongst them. Despite their initial misgivings, some of the Whitechapel residents warmed to their new vicar and his wife, whose high-profile presence soon earned her the nickname of 'Vicaress'.[33] Samuel soon learned to play down his official role: he rejected his clerical collar in favour of some 'ancient mufti clothes' and was often mistaken for an insurance salesman or, worse, an agent of that object of 'universal terror', a landlord in pursuit of outstanding debts. Once these misunderstandings were cleared up, however, residents began to talk more freely about their cares, concerns and aspirations.[34] In consequence, both Henrietta and Samuel started to see beyond the veneer of defensiveness constructed by their parishioners and, in turn, developed a genuine admiration for their resourcefulness and resilience.

In Samuel's biography, Henrietta recalled many instances – variously 'interesting, amusing, pathetic and tragic' – in which she gained new insights into the 'moral aristocracy' of these ostensibly joyless lives. An early instance of this was her re-appraisal of the 'dirty', 'unwashed' and malodorous Mr Marshall. Such was his devotion to his 'short, fat, shapeless' and 'coarse-featured' wife that one night he endured a rat frisking around their bed rather than disturb her sleep. Despite their meagre income – Mr Marshall hawked groundsel for a living – he and his wife had adopted four children abandoned by 'that low lot round at the Dosshouses'. Another family which lingered in Henrietta's memory were the Stuarts. The father, James, was a 'tall' and 'gaunt' figure, weakened by hunger but still ferociously independent. He and his 'miserably frail' wife had two children and a third on the way. James had tried to eke out a living by hawking broken quartz from a barrow but – as he put it – ended up as 'stony broke as [his] stock'. Near starvation, but too proud to accept charity, he agreed to limewash the vicarage cellars in return for food, clothing and a loan to enable the family to move out of the squalid and damp rooms in which they were incarcerated.[35] However, by no means all of the Whitechapel residents were as altruistic or independent as those cited above. People would turn up at the vicarage at all hours of day and night, thumping on the door, demanding alms and thundering with indignation when their requests were refused. Sometimes stones were hurled and windows were broken by these thwarted individuals and passers-by sympathetic to their plight. Usually, Samuel responded to such outbursts with habitual forbearance but once or twice his patience snapped. One manipulative and persistent applicant for relief must have been completely stunned when the mild, small and slight Samuel suddenly seized him by the collar and forcing a knee into his back, violently ejected him from the Vicarage.[36] As far as Samuel was concerned, this able-bodied man's begging was reprehensible enough, but it was his blatant dishonesty that pushed him beyond the limits of his patience. Deceit such as this reinforced Henrietta and Samuel's belief that the arbitrary giving of charity only exacerbated the lives of the poor:

> Indiscriminate giving of charity is among the curses of London. To put the result of our observation in its strongest form, I would say that the poor starve because of the alms they receive. The people of this parish live in rooms the state of which is a disgrace to us as a nation. Living such a life, they are brought into contact with soft-hearted people. Alms are given – a shilling by one, a sixpence by another, a dinner here and some clothing there … [Thus,] kind-hearted people by gifts of food and clothing are now educating another generation to lead this terrible life.[37]

The Barnetts' responses to their first year's observations of Whitechapel were still very much shaped by Octavia Hill's approaches to social reform. Living up to these principles, no matter how deeply held, caused Henrietta much pain. Not only was she aware that the residents' hearts were 'full of hatred' for herself and Samuel, she also sensed that they were regarded as 'hard and callous' by fellow charity workers less convinced by the COS ethos of encouraging self-reliance and support.[38] Indeed, few clergymen subscribed to such notions as they perceived them as running counter to a Christian spirit of generosity and compassion. For the first few years of their life in Whitechapel at least, however, the Barnetts continued in their steadfast belief that charitable handouts would ensnare the poor in their 'chains of idleness, carelessness and despair'. For instance, Henrietta lamented the number of very young people who came begging at their door – young people who had 'never been taught to read or write, or encouraged to believe that it is their duty to support themselves'. She was even more frustrated when families who they *had* helped towards a modicum of independence were dragged back down into helplessness by well-meant, but ultimately improvident gifts of cash and clothing.[39] Further reinforcement to the Barnetts' conviction that spiritual guidance towards self-help was the only salvation for the poor would have been garnered from the various tomes on political economy through which they ploughed in what little spare time remained for them. During the late 1860s and the early 1870s, the gloom-laden economics system based on Malthus' *Essay on the Principle of Population* (1798) was gradually displaced by the guardedly more optimistic theories of – amongst others – John Stuart Mill, the philosopher and social reformer. His *Principles of Political Economy* (1848) was instrumental in 'translat[ing] Malthusian pessimism ... into a vision of relative comfort and the idea of a world freed from crushing and elbowing'.[40] However, the attainment of such a vision was contingent upon the 'civilising' of the working-classes: in other words, the instilling of bourgeois values into the hearts and minds of what was perceived as a dangerous and volatile social group.[41] So, the iniquity to be challenged in society was not the poverty in which these people lived but the pauperism in which they allegedly wallowed: a state of drunkenness, debauchery and dependence.

To this end, Henrietta began to address her energies. Among her first successes were the Mothers' Meetings which she established in 1874. Right from the start, she was determined that there should be no financial or material gain for members – an exceptional state of affairs in working-class parishes. Rather, Henrietta resolved to enrich these women's lives by encouraging them to take an interest in 'matters which were or ought to have been important' to those responsible for a growing family.[42] She also attempted to kindle their curiosity about wider events in the world: as few of the women could read very well, she would buy illustrated newspapers and explain current affairs to them. This led on to discussions on 'public morals' and 'family ethics'. One of these evolved into a debate surrounding the wisdom of allowing teenage girls the freedom to mix with boys of a similar age, especially when such socialising often culminated in 'horseplay' and concomitant loss of 'maidenly reserve'. Henrietta seemed to hold boys responsible for instigating these shenanigans but as one older and wiser mother informed her:

> What we've got to remember ... is that there are worse girls always waiting for the boys. I'll agree to my girl losing something I'd rather she'd keep, if other mothers will let their girls keep my boys straight. There will be some 'larking' say what you may, but why bad girls is ... allowed at all beats me. The police are sharp enough over pickpocketing, but these sort of girls steal what's worth more than a boy's money.[43]

This observation was clearly taken to heart by Henrietta who, as will shortly be demonstrated, subsequently channelled much of her energy towards the taming of the 'wild girls' of Whitechapel. Nor were other women afraid to challenge her when she came out with one of her more ill-informed assumptions. Once, she and the mothers were discussing male drunkenness. As far as Henrietta was concerned, alcohol was a 'poison' and 'one of the worst evils ... which may bring our nation to disgrace and sorrow'.[44] Moreover, she asserted that 'men were what women made them [and] that every married woman could stop the drink, if she would have nothing further to do with a drunken husband'. Presumably this was a veiled reference to the withdrawal of sexual favours as well as domestic services. Whatever the case, it sparked hoots of derision from women who knew all too well what would happen if they took this line of action. As one 'little mother with a big family' commented, 'What about the example to the children if she refused to speak to her husband, when all the home-life had to be lived in one room?'.[45] Reactions such as these must have caused Henrietta to re-think some of her ideas on marital and family relations, but they didn't stop her from writing and publishing her views on domestic and family management. Her opinions on thrift, cleanliness and nutrition have already been explored in Chapter 3, but she also saw fit to hold forth on the subject of child rearing in her first book, *The Making of the Home* (1875). In this, she not only stressed the importance of children's physical needs – wholesome food, exercise, warmth, cleanliness and adequate rest – but also emotional and intellectual needs – love, security, play and stimulation.[46] To 21st-century readers, these may seem obvious, but the numbers of abused, filthy and half-starved children languishing on the streets of Whitechapel bore testimony to the ignorance of many young and inexperienced Victorian parents. Throughout her life, Henrietta's commitment to child welfare was deeply felt and sincere, but it has to be said that she would have been preaching to the converted at these Mothers' Meetings and through these publications. There must also have been a degree of wry amusement at a young (and childless) middle-class woman in her early twenties making proclamations about subjects in which she had no direct experience.

By the end of their first couple of years in Whitechapel, Henrietta acknowledged their limited successes – most notably with the older residents of Whitechapel and their 'self-respecting and hard-working' younger counterparts. However, she and Samuel were achieving less with the 'sad, downtrodden and ignorant' as well as the volatile and the violent.[47] For this reason, they considered moving out of the vicarage and into one of the 'worst of the courts' in the district. As Henrietta explained, their awareness that they could 'neither woo [these residents] to worship God nor break down their suspicion of man' made them moot the possibility of any step which would remove the barriers between themselves and their parishioners:

> Perhaps we should learn more of our neighbours if we shared their sufferings, and that, servant-less, we should realise the disadvantages of no copper, no oven, no sink, no water-tap, no lavatory, no cupboards, no coal-cellar, no bath, drunken neighbours, noisy children, a common staircase, a boltless front entrance, windows which would not open, doors which would not shut, and partitions which admitted every sound.[48]

In the event, this didn't happen. Samuel – perhaps rather conveniently – came down with a particularly intractable dose of phlebitis coupled with complications which puzzled the doctors.[49] Yet Henrietta's keenness to sacrifice the modest comforts of the vicarage and their self-imposed restricted income demonstrates the extent to which she was beginning to empathise with the psychological implications of the material deprivations suffered by these suspicious and resentful residents. Indeed, it was this burgeoning desire to have a greater understanding of their attitudes and beliefs which fuelled her determination to break down these barriers: first, by building bridges with the younger – and, she hoped, more malleable – generation of girls who ran wild in the courts and alleys of Whitechapel. Before embarking on this and other projects which would raise her profile in the community, Henrietta and Samuel took a much-needed holiday in Switzerland. They spent three weeks meandering and deliberating against the dramatic backdrop of the mountains, slopes and pine-scented valleys of Lucerne, Lauterbrunnen and the Wengen Alps. Henrietta, her spirits ground down by the smog and murky light of Whitechapel, positively luxuriated in the myriad crystalline lights and shadows playing on the snowy mountain tops. Thus reinvigorated, they returned to London freshly determined to achieve some lasting impact on the residents who had so far resisted their interventions.[50]

VI

Vice and Vigilance in Victorian London

Working the Streets of Whitechapel

Quite apart from the violence, crime and grime of Whitechapel, one of the most profound culture shocks for the 22-year-old Henrietta was her gradual realisation of the extent of sexual licentiousness which pervaded the entire neighbourhood:

> Slowly I learnt the truth. I had arrived at woman's estate in a condition of almost incredible innocence, and sins, now known, alas! to all play-goers and novel-readers of any age, were to me unimagined. To learn the facts of sex lawlessness through the channel of rude words and impure minds of the women in the underground Lock ward of the Whitechapel Infirmary made me ill, but I was absorbingly interested in the individual girls and never missed my weekly visit. [1]

These particular young women were incarcerated on what Henrietta delicately terms 'medical grounds'. Lock wards and hospitals served the sole purpose of treating those suffering from sexually-transmitted diseases – syphilis was especially virulent throughout East End London – although some would also have been subjected to brutal assaults by their partners, clients or pimps. Henrietta first learned of their existence through Samuel who, in his capacity as Guardian of the Poor, had been to inspect the Whitechapel Workhouse and Infirmary. Moved but also repelled by what he witnessed, he nonetheless encouraged Henrietta to visit these young women 'brutalised' by the 'dreariness' of their lives in such institutions.[2] Fuelled by an indomitable – if somewhat naive – optimism, she determined to first gain the confidence of these women and subsequently to relaunch them into respectable society.

The path of Victorian women philanthropists to the doors of their fallen and wanton sisters was already well-trodden. Some historians hold a benign view of their interventions: for example, F.K. Prochaska argues that these women's 'persistence, tact ... persuasiveness [and] willingness' posed a significant challenge to the '[m]asculine officialism' which had formerly dominated philanthropic reform.[3] However, other appraisals of middle-class philanthropy highlight the potential for the less altruistic pleasures of 'slumming' in the 'spice' of East End life.[4] To add to this confusion, there remained two conflicting strands of thoughts on issues of prostitution in Victorian society. Perhaps the most official line on prostitution was that it constituted the worst of the social vices contaminating London.[5] Clues to the utter contempt in which the inmates of Lock wards were held, and how these institutions were shrouded in secrecy, can be gleaned from an 1882 pamphlet outlining their nature and purpose:

> Lock hospitals are principally for reception and treatment of persons suffering from [venereal] diseases, the direct result of their own vicious indulgence. This is

why they enjoy so little of the liberality so lavishly bestowed upon other hospitals and infirmaries … Lock hospitals can never be open to the inspection of the public, nor can they ever be the objects of public entertainments, annual dinners, concerts, or bazaars. Their claims cannot specially pleaded from the pulpit or platform. Their work must be begun and carried on silently and unnoticed, save by the very few.[6]

It was further opined that it was 'natural' to assume that the female patients in these wards were nothing more than 'common prostitutes' whilst the male patients – far fewer in number – were merely 'guilty of some recent act of immorality'.[7] These male indiscretions, moreover, were implicitly excused by the enduring belief that men's sexual impulses were 'inherent and spontaneous' whereas women's *should* remain dormant.[8] Overt sexual desire in women was damned even further by insinuations that displays of such a 'raging fury of lust' were an 'obscene' manifestation of their 'insanity'.[9] As many 19th-century feminists fumed, such attitudes were typical of Victorian double standards in morality. Quite apart from the fact that at least some of these women would have been rape victims or infected by a promiscuous husband, many of these women simply had no other means of making a living.[10] As Victorian writer, Augusta Webster, made clear in her poem, 'A Castaway', prostitution was no more unscrupulous than any of the corrupt practices executed by so-called professionals such as lawyers, doctors and accountants.[11]

Henrietta was certainly repelled by the idea of prostitution but there is no reason to doubt the sincerity underlying her compassion for these young women and her desire to 'woo them' onto the 'self-restraining path which leads to righteousness'.[12] This suggests that she was influenced by alternative perspectives on prostitution prompted by the works of novelists and artists of the period. As Lynda Nead notes, their guardedly sympathetic portrayals of prostitutes as more victims than perpetrators of evil were held to be more 'eloquent' than 'a sermon or a book'.[13] More than that, the nuances embedded in a painting or characterisation and symbolism in a novel could awaken public awareness to the myriad social, economic and moral factors underpinning the so-called scourge of prostitution. For example, Alice, the hard-bitten prostitute in Dickens' *Dombey and Son* is allowed to articulate the wretchedness of her life before dying (fittingly repentant) of syphilis.[14] Indeed, Alice's fictional experiences were drawn from Dickens' own efforts at rescue work amongst London's prostitutes. And paintings such as Dante Gabriel Rossetti's 'Found' or William Holman Hunt's 'The Awakening Conscience' would have alerted the public to the possibility of salvation for these 'fallen' women.[15] Whatever the impulses which prompted Henrietta's forays into the sordid secrecy of the Whitechapel Lock ward, they would have been deeply disturbing experiences. Quite apart from the young women's recalcitrance and explicit references to their sexual antics, some of them would have been considerably disfigured. In its advanced stages, syphilis could leave its victims scarred by skin disorders such as pustules, chancres and ulcers: indeed, graphic and grotesquely exaggerated images of syphilitic patients were included in Victorian medical handbooks in order to deter men from the pursuit of salacious pleasures.[16] However, Henrietta did not shrink from her crusade. For the first few years, her work was carried out without any official acknowledgement, but in 1877 she produced a report for the Board of the Guardians of the Poor, onto which she had been elected in 1875. This report showed that in the previous year, 60 of these Lock ward patients had been discharged and helped towards a lifestyle more in keeping with Henrietta's standards. But of these women, only 12 were in a position to support themselves and their children. It is interesting to note that this report was never published.[17] This can only be interpreted as what Christina Pankhurst was much later to castigate as the intractability of that 'respectable silence over prostitution and venereal disease'.[18]

Given that Henrietta's recollections of her nine years spent working among the prostitutes of Whitechapel were published only five years after Pankhurst's outburst, her determination to foreground these young women's experiences shows considerable initiative and courage. Of all the women she cites, two are particularly memorable both for their own tenacity and Henrietta's steadfast belief in their potential. The first, Ellen Mather, was described – tongue-in-cheek – by Henrietta as an 'incorrigible pauper'. On first meeting her, Henrietta despaired of ever penetrating Ellen's 'half-closed eyes, sullen expression, set mouth, and general "don't care" attitude'.[19] Ellen, a patient in the Lock ward who had formerly been thrown out of the workhouse and into prison for insubordination, clearly held no aspirations for her future. She persistently resisted all Henrietta's overtures with a sulky silence until the latter offered to secure her release from the Lock ward if Ellen promised that she should 'never enter the workhouse again'. This promise was eventually forged, but not straight away – Ellen could be as stubborn as Henrietta. From these unpromising beginnings, however, a mutual friendship and respect blossomed:

> I could write a book on Ellen, her experiences, her temper, her clumsiness, her sense of humour, her intelligence, her incompetence, her scorn of most of her mistresses, and her appreciation of some, her shrewdness and stupidity, and through it all her great and permeating love. [20]

Ellen clearly adored Henrietta, but she wasn't in awe of her. For years, she sent her benefactor a gift and card on her birthday. One year, Henrietta 'decreed' that she was intending to refuse all presents in the future. Not to be thwarted, Ellen – 'chortling' with pleasure – gave Henrietta a 10 shilling note in order that she may 'help another girl' in wretched circumstances. She kept her promise to stay out of the workhouse, however. She worked in domestic service for a number of families and in her mid-30s became an under-servant at the home of Mr F.C. Mills, one of Samuel's colleagues. Here, the privations of Ellen's earlier years began to tell on her health. She developed consumption and, although near death, her shady past meant that no hospital was prepared to treat her. Mr Mills was fond of his servant, however, and arranged for her to be nursed in his home, even going so far as to put a Brett seascape in her room to keep her company.[21] Another young woman who was to cause Henrietta a mixture of exasperation and compassion was Selina, a 'dirty, hatless and almost shoeless' girl who lived chaotically between her own furnished room and 'dossing with her pals'. Henrietta suspected that Selina must have picked up some form of venereal disease, because she told her that before she could help her, she needed to go into the infirmary. Guessing that Selina would pay little heed to this advice, Henrietta told her to call at the vicarage later that day when she would make all the necessary arrangements for her admission. All through the evening, Henrietta sat in the cold and draughty hall waiting for Selina's arrival. Samuel, ruffled by his wife's dedication to this apparently hopeless case, went to bed and advised Henrietta to do likewise, but she refused, tormented by the idea of the girl turning up to find the vicarage in darkness. Hours

passed and her imagination was inflamed by the 'hideous human' noises in the street
– 'drunken songs, quarrelling, laughing, screaming' – which intensified her sense of
fear and hopelessness. Then, all at once, the door knocker sounded and Selina had
taken the first steps to making radical changes in her life.[22]

For the first few years of her involvement with the women of the Lock ward and
workhouse, Henrietta worked alone. After a while, she was joined by three colleagues,
Lady Monteagle, Mrs John Rodger and Mrs Frederick Greene. Between them, these
women extended their services to other parishes in poorer districts of London. Not
only did they personally supervise the aftercare of the women following their discharge
from Lock Hospitals and ward but they also arranged for their babies and children to
be fostered for as long as necessary. There would have been a modest fee for 'loving'
these often ailing children back into life, but there were plenty willing to look after them
without any payment, particularly if there was any suspicion of the natural mothers
reverting to their old ways.[23] And many of them did relapse into former habits – far
more than were persuaded into respectability. For, as Henrietta probably realised, the
tawdry attractions of a bright, aimless and carefree wantonness were perceived as
much more appealing than the rather more austere and disciplined lifestyle offered
as an alternative. Henrietta did not accept defeat easily, however. If she discovered
that one of her charges had rescinded on an earnestly made promise, she would set
off in pursuit of this miscreant and attempt to cajole her into submission. Often,
her reasoning would be met with refusal, but occasionally, they would tell Henrietta
of a 'younger' or 'less hardened' girl who may still benefit from these well-meant
interventions. It is also likely that her patchy success rate with these seasoned prostitutes
alerted her to the fact that prevention is preferable to cure. So, to this end, Henrietta
simultaneously turned her attention to the 'wild girls' of Whitechapel: already a rowdy
and rumbustious bunch but not yet completely off the rails.[24] Henrietta had already
had some experience of working with such wayward young girls whilst working in
Marylebone. At that point, she may have been out of her depth but now, a little older
and a lot more streetwise, she set forth with renewed determination to reform these
'rough and lawless maidens'.[25] Her line of reasoning was quite straightforward: remove
these girls from the dissolute environment of Whitechapel and place them in service
with respectable middle-class families. Here, they would learn the decorum, decency
and deference so lacking in the turbulence of their everyday lives. However, some of
them would already have been working. Amongst employment available for nimble-
fingered working-class girls and women in Whitechapel were the following: brush,
button and cigarette making, fur working, India rubber stamp machining, magic slide
lantern makers and spectacle assembling. These would have paid between 4s. and 14s.
per week as well as having the additional bonus of the camaraderie which flourished
between these groups of women as they guffawed, gossiped and grumbled through
their working days.[26]

It would appear that Henrietta regarded this raucous rapport with more than
a degree of suspicion – not least because she considered that older women would
corrupt their younger co-workers with their bawdy anecdotes and seamy experiences.
So she advocated more refined avenues of employment such as sewing, shop work or
domestic service. She was particularly keen to promote the latter as she argued that
'richer homes' would provide the advantages of 'good food and physical exercise' as well
as countless 'opportunities' for working-class girls.[27] Presumably, by 'opportunities' she

meant chances to assimilate middle-class morals and customs: table manners, modulated speech, modesty in dress, an orderly routine and the discipline instilled by a healthy work ethic. No doubt some working-class girls and women benefited from acquiring these refinements as they progressed from scullery maid (the lowest order of servant) to that most exalted of positions, the housekeeper. Many more, however, must have bitterly resented the hierarchical injustices of these middle-class homes and dreaded the drudgery of their daily lives: the ceaseless scrubbing, polishing, blacking, washing, fire-making, grate-cleaning, fetching and carrying necessary to maintain efficiency and order in the middle-class Victorian home. Unsurprisingly, some of the servants recruited from the ranks of Whitechapel's wild girls did indeed rebel against the perceived tyrannies of their employers. Instances of this insurrection abound in Henrietta's memories of her early Whitechapel days. One young girl, Kate, was 'jest [so] riled' by her employer's haughtiness that she seized the nearest missile and hurled it towards her. Unhappily, the 'missile' was the employer's baby. Julia, another reluctant recruit, threw a vengeful knife at her mistress whilst Clara, angered by her employer's superior manner, laid a fire under the floor of her attic bedroom and set light to it with a match purloined from the kitchen before sneaking away from the house for ever. Also amongst the catalogue of misdemeanours committed by these girls were pilfering, the use of foul language, inappropriate romps with male servants, 'borrowing' their mistresses' clothes and helping themselves to the contents of the drinks cabinet.[28]

Whilst Henrietta could not openly condone these acts of insubordination, the tone in which she recalls them suggests a degree of wry amusement and perhaps a sneaking admiration for these girls' irrepressible nerve. She was, of course, more aware than most of the wretchedness and despair which lay beyond their bravado. Indeed, some girls were rescued from 'disorderly' homes in which their mothers were encouraging them into crime and prostitution. Conversely, other desperate parents begged Henrietta to get their daughters 'right out of the neighbourhood'.[29] So, if she were to succeed with inducing these girls away from this 'evil environment', she soon realised that more formal monitoring was necessary before letting them loose onto employers unfamiliar with Whitechapel ways. To this end, in 1877 she established the Whitechapel branch of the Metropolitan Association of Befriending Young Servants. The purpose of this was for suitable volunteers to 'provide care and moral nurture' for these girls as well as guidance in matters of dress, appearance, leisure habits and personal relationships.[30] This, she reasoned, would not only serve to refine these servant girls but it would also serve to 'counteract' the 'undesirable' influences of their friends and families.[31] In order to inveigle support for this scheme, Barnett declared to prospective volunteers that it had been 'given to' them 'to hand over to some sunless lives a little of the joy which is so plentifully bestrewn around our own'.[32] For 21st-century readers and especially those sympathetic to Marxist perspectives, this is yet another instance of Henrietta's capacity for overpowering middle-class condescension. Yet no matter how misguided she may have been, she was at least tenacious in her commitment to these young girls. For example, records show that one, Elizabeth, was found no less than 11 different places to work before eventually giving birth to an unplanned – and unwanted – baby. Subsequently, Elizabeth spiralled down into an abyss of 'drink, indifference and idleness' and was ultimately discovered begging on the streets of London. But her story has a happier outcome. Despite her abject circumstances, a kind-hearted employer agreed that Elizabeth could come to live and work in her country home. Here, in a stable and caring environment, Elizabeth learned to give her own child the love and security lacking in her own. Others, however, were less fortunate. Their recalcitrance and disobedience often resulted in imprisonment, transportation and sometimes, the 'rope walk': a deceptively jaunty euphemism for the death sentences meted out for the most heinous of crimes. Alternatively, some of the girls, ground down by despair and disillusionment, succumbed to depression or mania and in extreme cases, committed suicide.[33]

In 1880, Henrietta – since 1876 a Manager of District Schools – turned her attentions to the plight of young girls raised in the austerity of orphanages and barrack schools. Of her campaigns against such institutions, more will be said in a later chapter. One of her greatest concerns was how ill-equipped these girls were to cope with life after leaving these places at the age of 14 or so. To address this, she used a legacy to adapt their recently acquired weekend home, Harrow Cottage on Hampstead Heath, into a 'Cottage Home' where the girls could receive three months' training before going into domestic service. Henrietta's former nurse, Mary Moore, was placed in charge of this establishment. No doubt Mary – along with Fanny, who 'hated dirty, noisy Whitechapel' – was relieved to move out to the pastoral and peaceful setting of Hampstead, but she certainly had her work cut out. Quite apart from their 'cold manners' and 'sullen tempers', these girls had no 'life skills' whatsoever:

> The ignorance of the girls raised in the barrack schools had to be experienced to be believed. Having walked out but seldom, and then only with hundreds of others, they had never shopped, and so they visited the greengrocer for a reel of cotton, went to the public house to buy a copy of *Punch*, dropped the stamps loose in the post box and expressed astonishment at seeing a bridge.[34]

Meanwhile, inside the house, these girls were a downright liability. Anxious not to replicate the institutionalised conditions of barrack schools, Henrietta would only admit three or four girls at any one time, and she went to great lengths to ensure that Harrow Cottage was furnished as a cosy and comfortable home. But confusion ensued. Having lived all their lives in a gas-lit institution heated by pipes, the girls were unfamiliar with the dangers of fires and neglected to snuff out candles because they couldn't fathom how to turn them off. One even managed to melt down a silver teapot by leaving it *inside* a piping hot oven. Yet Mary – for whom this was not the *first* experience of handling wilful and wayward girls – took it all in her stride. Showing remarkable forbearance, she 'took each into her large heart, and kissed and scolded and taught and reproved them all continuously'. The girls adored Mary and she clearly loved them back – possibly a little too much. In consequence, Henrietta appointed herself as responsible for dealing with those more serious transgressions deemed as 'beyond [Mary's] influence'.

No doubt the girls regarded the approach of each Friday with a certain degree of trepidation. This was when Henrietta and Samuel would arrive for a brief respite from the squalor of Whitechapel. Before taking a stroll over Hampstead Heath with her poodles and collies, Henrietta would discipline these miscreants. To her credit, she would encourage them to 'choose their own punishment' in order to promote the idea of self-discipline. Having given this due consideration, the girls would opt for something like 'going without sugar', 'getting up earlier', 'not taking the dogs for a walk' or – to Henrietta's amazement – 'an hour's gardening'. She had always assumed that this would be regarded as a treat.[35] As with the Whitechapel girls and the inmates of the Lock wards and hospitals, Henrietta's – and Mary's – efforts in Hampstead reaped a mixture of success and heartache. Letters treasured by Henrietta all her life bear witness to the deep gratitude and affection which lingered in the hearts of many girls long after they had left Harrow Cottage.[36] Some, however, were not so fortunate. Some were inadvertently placed in inappropriate employment and – not surprisingly – would abscond at the earliest available opportunity. As they were still under-equipped to deal with the vagaries of independent life, they were extremely vulnerable to exploitation from those more streetwise than themselves. Feeling entirely responsible for these missing girls, Henrietta agonised about them so much that she frequently became ill. Her worst fears were to be realised when she discovered that one young Cottage girl, long missing from her place of employment, ended up 'dying from the effects of her life': presumably, one prematurely ended by disease, drink or violence.

As well as providing training, monitoring and employment for these young girls, Henrietta was later to organise recreational activities to distract their factory worker counterparts from the tawdrier delights of the streets, music halls and gin palaces. The intention of these was to 'sweeten and raise character' and included girls' clubs, numerous guilds which promoted 'purity, honesty, temperance and mercy' and a gymnasium. The purpose of the latter was to encourage a wholesome outlet for girls' and young women's boundless physical energies. As a leaflet promoting these activities argued:

> All day rough, strong girls work in factories, their occupation often employing their hands only. Their homes are small and crowded, and their work hours being over, they only have the streets for exercise and amusement. The rough games there played tempt them to drink in public houses, and thence often to ruin.[37]

Such endeavours are likely to be perceived by modern readers as being steeped in sanctimony. It cannot be denied that their implicit purpose was to inculcate these young women with the leisure and recreational habits of the middle classes, such as music-making, singing, reading and voluntary work. But it is worth remembering that the leaflets produced to obtain funding, premises and volunteers would have been written in language contrived to cajole support from the more sober and respectable members of the middle classes. Henrietta would have known very well how to manipulate the language of Christian piety for these purposes and no matter how pious her written sentiments, she clearly had much fun working with these young girls. As she herself noted, official reports on institutions only reveal one layer of reality. What they do not express is the chaotic jumble of warmth, hilarity and exuberance with which they were infused: the 'wild whoops' of the girls' laughter, the camaraderie, the vibrancy of their street language, their fights – ferocious, fleeting but soon forgotten – and their guffaws of delight when Henrietta mimicked their accents and manners.[38] For all Henrietta's capacity for empathising with these young women's spirit and irreverence, however, she became less and less patient with those who persisted with their 'shameful' lives of sexual debauchery. In short, whilst she was resigned to the 'vicious, drunken and lawless' acts which peppered day-to-day Whitechapel, those who earned their living by vice were quite beyond the pale.

For Henrietta, the abundance of brothels in Whitechapel epitomised the very worst kind of human exploitation: unscrupulous men living off the immoral earnings of women who, in turn, ensnared and exploited men too weak to resist their salacious overtures.[39] Of course, this was a skewed perception and one by no means shared by all respectable Victorians. Indeed, almost twenty years earlier, that renowned chronicler of the London underclassses, Henry Mayhew, had recognised the extent of the exploitation of women in the sex industries that flourished in the 19th century. He defined brothels as 'houses where speculators board, dress and feed women, living upon the farm of their persons'.[40] Such a metaphor leaves little doubt about Mayhew's contempt for the rapaciousness of these 'speculators'. He also drew the public's attention to the hard economic facts which left women little option but to turn to prostitution. As one happily married woman put it, it was the only means by which she and her husband could be spared from sinking into 'a state of destitution'. Moreover, her husband was fully aware of the means by which she supplemented their income and escorted his wife to and from a 'notorious' East End brothel four or five times a week.[41] Nor were *all* brothels run by greedy and callous pimps, bent on exploiting the female sex. Others were managed by middle-aged women – often ex-prostitutes themselves. Whilst the morality of these madams may have been open to question, they did at least ensure that their girls were warmly clothed, well-fed, and – above all – protected from dangerous clients. Warnings about predatory or perverted punters soon spread around the informal network of communication between the brothels of the East End. Thus, such men were given short shrift by cynical and hardened madams who would have developed a keen nose for those with a penchant for aberrant practices. Given the violent, chaotic and abusive families from which they had drifted, many of these young prostitutes would have found their new homes infinitely preferable.[42]

Such justification would have cut little ice with Henrietta and, along with Samuel, she resolved to rid the district of brothels for good. Such a resolution anticipated the aims of the National Vigilance Association formed in the mid-1880s. Weary of the prevarication inherent in the debates on and investigations into prostitution, its founders mounted a crusade against these houses of ill-repute which, in as far as it resulted in their closure, was apparently successful.[43] However, the evangelical zeal which drove these campaigners caused them to be oblivious to the inevitable knock-on effects of their actions. Outlawing brothels did not put an end to prostitution: it merely forced it out of the sight of respectable society and into the murky alleys of slum streets and, by effectively removing the protection provided by pimps or madams, prostitutes became much more vulnerable to financial exploitation at best and, at worst, sadistic attacks which could leave them permanently disfigured. It has even been argued that the 1885 Criminal Amendment Act which made the keeping or managing of a brothel an offence was indirectly responsible for the most notorious wave of sex crime in 19th-century London: Jack the Ripper's spree of sadistic slaughter, which resulted in the mutilation and murder of five Whitechapel prostitutes between the late summer and early autumn of 1888.[44] The Ripper murders have persisted in capturing the public imagination right into the 21st century. Some of the intrigue is grounded in the fact that he – if indeed the murderer was a 'he' – remains unidentified. Suspects ranged between public figures, eminent doctors – the murders demonstrated a certain surgical precision – and, presumably employing similar logic, master butchers in the Whitechapel and Spitalfields areas. It is a measure of how much anti-Semitism persisted in Victorian London that there was a widely held assumption that the Ripper was Jewish. Such a supposition was reinforced by the lurid coverage of these crimes in the *Illustrated Police News* whose artists initially caricatured their elusive 'Whitechapel fiend' as an

Eastern European Jew. Later, however, these graphic representations of the Ripper transmogrified into an 'upper-class fop', complete with a fur-lined collar and a leather bag in which he secreted his surgical instruments.[45] Most of the ghoulish fascination surrounding the Ripper's crimes, however, sprang from the swift, scientific and sadistic means with which his victims were despatched. Nor was this fixation with this crime wave tempered by sentiment. For underlying the horror provoked by these attacks was a tacit consensus from self-respecting (and self-righteous) members of all classes that as all the victims of the Ripper were prostitutes, they were at least partly responsible for their own fate. Indeed, the Ripper himself may have been, like his 20th-century counterpart, the Yorkshire Ripper, a fanatic who saw it as his mission to alleviate the sexual licentiousness contaminating the East End.

Henrietta – clearly oblivious to how her interventions had effectively left women with little option but to ply their trade in the backstreets of Whitechapel – was intensely disturbed by the Ripper murders. As repulsed as she was by the visceral enormity of his actions, she was also sickened by the extent to which the Whitechapel residents wallowed in the grisly minutiae of these atrocities. Little children revelled in games of 'murder' whilst their mothers gossiped and gawped around the scenes of his crimes. For Henrietta, this gruesome preoccupation, further tainted by its apparent lack of pity, compounded her belief that these residents had been brutalised into such callousness by the degradation of their cultural and physical environment. So, in an effort to make these women 'feel ashamed of such talk, to exercise self-control in their gossip, and to range them on the side of order', she encouraged them to sign her petition seeking the help of Queen Victoria to improve the moral and cultural squalor of East End London:

To Her Majesty the Queen

MADAM, – We, the women of the East End, feel horror at the dreadful sins that have lately been committed in our midst, and grief because of the shame that has fallen on our neighbourhood. By the facts which have come out at the inquests, we have learnt much of the lives of our sisters who have lost a firm hold on goodness and who are living sad and degraded lives.

While each woman of us will do all she can to make men feel with horror the sins of impurity which cause such wicked lives to be led, we would also, your Majesty, beg that you will call on your servants in authority and bid them put the law which already exists in motion to close houses, within whose walls such wickedness is done and men and women ruined in body and soul.

We are, Madam, your loyal and humble servants.[47]

No doubt Henrietta had been particularly moved by the 'sad and degraded' details surrounding the case of Annie Chapman, the second of the Ripper's victims. In less turbulent times Annie, the mother of three children, had been married to a reasonably prosperous veterinary surgeon. Annie's increasing dependence upon drink had wrecked this façade of middle-class respectability and, following the break-up of her marriage, she turned to prostitution as a means of funding her alcohol addiction. Perhaps Henrietta felt that if the women of Whitechapel had rallied to support women like Annie rather than revel in the sordid circumstances surrounding their deaths, lives like hers may have been saved. But recent historians are more sceptical about Henrietta's campaign against the Ripper murders:

> Female moral campaigners like Barnett occupied a subordinate role within [the Ripper campaign]; they remained physically constrained within the female sphere and bent on keeping the neighbourhood women there as well … out of the earshot of salacious discussions of sex and violence, relinquishing public spaces and sexual knowledge to men.[48]

Certainly, Henrietta was disturbed by the macabre revelling of the Whitechapel residents as graphic details of the murders oozed relentlessly from the pages of the tabloid press. Whilst the particularities of street language and culture may appear trivial to Judith Walkowitz, for Henrietta they were deeply significant as they indicated an unquestioning assimilation of a culture of violence and cruelty. Moreover, Henrietta was no more contained in the 'female sphere' than any of the other women in Whitechapel. She had lived amongst these women for long enough to realise that 'sexual knowledge' was by no means solely the province of men. All she really wanted to do was make these residents stop and think about the wider implications of their gossip and games. In the event though, whether her interventions were conservative or innovative, they certainly paid dividends. Within a few years of the Ripper's brief but intense reign of terror, that 'furthest west … and blackest spot of the East End' saw the introduction of gas lighting, the re-invigoration of slum clearance and re-housing as well as – in deference to human sensitivities heightened by these vicious killings – a more humane approach to slaughterhouse practices.[49] No longer did the Whitechapel streets run with blood or resonate with the terrified cries of animals as they were herded to their deaths.

It is doubtful, however, whether these environmental improvements had any lasting impact on reducing prostitution. Indeed, the prevalence of venereal diseases following the outlawing of brothels suggests that it was, on the contrary, flourishing.[50] Nor, for that matter, did Henrietta's grass-roots intervention have much effect on the Whitechapel women's passion for gossip. What she clearly didn't understand was the subtext of this ostensibly shallow and sensationalist means of communication. As Melanie Tebbutt has pointed out, working-class gossip functioned – and continues to function – on many different levels. First, it had the capacity for making or breaking reputations which would have been just as great a self-regulating force as Henrietta's exhortations. Second, it provided a means by which women could keep up to date with the politics of everyday living and thereby analyse their changing roles within it. Finally, the slang and vernacular deliberately used by these women enabled them to maintain some 'dignity' and 'distance' from the middle-class condescension to which they were ceaselessly subjected. Indeed, whilst working-class women showed outward forbearance over what must have seemed like relentless encroachment into their lives, these well-intentioned visits were frequently a 'source of great amusement'.[51] Henrietta's attitudes towards sexual impropriety, frivolous pleasures and, above all, the extent to which the environment shaped such propensities, were to remain constant throughout her life. However, as the next chapters will reveal, her efforts at reforming housing, educational, social and cultural aspects of Whitechapel life were to cause her to re-evaluate some of the harsher judgements she had meted out when her idealism was shored up by a lingering youthful arrogance.

VII

✦◦✦✦◦✦

Sawdusty Shambles and Nests of Thieves

Housing Reform in Whitechapel

The slum clearance and re-housing schemes which were energised in the wake of the Ripper murders had been high on Samuel and Henrietta's list of priorities since moving to Whitechapel. Back in 1875 Samuel, appalled by the fact that 80 per cent of the residents lived in condemned housing, had argued that if:

> the gang of thieves and idlers who inhabit this quarter could be scattered, and good houses built, the boon would be immense; at present most of the rooms are what are called 'furnished', i.e. provided with a sack of hay, a chair and a table, and let at eighteence a night.[1]

As they were soon to discover, realising such a scheme was to be fraught with administrative and practical complications. First, the squalid hovels of Whitechapel would need to be officially condemned by a medical officer. Second, town councils would have to respond to this condemnation by demolishing them. Finally, building companies would need to be cajoled into buying the land and constructing more wholesome dwellings. Of these, the first was the most straightforward: Dr Liddell, the medical officer for the Whitechapel district, shared Samuel and Henrietta's horror at the disease-infested squalor in which people were expected to live and was only too happy to condemn their 'ruinous and insanitary' houses.[2] Samuel had also enlisted the support of Home Secretary Richard Cross by sending him a memorandum cataloguing the grime-streaked adversity of everyday life in Whitechapel. Deeply affected by these observations, Cross arranged a visit to Whitechapel where, guided by Samuel, he saw for himself the grim realities of living beneath the poverty line.[3]

The upshot of Cross's visit was his Artisans' Dwellings Act of 1875, which enabled town councils – in London, the Metropolitan Board of Works – to acquire dilapidated properties, demolish them and rebuild houses on the sites. This was a worthy attempt to address the housing problem but one later judged as 'a bungled disaster', in which a sizeable number of houses were demolished before any reconstruction plans had been mobilised. At the other extreme, the lengthy time lapse between the condemnation and demolition of some properties gave tight-fisted landlords a perfect excuse to spend even less than before on the maintenance or repair of these flimsy hovels. Alan Palmer deems Samuel as at least partly culpable for this shambles of a re-housing scheme. He singles him out from a number of 'over-zealous muddle-heads' and points out the fancifulness of Samuel's insistence that 'every court and alley between Fashion Street and Whitechapel High Street should be condemned'. This would have resulted in homelessness for over four thousand casual labourers, costermongers, dockworkers and lightermen: all from a notoriously 'difficult community to shelter'.[4] Gillian Darley also notes the 'utterly ineffective' nature of the Act:

> The flaw lay in the arrangement for compensation; landlords were effectively encouraged to run down their properties ... so as to receive compensation once they [were] deemed uninhabitable. The local authorities then failed to carry out their part of the bargain, which was to rebuild the housing to a decent standard. The overall effect was thus further to deplete the housing stock, and overcrowding and lack of sanitary facilities became ever more dire.[5]

Not surprisingly, Henrietta's version of events is somewhat more circumspect. She recalled the frustrations they experienced as the Metropolitan Board either started work it was unable to finish or – despite the recurrent outbreaks of fever and disease – ignored the medical officers' recommendations altogether. Another issue was the cost of land cleared of slums by the Metropolitan Board. As Samuel commented, this was offered at 'a price so high as to make the erection of artisans' homes impossible for builders expecting a fair return for their money'.[6] Henrietta was particularly outraged by her discovery that a single one of these condemned houses could generate up to nine shillings a week in income for their owners. As she puts it, such unprincipled exploitation 'roused an enthusiasm for housing reform' amongst the 'men and women who cared so much and worked so hard' to combat such injustice. Amongst these were Octavia Hill, one of her most steadfast volunteers, Emma Cons and the friend to whom Octavia was briefly engaged, the lawyer, Edward Bond. Between them, they also secured the support of the architect Elijah Hoole, who had designed model dwellings for Octavia, and of A.G. Crowder, Guardian of the Poor and stalwart of the COS, who was to continue 'peddling' its 'unreconstructed dogma' long after others had reconsidered its underpinning ethos.[7]

As Octavia recognised, the housing conditions in the East End of London were even worse than those in Marylebone. As she wrote in a letter to Samuel, 'I find the difficulties of management in Whitechapel greater than ever I anticipated, property and people being equally impossible to deal with in any satisfactory way'.[8] At least Octavia did have previous experience of securing and running housing schemes for seemingly 'unruly and hopeless' tenants. Indeed, since 1870, she had – with the assistance of numerous wealthy friends – bought numerous properties which were subsequently converted into blocks of housing supervised by middle-class 'visitors' (Octavia loathed the term 'rent-collector').[9] One of the most controversial of these was the purchase in 1872 of Barrett's Court, made possible by a donation of £7000 from her friend, the wealthy philanthropist Lady Julia Ducie. Already condemned, Barrett's Court was in an appalling state of dilapidation and fell well short of public health standards. However, Octavia managed to stave off the unwanted interventions of the Medical Officer of Health by effecting minor repairs and improvements. These included securing the front doors and issuing tenants with latch keys. The latter were frequently lost and the bolts which replaced them provided flimsy defence against drunks in search of shelter in stairwells and passages.[10] Despite its ill-omened origins, Barrett's Court was held in deep affection by many of its tenants. Indeed, when their homes were officially condemned in 1873, their 'grief at leaving their tenements was almost incredible'.[11] The tenants were a diverse bunch, ranging from 'very decent artisans' who were 'scrupulously clean' and respectable to 'idle, drunken ne'er do weels' who would rip down banisters for firewood and do a moonlight flit on Sunday nights – just before the rent was due. These were a minority, however. Largely due to the efforts of the witty and spirited lady visitors, Emma Cons, the Hon. Mrs Maclagan and, later, Henrietta, a genuine warmth developed between themselves and the tenants. The pretty and rosy-cheeked Emma was particularly courageous – and forceful. She would think nothing of intervening in street fights by prising the miscreants apart and sending them on their way with one of her legendary withering looks. She was also kind-hearted and – much to Octavia's despair – endearingly scatty where administrative niceties were concerned. Nonetheless, it was Emma's ability to create a rapport with her tenants which helped the somewhat starchier Octavia to soften her approach to these residents by treating them 'courteously and carefully'.[12]

The original buildings at Barrett's Court – later known as St Christopher's Place – were gradually replaced with model lodging houses for tenants who could be trusted to 'strive to live quietly, and keep their homes tidy and clean'. From this respectable community of artisans, communal activities flourished. In 1873, a working men's club was formed where men could smoke, talk, listen to concerts, read newspapers and books, and play games such as bagatelle, cards and dominoes. A year later, an Institute for Women and Girls was established. Here, classes were available weekly in needlework and singing as well as twice-weekly in reading, writing and arithmetic: it should be remembered that, as education had only become compulsory for under-12s in 1870, many of these women and girls would have had no formal education at all. In addition to these classes, lectures were given on topics such as childcare, cookery and dealing with infectious diseases. Alice, Henrietta's sister, was the Honorary Secretary and Treasurer of the Institute and – clearly sharing Henrietta's fondness for mathematical precision – maintained meticulous order in the Institute's books.[13] The successes of the Barrett Court scheme must have inspired Henrietta to circumvent the tangled impasse created by the Artisans' Dwelling Act. In the centre of Whitechapel was a collection of 'rickety dwellings' known as New Court. Not only were its deeds 'non-existent', its structure was 'rotten' and its reputation 'infamous': it was mainly populated by prostitutes, who were charged exorbitant rents by a 'disreputable' man whose claims to the ownership of the properties were tenuous, to say the least. Deeply affronted by such skulduggery and debauchery, Henrietta resolved to take over the management of these properties. In order to raise half of the funds needed to buy the alley, Henrietta sold her inherited jewels; Edward Bond agreed to donate the balance. Swiftly, the most incorrigible of the tenants were evicted, the properties patched up and subsequently let to those whose lapses into drunkenness and violence were only occasional. After the properties were finally demolished a few years later, the land was used for tennis courts.[14] Adjoining the land on which New Court stood was another piece on which A.G. Crowder arranged the construction of a block of model dwellings. Sanctimonious to the marrow, he had elevated hopes for its moral potential:

> The tenements will be ready in June and will accommodate about 50 families at an average rent of *2s. 6d.* a room. They will be under careful supervision, and we may expect that 50 families living respectably will have a great missionary power in the neighbourhood.[15]

These means of dealing with housing reform attracted the attention of the 'pretty, animated' and 'clever' Princess Alice of Hesse-Darmstadt. Princess Alice, the third child of Queen Victoria, quickly became disillusioned in her marriage to Prince Louis and channelled her energies into addressing the social iniquities in her adopted country of Germany. Through Colonel Gardiner, her mother's Equerry and member of the

COS, Princess Alice met Octavia Hill and – despite their differences in social status – a close friendship was forged.[16] On one of her visits to London, Princess Alice and Octavia drove out to Whitechapel where she met Henrietta and Samuel. This made a deep impression on the idealistic princess:

> [The Barnetts are] both the most self-sacrificing excellent people, full of their work and having the best influence over the poor and often deformed people under their charge. I believe the Court I was taken to see is one of the very dirtiest and worst in the East End. New Court is narrow, very dirty, [with] very low tumbledown houses.[17]

Alice was in turns moved and appalled by what she witnessed during this visit. She recalled the pathos of a tiny child languishing in bed, enfeebled by heart disease whilst his healthier siblings ran 'half-naked' amidst the filth and cold of their foetid room. She was haunted by the 'dear little faces' of the children incarcerated in the 'dark rooms' of Angel Alley – a 'horrid lodging house' frequented by 'disreputable' people.[18] Yet she was also heartened by the sight of Crowder's model dwellings, declaring that Henrietta must be 'proud and happy … to work so closely with such a man'.[19]

Meanwhile, other plans were afoot to improve – morally and structurally – other properties which blighted Whitechapel. In 1877, wealthy friends of the Barnetts funded the purchasing of four houses on Wentworth Street, formerly homes to inhabitants of a 'notoriously bad character'. Once again, these reprobates were seen off and, after the houses were put in good repair, they were let to a more respectable clientele. And by 1879, Samuel was able to record good progress in their striving for housing reform:

> About 1,000 people are now living in houses which are under the control of those whose object is their real good. Mistakes may be made and their actions misunderstood, but the fact that those who own their property are moved by a desire to be helpful rather than make a profit must have a distinct influence … The rents are collected by eight ladies who spend two days a week among their tenants. Punctual payment is enforced, chiefly because of the element of order and regularity it introduces into families, the cause of whose trouble is generally disorder.[20]

The sobering influence of these ladies on the messy chaos of these tenants' lifestyles is perhaps somewhat exaggerated. But at least Samuel did not resort to the flowery effusions of Oscar Tottie, one of the Barnetts' workers, who was most memorable for having rescued an 11-year-old girl from a 'house of ill-fame' and arranging for her to live in the country. The girl's mother, incandescent with fury, retaliated by hurling stones and abuse through the vicarage window. Having spent a day in the company of the antithesis to this foul-mouthed virago, the 'kindest', 'quietest' and 'courte[ous]' paragon of a lady visitor, Tottie concluded that the sight of these 'visions of delight', with their 'beautiful hair' and 'fair open faces' must have been as inspirational to 'the poor' as 'primroses in spring' were to the middle classes. But Henrietta, with her first-hand experience of rent-collecting, would have known better. Recalling all the fun they had with their dissolute tenants amongst all the difficulties these reprobates created, she questions this image of lady visitors as 'visions of delight'. For example, she cites the case of two would-be thieves, overheard plotting to rob Miss Busk, one of the rent-collectors, of her rent-bag, watch and chatelaine. This could have been construed as threatening. As Miss Busk was brave, buoyant and six feet tall, and her would-be assailants 'the usual size of pitiable, half-fed wasters', however, such schemes were doomed never to come to fruition. However, some of the tenants' circumstances demanded sensitivity and resilience in equal measures – no mean feat for young women still in their twenties:

> Desperately difficult situations had to be met. Drunkenness, immorality, dishonest withholding of the rent, 'away from home' – which meant prison – were not occasional but frequent incidents among the tenants. And the difficulty was ever the one of the mixture of good and evil: the wife so noble, the man so base; the woman drunken, the man industrious; the old couple worthy of respect; the younger members of the family disreputable.[21]

Kate Potter, sister of Beatrice Potter (later Webb), became responsible for the New Court dwellings in early 1876. Fleeing unhappiness in her personal life, the clever and highly capable Kate had begun working with Octavia Hill in October 1875. Whilst this experience had alerted her to the real suffering endured by the underclasses of London, she grew increasingly disenchanted with Octavia's austerity and aloofness. Conversely, after meeting Henrietta and Samuel during a Christmas party at the Potter family home, a lasting friendship flourished between this lively and enthusiastic young woman and the equally buoyant Henrietta. Realising that relations between herself and Kate were strained, Octavia recognised that Kate might be better placed working for the young and idealistic Barnetts. As she put it:

> I can't help thinking you would be very wise to see Miss Potter and interest her quickly. She is taking up one thing and another here with vigour and energy and naturally won't like to give up them for East End work when once she has begun them'.[22]

It can only be conjectured why Octavia found Kate's vitality so irritating, but it may have made her uncomfortably aware of her own depletion of energies. Certainly, by the summer of 1876, she had confided in a letter to her friend, Sydney Cockerell, that she felt 'completely knocked up' and 'fit for no place but home'.[23] Kate blossomed in her new role as rent-collector. She had the wit and intelligence to counter the sundry excuses offered instead of rent, coupled with a warmth and compassion which enabled her to delve beyond the resentment and suspicion which initially greeted her. She was also a valuable contact for the Barnetts: through Kate, they met 'hosts of her friends' – all of whom were willing to help in Whitechapel – as well as re-forging links with her sisters, Theresa and Beatrice. All these women came from materially privileged backgrounds and had a highly developed sense of social responsibility.[24] Kate stayed with the Barnetts until her marriage to the MP Leonard Courtney in 1882. Such was her attachment to Whitechapel that the wedding ceremony was held in St Jude's Church with the reception taking place in the schoolroom where the 'coster sat side-by-side with the Member of Parliament' and 'all the guests, however far apart in mental and social degree, were united in love and respect for the bride'.[25]

There were many other helpers, both for the supervising of the improved dwellings and for carrying out other social work in the parish. As Henrietta is the first to acknowledge, the 'hard and exhausting work' carried out by herself and Samuel 'was lightened' by the considerable number of their friends and acquaintances who gave so generously of their time and resources.[26] Much of this support was generated by the Barnetts' colleague, the witty and charismatic Rev. H.R. Haweis, who invited Samuel to

6 *The drawing
room at St Jude's
Vicarage*

speak to his largely middle-class congregation about their work amongst the poor of
Whitechapel. Moved by Samuel's account, many of Haweis' parishioners volunteered
their services. One young woman, 19-year-old Marion Paterson, was particularly inspired
by the young clergyman's words:

> It was so nice at Mr Haweis's this morning. He brought in a clergyman from the
> East End who talked to us about all the poor sinners in the wretched courts and
> alleys of his parish ... I want to go and be their friend. I know they are drunkards
> and a worse class of people than I have ever seen, but I would try so hard to
> help them if only Papa and Mamma will let me. ... I feel I must go to them. I
> know it will be hard work and most likely seem a failure and their lives will seem
> so dreadful to mix with, still I feel I can and ought to do it.[27]

Duly, Marion turned up at St Jude's Vicarage one Sunday evening. Henrietta, longing
for 'supper and peace' was irritated by the summons to meet this latest recruit and
even less impressed by the appearance of 'this girl of 19 whose childish face and
violet eyes spoke of innocency'. Deeming it 'foolish' of Mr Haweis to send 'such a
baby' to witness the evils of Whitechapel, she resolved that Marion's contributions
to their work would not extend beyond the tidying of their clothes cupboard. From
this inauspicious start, however, a lifetime's friendship grew between the two women.
Within the year, Marion had moved in with the Barnetts and she remained a member
of the household until Henrietta's death. Gentle, self-effacing and girlishly pretty, the
young Marion was in awe of the much more forthright and opinionated Henrietta.
Henrietta was struck in her turn by the 'uplifted ideals', 'sympathy' and 'self-surrender'
underpinning Marion's passionate desire to make a difference to the lives of the
degraded, the destitute and the downtrodden of Whitechapel.[28] So, very soon, Marion
was helping Henrietta with every aspect of Whitechapel life – including the taming
of its herd of wild girls – even to the extent of cleaning up those who were crawling
with head and body lice.[29]

Another significant figure in the Barnetts' lives was Pauline Townsend, who joined
them as a co-worker in 1877 and – after a shaky start – became their lifelong friend.

Pauline met Samuel at her interview for the post of secretary to the Metropolitan Association for Befriending Young Servants. Her youth, inexperience and crippling shyness meant that she was unsuccessful in her application. She had, however, clearly made an impact on Samuel, who was better placed than most to discern the earnest commitment burning under her tongue-tied diffidence. And, likewise, his 'pale face … soft brown hair … kindest eyes … gentle voice and courteous manner' endeared him to her. After the interview, Samuel suggested that Pauline may like to meet Henrietta, with a view to helping her with her parish duties. Pauline had already heard about Henrietta from her brother, and was more than a little apprehensive about meeting this 'learned lady' and her penchant for 'Aristotle and Pythagoras'. However, Henrietta's charisma – no doubt offset by the antics of her 'mischievous little dog' – instantly bewitched Pauline. For her part, Henrietta was more ambivalent. After meeting Pauline, she did not have any qualms about her capacity to work effectively but was not sure if she would warm to her on a personal level.[30] Quite what sparked her ambivalence here is unclear: perhaps she felt a little piqued by Samuel's instinctive affection for this young, earnest and unassuming woman. Or maybe she felt that Pauline's day-to-day proximity would encroach upon her growing closeness with Marion Paterson. In the event, her early misgiving proved unfounded and, for the next 22 years, Pauline spent four days of every week working alongside Henrietta and Marion in Whitechapel. Her photograph, along with those of Marion and Kate, were displayed on Samuel's mantelshelf until the day he died.[31]

Despite this network of influential, articulate and wealthy friends, State prevarication over slum clearance and re-housing persisted. As Henrietta acknowledged, the purchasing, repair and re-letting of 'tumbledown' rookeries may well have been 'morally valuable', but the Barnetts remained extremely frustrated about the excruciating slowness with which demolition and rebuilding was progressing. Even the long-suffering Samuel was beginning to despair:

> It is hard to write without passion, when one reflects on the deaths and the suffering, on the sin and shame which have been added to the sum of London's misery during the six years which houses condemned as unfit for habitation have been allowed to stand. If it is said that the cost of greater speed would have been too great, it might well be asked what other objects has the State in view which makes it too great an expense to preserve and protect its peoples? [...] My hope of one day having a parish with houses fit for people has grown very faint.[32]

The Barnetts' spirits were lifted a couple of years later when a group of their friends and colleagues jointly raised a sum of £36,000 – sufficient to found the East London Dwellings Company, a philanthropic building concern. Gleefully, Samuel began to make plans for re-housing those for whom securing the tenancy of clean and decent accommodation was the most problematic: the unskilled, casual and day workers who lacked the regular employment demanded by most letting agents and trustees. He also envisioned the building of common lodging houses for the very poorest of the residents, where they would not be subject to 'petty rules or unjust interference', nor deprived of the basic 'comfort and recreation' enjoyed by their more affluent counterparts.[33] Despite these initiatives – and further interventions from Richard Cross – other obstacles were to be negotiated before Henrietta and Samuel's hopes really began to materialise.

One particularly intractable problem was that land came on the market at short notice and with the minimum of advertising. This meant that the land could be snapped up and used for some commercial – and, as far as the Barnetts were concerned, unscrupulous – venture. For instance, two large public houses had materialised on cleared ground which would have been ideal for the construction of new homes. Henrietta soon became wise to this and, resolving to somehow purchase such land for more altruistic ends, contrived to keep her ear closer to the ground. In 1884, she and Samuel were enjoying a horse-drawn tour of England with Kate and Leonard Courtney. They had taken in sights from Oxfordshire through to Derbyshire and had trotted further north to the pretty little coastal town of Whitby, North Yorkshire, where they had intended to rest for a while before meandering back to London. However, no sooner had they unpacked their bags when a letter arrived informing the Barnetts of the impending sale of 'an important corner' of Whitechapel. So, with equal measures of alacrity and reluctance, the Barnetts uprooted themselves from the charms of rural England and caught the York train to London that very same day.[34] Back in Whitechapel, Henrietta hastily arranged their 'vicarious attendance' where the auction was to be held and very shortly, they were the stupefied owners of a 'great slice of [their] parish', one much larger than they had intended to purchase. Samuel was particularly shell-shocked – not least because it had taken every single penny of their savings just to pay the deposit. But Henrietta, irrepressible and optimistic as ever, was ecstatic:

> I recall my sense of triumph as, standing on a debris heap – dead cats, tin pots, and broken furniture accentuating the devastation – I realised we were king and queen in possession and that there need be no more delay.[35]

Certainly, the persistence of their efforts and interventions paid some dividends. Within three years, numerous blocks of dwellings had been constructed, replacing many of the cramped, higgledy-piggledy and foetid courts with tall, clean houses set in orderly and more spacious streets. Anticipating Henrietta's plans to make Hampstead Garden Suburb an attractive place to live for all, regardless of class or circumstances, one group of dwellings – College Buildings – was constructed with 'some regard to beauty' as opposed to the somewhat utilitarian facades of other replacements for the 'squalid courts' and their crumbling hovels. These are Samuel's words, but the sentiments are undoubtedly Henrietta's:

> Benevolence has had much to do with the erection of dwellings in the neighbourhood; and in the name of benevolence … some argue that decoration must be given up so that such dwellings may be able to pay. Probably this is a mistake in economy; it is certainly a mistake in benevolence. To treat one's neighbours as oneself is not to decorate one's own house with the art of the world, and to leave one's neighbour's house with nothing but drain pipes to relieve the bareness of the walls.[36]

Another initiative was to encourage 'self-government' amongst the tenants. On one level, the thinking underpinning this was steeped in Samuel Smiles' 'self-help' ethos, which was highly influential in late Victorian society, even if it did lie somewhat at odds with Henrietta and Samuel's professed subscription to Christian Socialist values.[37] On another level, however, this initiative was rather more altruistic. The frustrations of the previous 13 years had caused both Henrietta and Samuel to become increasingly disillusioned with the principles of the COS, not least because the only ideal it offered to the working classes was one of 'unrelenting thrift'.[38] Gradually, they had come to realise the extent to which tenants resented unwarranted interference and, in consequence, pursued two policies. The first of these was to accept that, provided the tenants paid their rent regularly and did not cause undue disruption to others, then the way in which they chose to live their lives was their own concern. The second was to involve the tenants in the management of their dwellings. This was intended to give them a greater sense of ownership and autonomy which, Henrietta hoped, would in turn engender senses of pride in and responsibility for their homes.

According to Henrietta, these new developments and their more relaxed regime meant that the earliest purpose-built tenement block to be erected in Whitechapel – the George Yard Buildings – became less popular. However, Crowder, the builder and owner of these, tells a different story. By 1883, he was grumbling that minimal intervention policies had resulted in his becoming 'disgusted with the state of [his] property' and the 'vicious, dirty and destructive habits' of those who lived there. In consequence, he felt increasingly 'obliged' to decline more and more applications for tenancy.[39] By 1890 it had been decided to refurbish the rooms of the George Yard Buildings and convert them into students' accommodation for the earnest young graduates keen to leave behind the leafy privileges of Oxford and Cambridge in order to live, work and study amongst the most deprived sector of the population.[40] For all Henrietta's glowing – if somewhat partial – accounts of housing developments in Whitechapel, there remained pockets of squalor throughout the parish. The virtues of the new developments which she extolled without reserve are also questioned by others. Not all slum clearance and building was carried out by those motivated by benevolence. During the 1880s, the slums of Whitechapel were also extended rather than alleviated by greedy entrepreneurs, who crammed poky terraces into the back gardens of houses vacated by those sufficiently wealthy to move to the more salubrious suburbs mushrooming around the outskirts of London during the second half of the 19th century. The rickety old rookeries, hastily (and flimsily) constructed during the 18th century to accommodate dock labourers were 'supplanted by new and worse ones with a greater concentration of families exposed to less light and air'.[41] Contemporary 1880s accounts are similarly ambivalent. In the first volume of his vast survey of life and labour in late-Victorian London, Charles Booth cannot deny the seductive appeal of Whitechapel's vibrant and diverse street culture: 'a veritable Tom Tiddler's ground, the Eldorado of the East, a gathering together of poor fortune-seekers … seeking their livelihood under conditions … on the middle ground between civilisation and barbarism'. At the same time, he also acknowledges the capacity of the new lodging developments to inculcate the 'principles of order, cleanliness and decency' into the 'lurid and intense' lives of their residents. However, he notes the lingering of Whitechapel's 'vile spots' and their infestations of 'horrible dens' which still remained to be demolished.[42] Perhaps he would have said even more had not he been a close acquaintance of the Barnetts. Indeed, Henrietta maintains that it was Samuel's early work amongst the poverty of Whitechapel which prompted the 'colossal' survey which would be forever associated with Booth's name.[43]

As well as concerning themselves with the housing of the Whitechapel residents, Samuel and Henrietta became increasingly aware of the need for open spaces such as parks and playgrounds for those whose lives were spent in cramped accommodation. This was by no means an original idea: many existing municipal parks in towns and cities all over the British Isles were the product of the branch of Victorian philanthropy which regarded such spaces as social necessities rather than luxuries. Finding space in the crowded and labyrinthine courts of Whitechapel was another matter. However, as early as 1875, Henrietta and Samuel arranged for a small piece of land behind the church to be cleared of its weed-choked debris and converted into a garden. The soot-stained wall which obscured it was replaced by freshly-painted iron railings, and trees and shrubs were planted in newly-spread topsoil. According to Henrietta, the people of Whitechapel showed 'great interest' in this project and this interest fuelled her hopes that such an oasis of light and beauty in their 'dark neighbourhood' would prove morally uplifting.[44] Not surprisingly, the people of Whitechapel did visit the garden, but rather than reflect amongst their sylvan surroundings, they got up to all sorts of mischief not foreseen by the idealistic young Barnetts. Courting couples would canoodle behind the shrubs, whilst young children would scramble around the fragile saplings and snigger at the amorous activities of their older brothers and sisters. No doubt the iron railings, too, would have provided an irresistible substitute for a climbing frame. Despairing at such antics, Samuel mooted the possibility of organising concerts in the garden, 'high-class' rather than the 'dance' music which he believed would further encourage the indulgence of sensual or sensationalist pleasures. A few years later, however, Henrietta and Samuel did concede that children needed some designated space where they could burn up some of their boundless energy.

By 1881 a playground had been established in Wentworth Street. It had swings and a slide, and the gravel on which it had originally been constructed had been replaced with tarmac: many children's knees, elbows or inadequately-shod feet had been grazed or cut by the rough and jagged stones surrounding the play equipment.[45] The smooth expanse of tarmac would also have provided an ideal space for childhood pastimes such as hopscotch, jacks and marbles, as well as skipping and ball games – or at least so Henrietta and Samuel imagined. Some children did use the playground, especially after the swings and slide were installed, but many more preferred to hang around the nooks and crannies of the cobbled streets which, despite their relentless fug of soot, cooking fumes, effluvia from blocked drains and sulphuric gases, had a vibrancy and an edge utterly lacking in any purpose-built playground. In these streets, the children could play football, scuffle and scramble around derelict buildings, cadge food from street traders and hassle toffs for spare coppers. On top of that, of course, the streets offered endless opportunities for petty crime for these sharp-witted young people. Many a young pickpocket would have honed their skills in the shadowy alleyways of Whitechapel, where an insider's knowledge of the topography would have ensured a slick getaway. En masse, these Whitechapel urchins were an intimidating bunch. A scandalised Walter Besant, social reformer and a friend of the Barnetts, observed their unruliness when they were let loose on a day trip to Hampstead Heath and commented that he had never heard 'language more vile and depraved' and further asserted that it was far worse than any he had overheard 'from any grown men or women in the very worst parts of the town'. Apparently, even some local workmen were shocked by the torrents of abusive expletives tripping from these children's tongues.[46]

Their behaviour wasn't much better in Whitechapel. In an effort to draw people to the Wentworth Street playground, Henrietta and Samuel cajoled the People's Entertainment Society into providing Thursday evening concerts throughout the summer months. Somewhat naively, Samuel hoped that people would sit and listen quietly to the music. Henrietta, however, probably rather more attuned to the residents' sense of fun, organised dancing at these concerts. Unfortunately, the more disruptive element of Whitechapel had other ideas. One Thursday evening, some energetic folk-dancing between volunteers and children swiftly degenerated into 'noisy horse-play' when a 'crowd of the abandoned girls of the neighbourhood' and their dissolute boyfriends interrupted the proceedings. Emboldened by drink, this 'lawless' mob lurched among the revellers and 'Bacchanalian' chaos ensued. Henrietta, resplendent in a white straw bonnet trimmed with terra-cotta ribbon which matched the embroidery on her dress and cape, had been dancing with a 'grubby little lad' and ended up treading on his tiny shoeless foot. She and Samuel tried remonstrating with these teenage renegades but their words had no effect on their gin-fuelled frolics. So, they ordered the band to stop playing, cleared the playground, locked the gates and made for home, not anticipating the reaction of the angry crowd. The thwarted revellers had blocked the pathway, forcing Samuel and Henrietta to walk in the road. Here, they were forced to endure howls and hoots of derision accompanied by a hail of stones hurled from all directions. Henrietta did at least have some protection from her 'thick straw bonnet' whereas the 'soft felt hat' which he had donned left Samuel much more vulnerable to these missiles. Fortunately, drink had marred the co-ordination of their assailants, so only a few of the stones went anywhere near their intended targets.[47]

This incident made the Barnetts realise that their 'neighbours were not yet fit for freedom', but it is a measure of their optimism and determination that they still pursued their attempt to open a larger public garden, Baker's Row Park, on ground formerly owned by Quakers. Money from various benevolent organisations enabled them to landscape the grounds, build a bandstand and set aside an area for children's recreation. Amidst much excitement and ceremony, this park was officially opened by the Prince and Princess of Wales in July 1881. The streets of Whitechapel were decked with bunting, flags and floral decorations and, as Henrietta recalled with some acerbity, self-important local businessmen and their equally bumptious wives 'fussed' their way to the best seats. Meanwhile, the more diffident local tradespeople made do with straining to catch momentary glimpses of their illustrious visitors, whilst the crowd of onlookers excluded from the opening ceremony made their presence felt by pushing, jostling, yelling and heckling throughout the proceedings.[48]

Generally, this park seemed to be more successful than the previous ones. The play area – possibly because of its relative seclusion – was frequently crowded with children. A court was also laid out for games of 'fives' and volunteers were enlisted to act as coaches and referees. The park benches proved to be popular with older residents – especially as they were suitably distanced from the noisy excitement of the playground. 'Delightful' as it was to see such use made of these facilities, Henrietta and Samuel would have been disappointed by the propensity of some residents to abuse them. Flowerbeds would be trampled upon, shrubs uprooted and saplings damaged, sometimes wantonly but more often accidentally as young people whooped and charged through the grounds. Rather than condemn them for such wilful disobedience, the Barnetts remained convinced that these residents were capable of redemption: partly through encouraging a pride in their improved homes and surroundings, but mainly through breaking down the all-too-palpable barriers between the social classes.

To this end, Henrietta and Samuel, like Octavia before them, arranged parties at the vicarage, where they hoped that the classes could meet on an equal footing. For Samuel, to 'entertain the poor' was an essential a religious service as visiting them and, indeed, the 'only justification for possessing houses, grounds and pictures'.[49] Perhaps not surprisingly, such sentiments provoked tirades of derision from those who perceived the Barnetts' largesse as a futile means of saving 'starving souls by pictures, parties and pianos'.[50] Nonetheless, these parties were held each month in the Barnetts' drawing-room at St Jude's. For those more accustomed to damp and squalid two-roomed hovels, the relative opulence of the Barnett household must have been akin to that of a Tsar's palace. For all Henrietta's professed indifference to worldly goods, the room was crammed with inherited paintings, ornaments and memorabilia from their various jaunts abroad, surrounding a motley array of furniture: a chinoise and chaise longue draped in silk and fur respectively, early Victorian armchairs, a damask-covered kneeling chair and Sheraton-style dining chairs. This eclectic mix of styles was interspersed with an abundance of exotic flower and plant arrangements which, according to one of the Barnetts' awe-struck visitors, evoked the 'fields and gardens and big skies' beyond the gloom and grime of Whitechapel.[51] Needless to say, by no means all the guests at the Barnetts' parties were overwhelmed by these unfamiliar surroundings. Neither was Henrietta any too impressed by the 'disagreeable and exhausting' aspects of these attempts to break down class barriers. Enduring the 'greasy heads' and damp, grimy clothing which smeared the William Morris wallpaper and damask covers was bad enough, but the guests' behaviour was even worse. Knowing the Barnetts' attitude to drink, they would make sure that they were well fuelled with gin before they arrived. The guests would then proceed to secrete food into their pockets, pinch flowers from Henrietta's carefully arranged displays, blatantly pilfer fruit and amuse themselves and each other by making 'unseemly noises' interspersed with ribald jokes and horseplay. These opportunistic reprobates also soon realised they could smuggle in friends who would masquerade as 'impromptu relations' or 'unexpected lodgers'.[52]

Rather than abandon the effort, Henrietta swiftly developed strategies to counteract such disruptions. Chairs and sofas were placed well back from the walls and their damask covers were replaced with washable Liberty cotton. Simple, buffet-style refreshments were served instead of grander, sit-down meals, and attempts to entertain the Whitechapel residents at these gatherings were all but abolished. As far as Henrietta was concerned, for a party to be successful, 'entertainment should be scanty'. Expanding on this belief, she asserted that 'vain' and 'shallow' 'songs or parlour tricks' provide the most pleasure for those who perform them and did little to address the mutual prejudices and suspicions which marred relationships between the classes.[53] Nor was she impressed by the propensity of some of her social peers to patronise the working classes by either 'playing to the gallery' – adopting vulgar and ribald East End ways themselves – or hosting these parties in their servants' quarters. One grand old lady entertained her East End guests in the stable-yard and, oblivious to individual preferences, had ready-milked and sweetened tea dispensed from watering-cans. It hardly needs stating that Henrietta was much affronted by such insensitivity [54] – and, of course, it ran counter to her principles underlying these parties. For what she really hoped was that the working-class East Enders would somehow assimilate the 'manners' and the 'self-restraint' of their philanthropic middle-class counterparts.[55] This determination to improve the cultural, as well as the environmental, circumstances of the urban poor was a major preoccupation of many eminent Victorians including, amongst others, John Ruskin and Matthew Arnold. Such thinking was to fuel Henrietta and Samuel's next venture to address the needs of the residents of Whitechapel.

VIII

Educating East Enders

Reforming Schools in London

In common with many other Victorian social reformers, Henrietta and Samuel were much concerned with matters of education for adults as well as children: what we would now recognise as 'lifelong learning'. For the Barnetts, education was not merely a matter of assimilating 'facts' and 'knowledge', but a much more holistic process by which prejudices could be challenged, self-esteem raised, passions ignited and potential realised. As implied in previous chapters, attitudes like this to education – particularly for the working classes – were quite radical. Such thinking underpinned the project for which Samuel and Henrietta are best known: the founding of Britain's first university settlement at Toynbee Hall, Whitechapel. Their intention was to create a place where Oxbridge students and graduates could live among and improve the lives of those less fortunate. It was named after Arnold Toynbee (1852-1883), the young and idealistic political economy lecturer who dedicated his brief life to developing an economic system which would benefit the poor. Deeply committed to working-class education and the co-operative movement, his optimism remained constant. Shortly before his death, he extolled the benefits of continuing education:

> Those who have had the most experience in manufacturing districts are of the opinion that the moral advance, as manifested for example in temperance, in orderly behaviour, in personal appearance has been very great ... The number of subjects which interest working people is much greater than before, and the discussion of the newspaper is supplanting the old, foul language of the workshop.[1]

Such optimism was shared by the Barnetts. On the day of Toynbee Hall's opening, Christmas Eve, 1884, Samuel outlined its aims to 'educate citizens in the knowledge of one another, to provide teaching for those who are willing to learn and recreation to those who are weary'.[2] Thus, volunteers became engaged in a diverse range of projects from the running of boys' clubs, the provision of legal aid, the organising of lectures and debates, and the arranging of art exhibitions and concerts. Others set themselves up as street patrollers and, anticipating the Mass Observation project of the 1930s, solemnly recorded nightly occurrences of drunkenness and violence.[3] In keeping with their philosophy on education, the Barnetts were determined to enrich people's lives practically, vocationally and culturally. Thus, classes ranged from the practical – first aid, carpentry, sewing, child care, domestic economy and woodcarving – to the vocational – book-keeping, arithmetic, building, nursing and shorthand – and the academic – classic and modern literature, foreign languages, philosophy and the sciences.[4] A few years after its opening, several debating societies and clubs were founded at Toynbee Hall. It was also used as a base by Charles Booth and his team of researchers as they worked on *Life and Labour of the People in London*.

The history and achievements of the Toynbee Hall settlement have already been well documented by a number of historians.[5] At the time of writing (December 2003), Toynbee volunteers are still devising innovative means of addressing the illness, unemployment, racial tension, drug abuse and overcrowding that continue to blight Whitechapel and its surrounding districts.[6] Without wishing to undermine its past achievements, Toynbee Hall has had its critics. Gareth Stedman Jones argues that, far from being a radical response to the social crises which erupted in the early 1880s, Toynbee Hall was – in common with the COS and Poor Law Reform – founded on rather more reactionary ideas and practices formulated during the 1860s as a response to what was perceived as the increasingly feckless and immoral habits of the urban underclass.[7] Carolyn Steedman highlights the paternalistic nature of the Workers' Education Association – inaugurated at Toynbee Hall – and argues that its underlying purpose was to dispel insurrection from the working classes by creating a sense of national identity through class harmony.[8] Similarly, whilst Melanie Tebbutt acknowledges the genuine sincerity behind many of the Toynbee Hall volunteers' eagerness to improve the lot of their working-class neighbours, she also points out how their offers of friendship were met with a polite, but firm 'refusal' from those sensitive to undertones of paternalism.[9] Paternalism – the altruistic use of property and the church – dated back to the feudal system of the Middle Ages. In the turbulent times of the 19th century, it was hardly surprising that refuge should be sought in what was imagined to be a more stable period in history: one in which each person knew and accepted their place in the social hierarchy. Thus, following the industrialisation and urbanisation of the 19th century, eminent Victorians such as Thomas Carlyle, Matthew Arnold and Benjamin Disraeli formulated the principles of paternalism into a new social theory:

> The paternalists saw a simple solution to *all* the social problems of the time. Through the efforts of the landed property owners and the Church, they would lead a moral and spiritual regeneration of the nation which would create a more Christian and stable society … If the growth of manufacturing continued then the owners of urban property would also realise their duties and act as model mill and mine owners. Moral decay, and its outward signs … of crime, vagrancy and prostitution, would disappear under the influence of the Church which would be responsible for the education of the people.[10]

Such thinking was to inspire 19th-century factory and mill owners like Sir Titus Salt, who built a model village named Saltaire for his workers at his wool mill near Bradford, West Yorkshire. Other similar settlements were soap manufacturer Lord Leverhulme's Port Sunlight near Liverpool, chocolate manufacturer George Cadbury's Bourneville in the suburbs of Birmingham and his northern counterpart Joseph Rowntree's New Earswick on the outskirts of York. Whilst the Barnetts were not sufficiently wealthy to provide such largesse, they saw it as their responsibility to share their knowledge, values and attitudes with others less fortunate and, through the Toynbee Hall initiative, to encourage others in privileged circumstances to do likewise.

Samuel Barnett's achievements during his 22 years as Warden of Toynbee Hall are meticulously – and loyally – recorded by Henrietta in his biography. Like his wife, he believed that people learned 'indirectly' and therefore took pains to ensure that the

7   *Toynbee Hall, Whitechapel*

'sleeping energies' of students were roused by the 'cultured', whose 'various good and elevating influences' would teach them the 'better reasons which make life worth living'.[11] It has to be said, however, that most of the students were either lower middle class – the growing numbers of aspiring junior civil servants, clerks, primary schoolteachers and shop assistants – or 'steady' and 'thrifty' working-class men. Henrietta was less than impressed by some of the early Toynbee students:

> They were very trying … young ladies whose affectations when 'seeking culture' made one long to shake them; prigs who quoted Browning on all occasions; excellent persons whose little learning made them mad – with conceit; pretentious youths who patronised all who had not read the few books they had perused, and who killed by bad manners the belief that education made equality.[12]

Henrietta was never one to suffer fools, but such youthful pretensions may also have served as an uncomfortable reminder of her own predilections towards pomposity in her earlier years. More than anything else, she must have been frustrated that their efforts to make education accessible to all seemed only to attract this dilettante lower middle class. In fact, some appeared to use the classes as a dating agency: 'silly and wilful girls' would distract 'enamoured youths' and, on one occasion, this resulted in the elopement of two students. Untrained and inexperienced volunteer teachers inevitably experienced discipline problems: failure to defuse a quarrel ended up with half a class 'alienated' and the entire course in chaos. There were also instances of 'financial dishonesty' and what Henrietta darkly refers to as the 'undue influence' of one of the volunteers . Meanwhile, problems frequently occurred on a logistical level. Rooms were double-booked; classes had to be cancelled when volunteers defected to paid employment; philosophical debates were sabotaged by uproarious children's parties held in adjoining rooms; overcrowding was sometimes so acute that the volunteers were forced to use their bedrooms for tutorials and seminars. Such unorthodox use of rooms infuriated the staff who were lumbered with the weekly washing of counterpanes made grubby by this constant influx of unexpected guests.[13]

Many of the volunteer workers were very young – barely out of their teens – and most had led sheltered lives well away from the volatile and vibrant environs of Whitechapel. Samuel – by then aged 42 – did his best to act as a father figure to these young men and formed close and lasting bonds with many of them.[14] Early on, it had been decided that there were to be no women settlers at Toynbee Hall. According to Henrietta, the reason for this was that young, intellectual men had only just joined 'the ranks of philanthropists' – previously the domain of middle-class women – and Samuel felt that they would be intimidated by the presence of these more experienced females. Judith Walkowitz, the feminist historian, is more cynical. She sees this as a Victorian revival of chivalry: male theorisation, appropriation and control disguised as benevolence.[15] Certainly, even by 1897, Samuel was still reacting with alarm to the 'many women – too many' who had become involved with other settlements and remained adamant that Toynbee Hall should be exclusively male.[16] This suggests his own intimidation by these women but perhaps his unspoken fear here was that a female presence in his hothouse of earnest commitment, academic rigour and debate may have ignited passions other than those for social reform. As John Tosh has pointed out, several leading figures of the 19th century – amongst them, Thomas Carlyle, Alfred, Lord Tennyson and Robert Browning – expressed their concerns about male sexual energy and what they saw as its potentially destructive nature.[17] Against the advice of those who advocated the employment of male servants only, young women were employed as housemaids and kitchen assistants. They were supervised by a formidable middle-aged housekeeper but, inevitably, some shenanigans occurred between these young women and those volunteers who were not as earnest, committed and sober as the Barnetts had anticipated. One way to sneak into the servants' quarters was for the men to offer to carry heavy trays or fetch coal. Any servant found colluding with these illicit liaisons would have been dismissed, whilst the miscreant young men were merely 'dealt with' by Samuel.[18] Of course, there was one exception to the 'men only' rule at Toynbee Hall: Henrietta, who managed the house and staff for 17 years.

Henrietta is circumspect about the time spent as the glorified housekeeper of Toynbee Hall. In her husband's biography, she maintains that she took a great deal of satisfaction in the efficient running of domestic affairs. Her exacting standards clearly caused dissent amongst the Toynbee residents, however. A sub-committee was formed amongst these young men who, on no less than three occasions, 'volunteered' to take over her duties. Henrietta duly complied on each occasion. However, she must have managed to thwart their efforts because she recounts (with a certain glee) that 'three times, a chastened sub-committee' came grovelling back, begging her 'to resume the reins of government'. And 'chastened' was something of an understatement, given the unctuous tones of a letter she received, 'very sincerely', from Ernest Aves, the Honorary Secretary of the Committee. In this, he informed her that a 'special vote of thanks' had been recorded 'for the time and care bestowed upon the management of the house' as well as her 'invaluable help' with the financial administration of

Toynbee Hall.[19] No doubt Henrietta gleaned more than a brief glow of satisfaction from this and other ingratiating gestures from the men of Toynbee Hall. She was also very much aware of the fact that she was the only woman in a community of 75 men – a community steeped in a hyper-masculine collegiate culture that, despite surface politeness, would not have placed too great a value on her 'feminine' touches. Rather, these would have been perceived as an unwelcome interference by men who thought their innovative lifestyle would allow them a legitimate escape from the stifling boredom of domesticity.[20] As one resident commented, Henrietta was the 'unexpected element' at Toynbee Hall who bought a 'touch of womanly refinement which corrected bachelor habits … and male roughness'.[21] Some would have deeply resented this – and not just the wayward heterosexual young men. This bookish and (almost) exclusively male environment also appealed to gay intellectuals who had rejected the competitive and cut-throat entrepreneurial world of their fathers. Notable amongst these men was Charles Ashbee, the architect and socialist, who had alienated his father, Henry, by refusing to join the family business after graduating from Cambridge. Initially, Henry Ashbee had been a devoted and hard-working husband and father but, disillusioned by his son's rebellion and resentful of his wife's widening social circle, he transmogrified into a patriarchal tyrant who became infamous for his obsessive collecting of Victorian pornography.[22] Appalled by his father's hypocrisy, Charles railed against the oppressions suffered by married women and was highly sympathetic towards the 'new women' of the late 19th century – those who had rejected marriage in favour of financial and emotional independence.[23]

However, Charles was also a staunch supporter of those 'companionate' marriages identified by John Stuart Mill in 1867:

> Women and men are, for the first time in history, really each other's companions … In former days a man passed his life among men … with men alone did he consult on any serious business; the wife was either a plaything or an upper servant. All this, among the educated classes, is now changed … The women of a man's family are his habitual society; the wife is his chief associate, his most confidential friend, and often his most trusted advisor.[24]

As one of the Toynbee residents observed, this was precisely the 'ideal of married life' displayed by the Barnetts' relationship, in which he saw Henrietta as 'an equal partner in work and thought'. He also noted the symbiotic nature of their marriage, asserting that 'together they did what neither could have done apart'.[25] The historian Seth Koven also highlights the 'subversive complementarity' of the Barnetts' personal and professional lives. Contrasting Samuel's 'gentleness' and deference with Henrietta's 'boldness' and audacity, he concludes that their marriage was one which 'respects and encourages individuality' at the same time as it 'create[ed] harmonious and productive solidarity among unlike types of people'.[26] This may well have been the case, but as feminist historians such as Mary Poovey have pointed out, Victorian women still 'remained limited by the way in which the female sex was defined and positioned'.[27] Indeed, despite the middle-class woman's higher profile in the world of work, she was still expected to behave with the decorum and modesty deemed appropriate for her sex. For the outspoken, quick-witted and spirited Henrietta, such expectations must have been extremely irritating. These frustrations are understated in her biography of Samuel, but they haunt a fragment from her personal papers:

> I must remember I am the Vicar's wife and *owe* it to him to take as my *first* duty to do a wife's part, and be his helpmate in his work … I must not push things, suggest and leave it to God to do the rest by his Holy Spirit … I resolve to preach devotion and duty … to help folk to *do* their own work, and not to criticise others.[28]

Implicit in this self-rebuke are the various tensions between Henrietta's 'feminine' sense of duty as a wife and her 'masculine' impatience at the incompetence of others. There is also a vague hint that her faith in religion was declining after almost fifteen years of witnessing first-hand the brutalising and degrading effects of poverty. Indeed, it was around this time that Octavia Hill, discerning Henrietta's 'want of real affection for the Church', told Samuel in no uncertain terms that he should rectify this shortcoming in his wife.[29] It is doubtful that she would have taken much notice even if Samuel had followed Octavia's advice. So, whilst Samuel remained deeply committed to spiritual redemption for the tainted souls of Whitechapel, Henrietta's determination to educate hearts and minds became ever more apparent.

Henrietta's ability to exert more influence in the public arena was facilitated by changes in legislation that had been implemented over the previous decade or so. The Municipal Franchise Act 1869 had enabled women's participation in local government and, more significantly, following the 1870 Education Act, female involvement in the running and representation of School Boards was both intended and encouraged. As Jane Martin observed, the reasoning behind this was that middle-class women, childless or otherwise, were perceived as the 'saviours of the nation's children'.[30] Something Henrietta had learned from her past attempts to enrich and improve the lives of Whitechapel's young women was the extent to which they resented middle-class interference. She also realised the extent of the irreversible damage done by the Industrial schools from which these young women had graduated. So, in addition to her involvement with housing reform, rescue work and her Toynbee Hall responsibilities, Henrietta became ever more committed to challenging the iniquities of these institutions at root level. She had been inspired by the tireless efforts of Jane Nassau Senior, who several years earlier had helped the young Henrietta stun her 'shouting, angry and fighting' mob of pupils into silence by singing to them.[31] As an Inspector of Schools, Mrs Nassau Senior was appalled by the conditions in which many orphaned and unwanted children were incarcerated and began a 20-year campaign against them.

Industrial – or 'Barrack' schools as they were frequently disparaged – were offshoots of workhouses. They catered for homeless children, those from disorderly homes and those who had been caught begging. They were huge institutions: Forest Gate, the school which so appalled Jane Nassau Senior, held almost 600 children aged between three and sixteen. The purpose of these schools was to provide a rudimentary drilling in literacy and arithmetic, alongside training for menial work in adult life. The regime was austere, to say the least. All the children wore a uniform – any that happened to fit as they had no clothes of their own. This would be changed weekly. Rations of food were dependent upon the age of the child – size, physical health and, indeed, appetite, were not taken into consideration. The children were not called by their names and had no toys, personal possessions or any recreational activity. Once school was over, the girls were put to the endless scrubbing of floorboards, whilst the boys were turned out into the yard, where they would half-heartedly engage in scuffling among themselves or perhaps bully their smaller or duller-witted peers. Most oppressive

8 *Henrietta and Samuel at the founding of Toynbee Hall*

of all was the heavy pall of silence which hung over these institutions: silence was compulsory during meal times as well as lessons. The girls were not even allowed to relieve the monotony of scrubbing the floors by chatting and joking. Instead, they were placed in serried ranks yards apart from one another. Discipline was 'ruthless' even by Victorian standards: children were routinely beaten for the most minor of disobediences and habitual offenders were strapped into the much-feared 'restraining' chair. As its name implies, this was a terrifying contraption in which children's wrists, arms and legs were fettered in tight leather straps.[32]

Following Mrs Nassau Senior's emotive report, Henrietta – as a member of the school's Board of Managers – mobilised a 'delightful group of ladies' to tackle the iniquities and inhumanity of this institution. She also took responsibility for appointing compassionate members of staff, 'noble characters' who were prepared to sacrifice their own comforts in order to bring some hope and colour into these wretched children's lives. And over the next few years, several improvements were made. Playing fields and gardens replaced the Spartan cobbled yards; recreation rooms were filled with toys such as rocking horses, dolls' houses, climbing apparatus and board games such as bagatelle, draughts, lotto and tiddlywinks; previously bare walls were colour-washed and hung with paintings; the lofty rooms were 'brilliantly lit' and even heated with hot-water pipes. The children were called by their first names and were allowed to keep personal possessions such as small toys and books. Conversation was encouraged at mealtimes and, whilst there was little improvement in the food served, children were at least given some choice over the quantity provided. Not content with merely appointing new staff and instigating these changes, Henrietta and Samuel made frequent (and unexpected) visits to ensure these standards were maintained.[33] Despite these changes, Henrietta remained uneasy. During her many trips abroad, she became intrigued by alternative approaches to education and was particularly impressed by the system in Japan where the development of each child's individuality was considered paramount. Never one to rest on her laurels, she came to appreciate that:

> Though the school as a school was excellent, the system was wrong. The keynote of character development is love, and that was missing. No-one can love 600 children, each one of whom needs the comfort and stimulation of personally rendered affection ... With the experience of other nation's educational standards, the evils of herding children together, divorced from the influences which train resource, and deprived by discipline of the power of choice, took their true place in the list of our national wrong-doing.[34]

The trouble was, it was difficult to dismantle a system which, especially with its improvements, had engendered a great deal of approval and goodwill from the various Guardians of the Poor associated with Forest Gate and other, less enlightened 'Barrack' schools. Henrietta became increasingly scathing about their lack of insight and was infuriated by one 'comfortable' woman who 'radiated' with satisfaction at the sight of hundreds of children, oblivious to the pathos underlying their 'painfully clean and depressingly tidy' appearance. Such attitudes made her despair of ever alerting a complacent public to the iniquities of a system which, however well organised and efficient, deprived children of 'freedom, joy and individuality'.[35] As she later put it, 'what child so drilled can gather the strength which holds impulse and passion in check?'.[36]

In the event, the public's awareness of the potential for cruelty and neglect in the regime of 'Barrack' schools was gradually awakened by three separate tragedies. The first of these was at Hackney Pauper School, where it emerged that Ella Gillespie, one of the officers, was systematically abusing the children in her care. She would beat them with stinging nettles, make them kneel bare-legged on hot water-pipes and repeatedly crash their heads against the stone walls until blood ran from their noses and ears. What made this even worse was that her fellow officers were well aware of her cruelties but did nothing to stop her. Gillespie was sentenced to five years' penal servitude for her crimes. The school Guardians, as well as the general public and the press, were naturally deeply shocked and saddened by these revelations. However, they were reluctant to blame the system *per se* for these occurrences, preferring instead to cite sloppy management as being responsible. The second occurred at the school of which Henrietta was a manager. On New Year's Eve, 1890, worshippers were making their way home when they noticed a fug of smoke and flame around the school. They rushed to help, but the overcrowding, combined with the school's labyrinthine corridors and its lack of fire exits, meant that 22 children were either choked or burned to death. Many more suffered terrible injuries: emotionally as well as physically. An inquest was held in which pertinent questions were asked, bravery was commended and condolences were doled out but as Henrietta put it, no one thought to 'put the saddle on the right horse, and to declare that the *system* was wrong': a system which condoned the 'massing' of children in such dangerous conditions. What depressed her even more was the passive acceptance of grief-stricken parents, too ground down to rail against the senseless deaths of their children, who had been forcibly removed from 'bad' homes to a place of alleged safety.[37] Four years later, another disaster occurred at the same school. One scorching hot day, a maid noticed that the meat set aside for the children's lunch was putrid and covered in flies. Indignant, she pointed this out to an official, who took no notice at all, informing her in no uncertain terms that it was none of her business. The meat was subsequently served to the children and within hours, 141 children had succumbed to violent stomach cramps and raging temperatures. Of these children, two were to die frightening and painful deaths. Once again, a travesty of an inquest was held in which all were about to be exonerated when Henry Elliott, a member of the school staff, interrupted the proceedings by stating that he had 'something to say'. His revelations were startling. According to Henry, the children were routinely fed on the officers' waste instead of fresh meat and that the dietary table was often broken. Such was the seriousness of his allegations that the Local Government Board was obliged to hold a separate inquiry. All of Henry's allegations were proved to be well-founded but, beyond a 'mild rebuke', the Local Government Board took no action against the school superintendent responsible for these discrepancies. However, Henry – whose only 'crime' had been to blow the whistle on these malpractices – was swiftly dismissed from his post.[38]

That would probably have been an end to the matter – if the press and the highly influential *British Medical Journal* (BMJ) had not picked up on the issue. Incredulous at the Local Government Board's conclusion that the circumstances leading to the food poisoning had been 'accidental' and 'unprecedented', the journal asserted that the only accidental aspect of the case was the 'discovery of the evil' inherent within the system. No doubt fuelled by Henrietta's indignation, her brother-in-law and esteemed contributor to the BMJ, Ernest Hart, began a rigorous inquiry into *all* Barrack schools. This culminated in the formation of a Departmental Committee to 'inquire into the condition of Poor Law schools'. For the next two years, Henrietta (the only woman on the committee) worked ceaselessly with other members to unravel and expose the iniquities enmeshed within the system of all state-supported boarding schools. As well as meeting on a regular basis, the members of the committee visited all manner of these schools throughout London and the provinces. Then there was the gargantuan task of preparing the final report on their findings. Despite numerous personality clashes, internal wrangling and dissent, it was finally finished in February 1896. Samuel was delighted, not least because he had been the source of tireless 'counsel and comfort' to Henrietta as she threatened to crumple under the conflict and controversy generated by such harrowing work:

> [The report] really is a great triumph for my wife, and one she deserves. She has done most of the work, thought out the recommendations, executed the form and ... by a mixture of tact and temper, has made the men sign. If one thinks of the opinions with which some started, the change is wonderful.[39]

The report was published on 3 April 1896 in *The Times*. It was an angry and impassioned document which not only exposed the disease and adversity endured by children herded together in these institutions, but also railed against the 'criminal self-satisfaction' and 'wicked indifference' of those so-called Guardians of the Poor and Local Government officials who chose to turn a blind eye to such iniquities.[40] Thus shaken out of their complacency, these officials were incandescent with fury and responded by showering a tirade of personal attacks on Henrietta, who was variously accused of lying, exaggerating and disloyalty to her Board of Guardians. Her first reaction was to respond to these venomous outbursts with some well-chosen retorts of her own but – much against her will – Samuel persuaded her to keep quiet.[41] Others, however, were prepared to speak on her behalf: Ernest Hart was particularly incensed by these savage criticisms directed at his sister-in-law and determined to keep the plight of these children imprinted upon the public consciousness. As a result of his relentless campaigning, the State Children's Association (SCA) was formed in November 1896. The prime objective of this organisation was to ensure that children cared for by the state were nurtured as individuals. As far as its supporters were concerned, it was ludicrous that the state – unhampered by the factors which led to child neglect within the home – should perpetuate the suffering of children in its care. As a result of Hart's interventions, issues of child neglect and abuse gained unprecedented coverage in the media and hence became firmly imprinted on the public conscience. This no doubt took its toll on Hart, who died the following year aged sixty-two. The BMJ acknowledged his achievements thus:

> In Mr Ernest Hart the children have lost a friend; one never so persuasive as when pleading for the helpless, never so eloquent as when stirred by injustice to the weak. His interest in the State Children's Association and its aims was practical and persistent, and it should not be forgotten that to Mr Ernest Hart's fearless energy is owed the earliest arousing of public attention to the evils connected with Barrack schools, and the demand for radical reform.[42]

Through these demands for 'radical reform' emerged two new education systems to replace the now-notorious Barrack schools. The first of these was 'Village Communities': groups of purpose-built cottages surrounded by flower beds and lawns. Between twelve and twenty children would live in each of these cottages, all supervised by trained staff. Middle-class visitors to these communities were impressed by their attractive layout, the clean, tidy and well-disciplined children and the absence of the diseases which had blighted the overcrowded Barrack schools. Yet such an ambience had a price. The reason the children appeared so orderly and well-behaved was that they were subjected to endless physical drilling, a means of control used in schools since the middle of the 19th century. Such a method of discipline had evolved through the concerns of Sir James Kay, the first secretary of the Committee of the Privy Council on Education, and his colleagues on the Poor Law Commission, Edwin Chadwick and E. Carleton Tufnell. Convinced that 'pauperism' was the result of 'inherited and inbred moral shortcomings' rather than the consequence of unemployment and overcrowding in a turbulent economy and environment, Kay argued this degenerate sector of society needed to be taught 'the habits of industry' as early as possible. As he put it, if 'workhouse children grew up educated in reading, writing and arithmetic only, they would be unfitted for earning their livelihood through the "sweat of their brow"'.[43] However, if they were trained via military-style drill, the benefits would be two-fold. First, this training would instil order amongst huge groups of unruly children, haphazardly herded together. Second – and this particularly appealed to Chadwick, the first Poor Law Commissioner – the children's health would benefit from such regular physical exercise.[44] Such an ethos lingered in schools throughout the rest of the century and into the early part of the next. In 1894, a teaching manual proclaimed that:

> the class at drill should be a mere machine, actuated only by the will, and at the word, of the teacher … Every order should be given smartly; and its execution with unhesitating promptitude should invariably be as rigorously demanded.[45]

Whilst such rigid training may have been necessary as an initial means of establishing boundaries in huge institutions – some newly incarcerated children were not above trying to burn down these instruments of oppression – it was hardly warranted in smaller and more intimate institutions like the Village Communities. As Henrietta and Samuel both agreed, such means of discipline may produce robust physical health but these children's coercion into blind obedience was certainly not conducive to the development of the self-reliance, independence and initiative needed in adult life.[46]

So, another system grew from the SCA's demands for the nurturing of children living under the care of the State: 'Scattered Homes' were rented houses dotted around working-class communities in cities throughout England. In each of these homes, up to twelve children of varying ages were cared for by a housekeeper chosen for her warmth and maternal qualities. Bedrooms would be shared by no more than four children, and one single-bedded room was reserved for any child who was ill. As well as helping to prevent the spread of disease, this enabled an ailing child to have the space, peace and quiet necessary for recovery. These 'State' children were not educated separately, as they would have been in Barrack schools or Village Communities. Instead, they attended the local elementary schools along with children cared for by their own families. In consequence, they became integrated into their local communities, making friends outside their homes and learning the resourcefulness and resilience necessary for adult life. Whereas in Barrack schools or Village Communities the children would have had no day-to-day responsibility for chores, cooking or running errands, in Scattered Homes, the housekeeper would encourage – and expect – her charges to help with all the sweeping, dusting, mending, cooking and washing generated by such a large household.[47] As well as the children benefiting from the relative freedoms inherent in the Scattered Homes system, the housekeeper, too, would be a fully integrated member of her community, able to mix with neighbours and to become involved in local activities. Much has been implied about the austerity, coldness and even sadism of the staff in institutions such as Barrack schools and Village Communities. However, it is worth remembering that they themselves were isolated and incarcerated within the same system, and it is perhaps not surprising that their own simmering resentment and frustration occasionally erupted into anger and violence. Teachers during the mid- and late 19th century also lived in abiding fear of the demands inflicted by the Revised Code, an 1862 Act of Parliament which deemed that schools should be paid by 'results' – the success rates of children sitting an annual 3Rs (reading, writing and arithmetic) examination – as well as records of 'satisfactory' attendance:

> For more than one generation of teachers and scholars [...], the daily routine became an unremitting grind in the 3Rs, with constant repetition and rote-learning the normal methods of instruction. Individual initiative was crushed as teachers endeavoured to meet the conditions of the [Revised] Code and discipline was severe.[48]

So the children from the Scattered Homes would still have been subjected to a certain amount of mental and physical drilling whilst at school, but at least their leisure time was not so regimented. Similarly, it should be noted that by no means all working-class children remembered their schooldays as cruel, harsh or oppressive. As Jonathan Rose has argued, a sizeable number were grateful for the discipline of the classroom which, for all its shortcomings, did provide a degree of stability, security and consistency often lacking in the chaos of their home lives. Plenty also acknowledged that without the learning by rote from the admittedly tedious textbooks of their youth, they would not have had the fundamental skills which they later used to discover the pleasures of learning for themselves.[49]

Henrietta strongly supported the blend of freedom and responsibility enjoyed by children in the Scattered Home system, but remained concerned about the injurious effects of the urban environment on the children's physical health. Indeed, another project which flourished during the Barnetts' years at Toynbee Hall was the Children's Country Holiday Fund. This had actually laid its roots several years earlier. In 1877 Samuel, stressed and exhausted by the demands of his first few years in Whitechapel, arranged to cover church duties for Canon Shuttleworth in Wadebridge, a tiny village in Cornwall. With the heady scents of its moors, the savage beauty of its coastline and its flower-strewn woods, it provided the perfect antidote to the grime and grind of Whitechapel. The 'church duties' proved none too taxing either. Most days, Henrietta and Samuel would spend the mornings reading some improving tome and, after lunch, would pack up their two-wheeled cart with a picnic basket, oats for the pony and sketching materials before heading off to explore the countryside. They were soon joined by guests, equally seduced by the idea of this refreshing alternative to urban toils. Octavia Hill, deeply despondent after the end of her romantic liaison with Edward Bond, was the first to arrive and was cajoled out of her despair by the variety of frivolous pursuits dreamt up by Henrietta.[50] A week or two later, Alice and Ernest Hart arrived with their horses and carriages. These close friends and family were shortly followed by 'more and more guests, rich and poor; gentle and simple' – in other words, a hotchpotch of more casual acquaintances, such as workers from Whitechapel and their children who, intoxicated by the scope and space of these unfamiliar surroundings, drove Henrietta to distraction with their 'uncontrolled laughter and lawlessness of habits'.[51] Nonetheless, perhaps recalling the freedom and pleasures of her own country childhood, she did recognise the extent to which these children, stunted by their urban upbringing, blossomed amongst the air, light and space of the beaches and surrounding woodlands. Her first thought was to arrange for th ese somewhat irksome guests to stay with local families rather than at their vicarage. This less than altruistic impulse was soon supplanted by the idea that children much less privileged than their current visitors may also benefit from a break at the seaside or in the country. To this end, she and Samuel wrote to the *Guardian* encouraging the clergy in the Home Counties to promote this scheme among local parishioners willing to give city children a holiday in rural surroundings.

Just a few weeks later, nine sick children were duly provided with a fortnight's holiday in the Sussex countryside and by 1880 more than 400 children were to benefit from the country holiday scheme. Four years later, this local project grew into a national association, the Children's Country Holiday Fund (CCHF), which soon inspired similar schemes in settlements throughout England, Europe and the United States.[52] Indeed, as Martha Vicinus notes, the CCHF was one of the most popular projects organised by settlement workers. Instead of the clergy organising these placements, middle-class women volunteers would enlist support from their network of friends in the country to locate suitable premises for children from urban slums. Meanwhile, more case-hardened volunteers were recruited in order to weed out applicants whose bed-wetting, body lice or potential delinquency threatened to bring the scheme into disrepute. Nor were these holidays free: most families had to contribute to costs, which were only partially subsidised by the CCHF. Thus, the children most in need of a change from the poverty, disease and squalor of their daily lives became the least likely to benefit from such a scheme.[53] For their more fortunate counterparts, these holidays would have been something of a culture shock. No doubt their hosts, too, would have been more than a little alarmed by the sight of pasty-faced and undersized ragamuffins clambering out of the train windows, too impatient to wait for the guards to release them from locked compartments. Once unpenned, they would scuffle and scrap on little branch line platforms until volunteers herded them into some sort of order before distributing them at their allotted garden gates. Inevitably, there were conflicts: pecking orders were soon established between Cockney invaders and village urchins keen to protect their turf, and some of the country hosts were stunned by the string of expletives which peppered the speech of wide-eyed mites as young as six or seven. Any miscreant who filched plums, wrecked fences or tormented animals was swiftly despatched back to the city slums. Equally, the town children were nonplussed by the harmony of their host families, who *never* fought, swore or drank themselves senseless – even on Sundays. More often than not, these holidays were a success. The city children – despite their apparent puniness – *always* won the cricket matches organised by CCHF volunteers and they soon got the hang of games played by country children for generations. Instead of hanging out on street corners playing football, gambling with halfpennies or chalking out games of hopscotch on urban pavements, they learned to fish, fashion hoops from discarded barrels and make skipping ropes from lengths of abandoned twine. Meanwhile, CCHF officials, anxious that their urban charges should gain educationally as well as socially from their holidays, attempted to foster their interest in nature study. This led to numerous misunderstandings: a hammock stand was taken for a 'sparrer perch' and some unfortunate frogs met an untimely end when they were 'posted' into a letter box along with 'plenty of grass an' stuff for 'em to eat'.[54]

Notwithstanding these incidents, most of these city children returned home energised and sunburnt, laden with the flowers, fruit and eggs heaped upon them by their country hosts. The luckiest had parcels of freshly-baked cakes, biscuits and bread thrust upon them, but it is doubtful whether these gifts would have lasted much beyond the next station. Their memories of their country holidays were varied: some recalled the snowy-white sheets of the country bedrooms, while others were intrigued by the animals. Cows were described as 'oblong' with 'large, thoughtful eyes' whilst pigs had bodies 'made of pork, bacon and dripping'.[55] And some children were bereft when they had to leave their pastoral idyll. As one little girl put it, 'as I sit at school I always imagine myself roaming in the fields and watching the golden corn, and when I think of it, it makes me cry'.[56] For Henrietta, such poignant testimonials convinced her of the 'joyless[ness]' of urban children's lives:

> And those tears will find companions in the hearts of those which ache for ...
> our town children, weighted by responsibilities, crippled by poverty, robbed of
> their birthright of innocent fun. The ecstatic joy of children in response to such
> simple pleasures tells volumes about their drab existence.[57]

Tears would not have been universal, however. As subsequent recollections of children evacuated to the country during the Second World War have shown, many pined for the grimy vibrancy of city life. And country life – especially in the 19th century – was by no means the idyll that Henrietta imagined. It was not uncommon for some

9 *Henrietta and Samuel after ten years' work in Whitechapel*

country dwellers to be even more strapped for cash and basic comforts than their urban counterparts. More particularly, the children of agricultural labourers were often deprived themselves of the 'simple pleasures' of rural life because they – like city children – were expected to work as soon as they were old enough to help to scratch a living from an increasingly impoverished environment.[58] Nevertheless, Henrietta's enduring faith in the redemptive and regenerative powers of the countryside was later to fuel her most innovative and ambitious alternative to the 'artificial machinery' of Whitechapel: the development of a Garden Suburb at Hampstead.

IX

Brave New Worlds

Travels round the Globe

T he intensity of their efforts at moral, social, housing and educational reform frequently left Henrietta and Samuel beside themselves with nervous exhaustion. But they were able to take frequent short holidays in various locations throughout the UK. Cornwall, the Channel Islands, the Yorkshire Moors and South Wales were particular favourites. However, in March 1879, Henrietta became seriously ill with pneumonia and her recovery was delayed by what she terms as a 'long trying summer' in Whitechapel.[1] Her doctors advised a complete break and so, in November 1879, Henrietta and Samuel sailed from Liverpool to Egypt for a six-month holiday. Leaving their parish in the care of the Reverend Brooke Lambert, formerly the vicar of St Mark's, Whitechapel, and Marion Paterson, Henrietta and Samuel were accompanied by Kate Potter and were to be joined by Kate's sister, Margaret, when they arrived in Cairo. On disembarking, they were somewhat disconcerted by the unexpected presence of Sir Herbert Spencer, the Social Darwinist philosopher.[2] Apparently, the Potters had been concerned for his health and suggested that he may like to accompany Margaret on her travels. It was more likely, however, that Spencer had outstayed his welcome at the Potters' home. As the party was soon to discover, he was irascible, pig-headed, misogynistic and self-opinionated. Even the normally tolerant Samuel was irritated by his narrow outlook, his pomposity and, worst of all, his rudeness. Several academics, learning of Spencer's presence, eagerly sought out his company. Spencer dismissed them with the shrivelling proclamation that 'Je n'aime pas les introductions qui ne viennent a rien. Bon jour'.[3] The blight cast by Spencer on this holiday can only be imagined. He became more and more difficult by the day, grumbling about the heat, Egyptian culture, fellow guests and the effects of local cookery on his digestive system. Even the coffee grounds were deemed too fine as a result of the 'barbarous' method of grinding them with a pestle and mortar. The party must have been relieved when, after five weeks, Spencer announced he had decided to leave on account of a nervous debility exacerbated by his unfamiliar surroundings and – no doubt – the ill-disguised irreverence of his young companions. As a Christian Socialist, Samuel had been particularly riled by the right-wing racism and irreverence which imbued Spencer's denouncement of Egyptian culture and religion. He was deeply dismissive of its people's lack of sophistication, want of ambition and, above all, worship of 'dead ancestors' which, for him, represented a blind faith in the religious ethos which threatened his evolutionary theories:

> Savages dream of their dead ancestors. These ancestors seem to them to be alive, inhabiting the original seat of the race. They make offerings to these ancestors, the ancestors become to them gods, and hence the whole religious fabric.[4]

Henrietta was more rattled by Spencer's refusal to be moved by the richly textured history of the Nile and the 'hundred thoughts and pictures of the lives, joys, pains of the multitudes who had lived by it, on it, for it'. Whilst she and Kate were mesmerised by such reflections, the cantankerous Spencer looked at the river with his habitual cynicism and dryly noted that 'the colour of the water hardly vouche[d] for its hygienic properties'.[5] Nonetheless, the 28-year-old Henrietta was still sufficiently charitable to feel a modicum of pity for this 'lonely, unloved and unloving old man'. Recalling her reading of *Middlemarch*, she declared that he was a 'Casaubon without even a Dorothea'.[6]

However, their relief was to be short-lived. On 4 January a telegram arrived announcing the imminent return of this dour old cuckoo to their nest. Spencer, feeling in better spirits, had hitched a ride with a party sailing towards Karnak. He certainly didn't approve of their riotous behaviour: gaming, betting and heavy drinking, to name but three of their vices, but that didn't stop him from making free with their hospitality for 10 days. After re-joining the Barnett party at Karnak, he accompanied them southwards to Philae. On the way, the voyage became rather more eventful than it had thus far. Whilst negotiating the rocky islands of the Cataract, a sail snapped and their boat bumped onto a sand bank. Henrietta was enthralled by the ensuing rescue operation, which involved hordes of men variously pushing and dragging their boat from the bank and through the wind and rocks until, at last, the boat was freed into the less turbulent and treacherous waters beyond. In contrast to Henrietta's fascination with this medley of men, sea, rocks and wind, Spencer was aghast at what he perceived as the chaos of this rescue operation and the cacophony of voices which accompanied their efforts. Philae, too, held little pleasure for him. He stumbled over the crumbling granite pathways, teetered over the rock pools and was troubled by the constant presence of sand in his shoes. Spencer was also riled by the antics of the ever-present swarm of curious – and high-spirited – little boys who followed these English travellers as they explored the area. By then, Spencer had managed to pick up a few Arabic words: all of them either declamatory or defamatory. He would fire tirades of these expletives at these little boys and punctuate his outbursts with furious wielding of his umbrella. This caused the young rascals to scatter and, no doubt dissolving into helpless mirth, they would spring across the rocks only to re-congregate a few moments later.[7] Nor did he have any sympathy for the weak and ailing children whose parents were besieged with advice from Henrietta and Kate whenever their boat moored near a village. The two young women would bathe these children's eyes, or clean and dress their wounds, whilst Spencer would watch aghast that anyone would waste their time and energies preserving the health and lives of these 'barbarous' scraps of humanity.[8]

After a couple of weeks, Spencer decided he'd had enough. So must have his hosts, but they remained sufficiently solicitous to arrange for him to return to the relative comforts of Cairo in the company of a doctor. This left the Barnetts and the Potter sisters free to savour the cultural and environmental kaleidoscope of Egypt unhampered by Spencer's relentless gloom and grumbling. They drifted on down a windless Nile, banked by scorching yellow sands and lupin-strewn hills which glowed blue, emerald and purple in the vibrant sunshine. Henrietta, always fascinated by the magical interplay between light and landscape, was enchanted by these exotic sights and spent hours daydreaming on a couch watching them drift by. She was clearly re-invigorated by this cultural and environmental contrast to Whitechapel. According to Samuel, she was in 'splendid health' by the middle of January: certainly, her spirited mischievousness had re-established itself. Interrupting the dutiful Samuel, who was engaged in eulogising about the temple at Aboo Simbel in a letter to his mother, Henrietta bounced into the room opening and closing windows and philosophical debates alike before 'dragging' her husband back in his chair, ruffling his hair and showering him with a swarm of kisses that he likened to 'a concentration of flies' feet' which left his mind 'somewhat distracted'.[9] The Barnetts celebrated their seventh wedding anniversary in the brilliant sunshine of Aboo Simbel. Their table in the ship's dining room was bedecked with flowers and sweetmeats and the captain made a 'wonderful' speech in their honour. After lunch, they lazed in the shade sipping iced water and, later on, the ever-inventive Henrietta devised a new game to amuse everyone. Between the hills surrounding Aboo Simbel, there were dunes of soft, golden sand. Henrietta decided that they would all climb up them – an arduous task which would have taken around 35 minutes – and then, clinging tightly to each other, hurtle down as quickly as possible. What the ship's crew made of this ostensibly respectable English party whooping, leaping and skidding down these golden drifts can only be conjectured, but Henrietta's exuberance was infectious. Before very long, these sailors were also scrambling up the dunes and propelling themselves downwards in a glorious tangle of arms, legs and laughter.[10]

Soon though, the enchantment of the Nile was diminished by the discomforts of sailing coupled with the stifling heat. Thus, they stopped off more frequently to explore the little towns and villages dotted along its banks, but there were usually besieged by a muddle of locals peddling a bewildering mixture of goods: a multitude of jewelled bracelets, rings, silver beads and clothes jostled alongside ornamental spears and knives glinting in the bright sunlight. Even the normally forbearing Samuel was disturbed by the sight and sounds of these hawkers: their cacophony of 'wild shrieks' and their sheer multitude was all too much for him to bear. Henrietta was more resilient. Any nonsense from 'yelling and fighting mobs' hassling her for 'Baksheesh' was dealt with by swift and sharp blows from her umbrella. A letter to Marion Paterson reveals how utterly bewitched she remained by her surroundings. Ignoring the 'demonical voices' pestering them at every turn, she revelled in the sweet-scented medley of lentils, corn, beans and lupins shimmering in the sunlight. She was also enchanted by the birds and animals of this strange and beautiful land: buffaloes, sheep, donkeys and goats lazily grazing among the grass while flocks of larks, sparrows, white ibis and hoopoes flitted and swooped above the cornfield. Most of all, she was beguiled by the Egyptian sunset and the speed with which darkness fell:

> Sunset already and we four miles from home. What an after-glow, pale blue-grey over the mountains, crimson here fading into yellow which (greenless) fades into blue, and this is the east. In the west, yellow-orange, with soft greens till the arch meets overhead, a perfect symphony of colours. Gone! And how dark.[11]

In March 1880, the Barnett party returned to Cairo, where they were joined by Alice and Ernest Hart. Together, they visited the Pyramids and the Sphinx before moving on to Alexandria, Greece and, finally, Italy. By the time they arrived in Italy, the party were tired of travelling and looking forward to returning home: Samuel, in particular, longed to see his mother again. Yet the 'antiquity, the beauty and the power' of Italy's art and architecture invigorated their jaded spirits and they were once again uplifted by these enduring monuments to religious faith. However, Henrietta was also overwhelmed by the huge chasm between the awesome splendour of Rome, Florence and Milan and the 'ugliness, smells, poverty and degradation' of the East End to which they were soon to return.[12] Whilst she and Samuel had witnessed much deprivation on their travels through Egypt, they both reached the conclusion that its rural dwellers were much more content than their urban Western counterparts:

> With all the misery which Western people are fond of noticing here and which is forced on their notice, I still deliberately think that the people are happier and cleaner than ours. They are certainly more honest and peaceable, though of course this may be at the cost of those qualities which make our people push and strive.[13]

For the Barnetts, then, holidays were by no means regarded as an excuse for the mindless frolics enjoyed by the shallow aristocracy in resorts such as Le Touquet, Nice or Biarritz. Rather, as F.M.L. Thompson puts it, for the more earnest members of the comfortable middle classes, like Samuel and Henrietta, holidays were intended to have a 'serious purpose': one imbued with a 'moral force' from which they would return 'mentally, spiritually, and physically refreshed and enriched'.[14] Clearly this holiday did make them reflect on the contrasts between Eastern and Western cultures and beliefs. Uncommonly for his time and mores, Samuel did not assume the Western way of life to be inherently superior: indeed, Samuel asserted quite plainly that whilst Egypt was much in need of civilisation, it should be developed by the Egyptians and not by Europeans.[15] In turn, both were much impressed by the lack of resentment displayed by its poorer inhabitants. Equally, they were perturbed by the European aspirations of richer Egyptians such as their guide, Ali, who had proved to be unfailingly obliging and utterly charming throughout their entire stay. Visiting his home, they expected to find divans, Eastern ornaments and Persian rugs. Instead, Ali had furnished and decorated his home with typically English carpets, wallpaper, chairs and tables. For the Barnetts, this suggested that he was aspiring to materialist Western values as well as tastes. It is likely that Henrietta and Samuel worried that the adopting of such values by he Egyptian middle classes would in time begin to breed resentment among their poorer counterparts. On the other hand, rather than taking several wives, Ali had just one – with whom he was very much in love. Not surprisingly, the Barnetts were happier with this predilection towards Western customs.[16]

This moral, intellectual and spiritual replenishment did not come cheaply. Henrietta makes no mention of what this six-month trip cost or, indeed, how it was funded. However, it must have been her share of the Rowland family fortune which enabled them to travel for so far and so long in such lavish style. The outlay on a Thomas Cook six-week package cruise down the Nile in the 1880s would have been about £300, so the Barnetts' trip must have cost in the region of £2000. This was at a time when Samuel would have been earning around £25 per month.[17] Henrietta must have had a pang of conscience about their good fortune as she revelled in the arts and architecture of Europe: she determined that other charity workers in Whitechapel would have similar opportunities to re-ignite their ideals and, to this end, she decided to encourage them to form a Travellers' Club through which they could organise short and lower-cost trips to Europe. Eight years later, a party of 80 Whitechapel workers left for an educational trip to Italy subsidised by Sir Henry Lunn (the founder of what is now known as Lunn Poly Travel). Lunn was willing to subsidise this trip because it gave him the inspiration to organise similar tours for an earnest rather than a pleasure-seeking clientele. By the late 1880s, such 'improving' package holidays were widely regarded as 'ludicrously shallow, vulgar and meretricious' by an upper class no doubt anxious to preserve art and architectural treasures for themselves.[18] It is to Henrietta's credit that she rejected such snobbery and strove to make art available – and accessible – to all.

Henrietta's passionate belief in art's redemptive powers fuelled what ultimately became the Whitechapel Art Gallery. Soon after their return from Egypt, it was suggested by Mr Stockham, a retired soldier and Whitechapel worker, that the plethora of artefacts gathered on their travels should be exhibited to many, rather than just the few of the Barnetts' immediate acquaintances who had seen them at St Jude's Vicarage. This suggestion immediately inspired Henrietta to far greater things. Drawing on her wide circle of well-heeled acquaintances, she swiftly amassed a collection of paintings and *objets d'art* from friends, museums and galleries, which she assembled into the first of many annual exhibitions in the Whitechapel school halls. This was in 1881, only a year after their return from Egypt. By 1882, Samuel's decision to open these art exhibitions on Sundays had generated considerable controversy and vociferous dissent from those who believed such an act constituted blasphemy of the direst order. Appeals were made to the Bishop of London but Samuel pre-empted these by reminding his superior that he himself had deemed the parish the 'worst in London' and its inhabitants were therefore not likely to be receptive to the 'preaching of a Puritanical Sunday'. Conversely, he argued that exposure to the moral and spiritual narrative of paintings would connect with these people's souls in a way which sanctimonious admonitions never would.[19] The Bishop was duly convinced and exhibitions were held annually in the schools until March 1891, when the Whitechapel Art Gallery was opened. As well as showing the work of established artists, there was space for modern art, museum artefacts representing the development of trade and industry, and a gallery dedicated to the artwork of local schoolchildren.[20]

How well the people of Whitechapel *really* responded to the Barnetts' attempts to awaken their aesthetic sensibilities can only be conjectured. Henrietta, however, remained steadfast in her belief that art 'was good' for the poor. Extolling the morally uplifting subject matter of Richmond's 'Sleep and Death', she maintained that:

> such a picture … which depicts the strong, pale warrior borne on the shoulders of Sleep, while being gently lifted into the arms of Death – simple in colour, pure in ideas, rich in suggestion – is good for the poor to see. Death among them is robbed of none of its terrors by the coarse familiarity with which it is treated; with them funerals are too often a time of rowdiness and debauch. But death thus shown to them is a new idea, which may produce, perhaps, more modesty about the great mystery of our existence.[21]

From Henrietta's perspective, it may well have seemed that the working-class funerals in Whitechapel were devoid of any decorum or dignity, let alone an acknowledgement of any spiritual significance. Yet, as J.F.C. Harrison points out, many poorer Victorians took great pride in organising a 'good send-off' for their deceased relatives. Thus, funerals were 'important social occasions' which were prepared for years in advance via subscriptions to the Burial Club. The pay-out from these insurance organisations would enable the bereaved to lay on a decent wake complete with ham, ale and

10   *The Whitechapel Art Gallery*

cakes. For those who had not had the foresight (or the financial means) to insure themselves against funeral expenses, a pauper's burial was the only alternative. Such was the indignity of this that it is hardly surprising that grieving relatives ended up numbing their shame and misery in the local ale houses or gin palaces.[22] The other point overlooked by Henrietta was, of course, that in order to appreciate the nuances of these artistic depictions of death, it was necessary to have what Pierre Bourdieu has famously termed 'cultural capital' to decode the symbolism within them.[23] She had written catalogues to accompany the Whitechapel exhibitions, but as much of the population remained unable to read, these were of limited value.

Whilst Henrietta's efforts may have been somewhat misguided, she did at least attempt to share her experiences, souvenirs and reflections of her holiday in Egypt in a positive way. Clearly, this time out from the emotional and physical demands of Whitechapel left her newly determined to persist with the housing, social and educational reform issues which had preoccupied her since the age of seventeen. However, the three years which were to follow were beset by personal sorrows and trials. On 6 November 1880, just months after they arrived home from Egypt, Samuel's adored mother died. He was devastated by this loss and almost paralysed with grief. His only comfort was that Mary died unexpectedly, without any illness or suffering. Nonetheless, he plunged into a deep depression which was made worse by his father's constant demands upon him. 'Unloved, lonely, and losing health', the ever-irascible Francis senior would summon his elder son at the 'shortest notice', which meant that Samuel had to drop his own considerable commitments, rush down to Clifton and pander to the older man's morbid obsessions with his health. These forays into the 'grey world' of his father's miseries and grievances were to continue until 27 December 1893, when his father finally died after suffering a massive stroke a few weeks earlier. This must have been a huge relief. As Henrietta candidly put it:

> My husband mourned for him as dutiful men do mourn at the death of their parents, missed him by the relief of a great weight, but the loss was not touched by grief, and indeed his work and plans had been so seriously interrupted that to return to Whitechapel and take up his responsibilities was an immediate duty. For his mother, he never ceased to grieve, mentioning her in the delirium of his last illness, and 6 November was always kept by us both with some evidence of reverence to her memory.[24]

No doubt Henrietta was also secretly relieved at the demise of her cantankerous old father-in-law, as much of Samuel's Whitechapel workload had fallen to her and Marion during his lengthy absences. She does, however, acknowledge that old Mr Barnett may have – privately – taken much pride in his son's achievements. After his death, they were clearing out his papers when they came across a copy of Samuel's first sermon, preached at St Mary's, Bryanston Square, on 9 February 1867. It had been copied out in Francis' 'clear business hand' and, for Henrietta, encapsulated the 'affection and capacity for devotion' that he had been incapable of expressing outwardly.[25] Old Mr Barnett would not have been alone in his style of distant and aloof parenting. In the mid-Victorian era, the father of the middle-class home was expected to be a remote figure: a disciplinarian who set an example of stoical and unyielding masculinity to his sons. Given Mary Barnett's predilection for over-indulging her sons, Francis Barnett probably felt the responsibility of Victorian *paterfamilias* weighing even more heavily upon his shoulders.

In turn, the extra responsibilities borne by Henrietta during the 1880s continued to affect her physical and emotional health. She does not dwell on the details of these, but Samuel's letters to his friends frequently bear witness to his beloved Yetta's bouts of ill-health. During these, her energy levels would plummet, leaving her lethargic, depressed and physically debilitated. Quite why Henrietta was so susceptible to these illnesses is never made clear. Obviously, she always worked at a frenzied pace and often inspired – and possibly intimidated – others with her sheer determination to overcome the most intractable of obstacles. As one Toynbee settler of that period recalled, Henrietta's 'irrepressible will was suggestive of the stronger sex' and there was always something 'maverick, dominating, Roman about her, which is rarely found in women, though she was capable of deep feeling'.[26] In these observations lie clues to the contradictions within Henrietta and the inner conflicts they created. On one level, she had clearly maintained a profound sense of social responsibility and the audacity to cajole or coerce others into helping her achieve the seemingly impossible. She also appeared to have unlimited supplies of energy and self-belief, as well as enthusiasm for, and commitment to, a diversity of projects. On another level, this public display of confidence and competence probably masked inner turmoil and disappointment over her personal life. It would be prurient to speculate too closely on the extent of the intimacy between her and Samuel, but it is not unreasonable to expect that a woman as passionate as Henrietta would be capable of powerful sexual desire, even if she did not recognise it as such. However, as she delicately puts it, Samuel was 'daintily sensitive on sexual relationships' and, indeed, deeply wary of any adrenalin-inducing experience, such as sailing on rough seas or involvement in the most minor transgressions of the law.[27]

This is not to question Samuel's unending adoration – and admiration – of Henrietta or, indeed, to dispute her affection and respect for him. Yet Freud would have argued that much of Henrietta's achievements arose from her sublimated libido: the channelling of her considerable life force (a euphemism for sexual energy) into socially acceptable or creative pursuits, such as her philanthropic ventures or the sketching and paintings she produced while on holiday. Indeed, it was Freud's belief that the world's most artistic, creative and innovative endeavours were generated by the sublimated libidos of poets, philosophers, artists and engineers. He also warned that denial or repression of innermost longings and desires could have dire consequences for both emotional and physical health.[28] Henrietta was perfectly aware of the processes of repression and denial, even if psychoanalysis had not then been formulated. Years earlier, she had opined that whilst there was nothing wrong with friendships between women and men, 'every girl will know the sort of thoughts she ought to drive away, and the sort of ideas on which her mind should dwell'. In the same book she had proclaimed that 'it is often people's own fault if they get ill, and so they ought to be blamed, not petted'.[29] Needless to say, she did not apply this somewhat harsh generalisation to herself and indeed, whenever she was ill, Samuel's letters indicate that she was doted upon by all around her. Also, if, as suggested earlier, Henrietta's bouts of illness were related to her menstrual cycle, then her accompanying depression on reaching her mid- to late thirties may have been caused by her repeated failure to conceive a child. In the event, Samuel and Henrietta were never to have children but, whilst that may have been a huge disappointment, it is likely that Henrietta would have found motherhood a somewhat stifling experience. As she had discovered, it was hard enough for a married woman to have a life beyond the home. A woman with the responsibilities of rearing children – even with the help of servants – would have been even more restricted. Perhaps her memories of her Aunt Sophey's resentment at having to look after a brood of unruly children still lingered, too: despite publicly extolling the virtues of motherhood for *other* women, Henrietta consistently made her antipathy towards noisy, troublesome children – especially boys – abundantly clear.[30]

Whatever the reasons for Henrietta's increasing tendencies towards debility during her 30s, the cumulative effect of this was in 1889, when she was afflicted by a severe attack of pneumonia which left her dangerously weak. Her recovery took much longer than usual and, fearing for her life, her doctors recommended another lengthy stay abroad. This time, the Barnetts decided to take a 10-month world tour. Together with Marion Paterson and a trained nurse to help care for the still-fragile Henrietta, they set sail from Tilbury Docks to India on the SS *Peninsula*, a luxury 5000-ton vessel carrying (for the most part) wealthy tourists hell-bent on savouring luxuries on a global scale.[31] Characteristically, the Barnetts had rather more worthy schemes in mind and thus distanced themselves from these dissolute pleasure-seekers. Moreover, Henrietta's diaries reveal that she and Samuel had reached an age (39 and 46 respectively) when they were too old to socialise with their fellow travellers. So, whilst many of the holidaymakers slouched in bars, smoked and gambled to pass time as the ship steamed over an untypically smooth Bay of Biscay and a rather more turbulent Mediterranean, the Barnetts read or studied the star formations which lit up the night skies. Their first sight of land was Gibraltar, scintillating in the early morning light as the ship sailed into the harbour. Her torpor instantly forgotten, Henrietta cajoled Samuel and Marion into cramming in as many sights as possible during their brief stay on the island. This newly reactivated spirit of adventure almost resulted in the ship leaving without them. As Henrietta admitted, her zest for exploring meant that 'three rather alarmed passengers were hauled up the side of the already moving ship'. From Gibraltar, they sailed towards the Gulf of Suez, another sight which dazzled Henrietta with its sublime beauty. Sketching this scene, she was once again irritated by the apathy of her fellow travellers who, seemingly oblivious to their surroundings, carried on playing games, reading or dozing the time away. Nor was she impressed by their indifference as one of the ship's seedy boys – stoke hole workers – was buried at sea following an accident. As she noted in her travel diaries, 'the dinner went on, no one knew or if they knew, no one noticed – corks flew and laughter pealed. Is this not a picture of the world in miniature?'.[32] Yet, if Henrietta was becoming increasingly disillusioned about the lack of scruples among the social world, then the natural world still captivated her. As the SS *Peninsula* sailed towards India they crossed the Red Sea, which she deemed 'maddening by its elusive beauty', whilst the Indian Ocean, 'aflame with colour', also revitalised her spirits.[33]

The Barnetts were to spend four months in India, travelling around major cities such as Bombay, Delhi, Ceylon, Calcutta, Darjeeling and Madras. Henrietta's first impression of India was that it was 'hot and wonderful – a veritable fairy land'[34]. She was also pleased to discover that, despite the dry and dusty climate, the roads were 'well-made, well-watered and smell-less'. However, after a few days, she became less enamoured of these unfamiliar environs. For a start, all the living and sleeping accommodation was located on the ground floor and Henrietta, terrified of snakes all her life, lived in constant trepidation that one of these creatures would come slithering in unawares. The novelty of the heat soon wore off, too. Such was its intensity that women could only bear to wear the finest white muslin, whilst men needed to change their linen shirts every few hours. It became a little cooler after sundown, but dawn and dusk were blighted by the overbearing stench of burning cow dung. As far as Henrietta was concerned, this smelt far worse than the foulest smog which had engulfed Whitechapel.[35] Before leaving for India, the Barnetts had arranged to meet numerous English dignitaries and missionaries, as well as Indian religious leaders. Through these connections, they came into contact with the numerous medical, social and educational reform projects instigated – some would say inflicted – since the beginning of British rule in 1858. As far as Henrietta was concerned, these people were doing sterling work:

> Thus we gained some knowledge of that fascinating, absorbing, disappointing, alluring, glorious portion of our Empire, and the result of our experience has been to speak more doubtfully of its problems and more admiringly of its official servants – that splendid body of men who, loving truth and pursuing justice, accept service away from home in terrible climates, where misunderstandings are prolific and the sense of duty achieved is, in the majority of cases, the sole reward.[36]

Henrietta's perceptions of Indian cultures, religions and British rule, however, were skewed by her resolutely colonialist mentality and her largely unquestioned assumption that the western mores were superior to those of the east. She reserved her highest esteem for 'highly cultivated' and 'educated' Indians such as Mr and Mrs Surabji, Hindu Christians [sic] who ran a school for 'all classes' in Bombay and who communicated the 'purest English', or those deferential 'native gentlemen' who responded 'courteously' to Samuel's questions in 'excellent English'.[37] Other Indians, she observed, 'kept themselves to themselves' but who were, '*of course*, submissive to the English'.[38]

Yet what Henrietta interpreted as acquiescence was more likely to be resistance to – as well as resentment of – this imposition of British culture on a land already rich in its own religions, heritage and history. After all, it was only around thirty years since the most violent and damaging incident in Anglo-Indian relations: the Mutiny in which Indian soldiers rebelled against their Sahibs (British officers). This uprising was brutally quashed by British Imperialist forces. The apparent cause of this rebellion was that soldiers in the Indian army suspected that their gun cartridges were greased with animal fat. This was deeply offensive to both Hindus and Muslims. For Hindus, the cow is a sacred animal, whilst for Muslims, pigs are unclean. It was also, however, a manifestation of much wider disaffection with British rule:

> The causes of the Mutiny were constitutive to British Imperialism itself, to an army largely staffed by natives and officered by Sahibs, to the anomalies of rule by the East India Company. In addition, there was a great deal of resentment about white Christian rule in a country of many other races and cultures, all of whom most probably regarded their subservience to the British as deeply degrading. It was lost on none of the mutineers that numerically they vastly outnumbered their officers.[39]

As Said also reminds us, Indian and British accounts of the Mutiny are sharply divergent.[40] The one the Barnetts would have been familiar with was the version in which a lawless mob of cruel and savage natives butchered not only the Sahibs but also their wives and children. So, it was likely that they would have perceived the swift and bloody retaliation from the 'superior' civilisation of the British as necessary to instil subordination among these restless and excitable insurgents. Of course, their personal experiences in Whitechapel of resentment simmering in a volatile working class had made them extremely wary of outbreaks of mob violence. Another aspect of Indian culture which disturbed Henrietta was what she regarded as the wholesale oppression of middle-class Muslim women. A lifelong champion of women's abilities, if not their rights, she was staggered to discover the extent to which they were subordinate to men. Perhaps recalling her own lack of education, she was particularly indignant that these women were shrouded in ignorance. None could read or write, they were not included in conversations and, if they left the home, they were incarcerated in a heavily-curtained carriage from which they could see nothing. Henrietta was also horrified to discover that young girls were considered to be of marriageable age when they were only 12 and, moreover, that their sole purpose within marriage was to fulfil their husbands' desires. That said, she remained respectful of the Muslim faith. On this she commented that, had it not been for its degradation of women, 'as a form of worship, there [could] hardly be anything finer'.[41]

For one supposed to be recovering from a serious illness, Henrietta's itinerary in India was hectic, to say the least. As well as visiting schools, colleges and mission settlements, they had numerous social engagements to fulfil. Indeed, in Delhi, Henrietta became completely exhausted by the endless round of sightseeing punctuated by relentless dinner parties, and so took refuge in bed for a few days. After she had rallied, she, Marion and Samuel went to spend some time at the Cambridge Mission Settlement, where six of their English acquaintances lived and worked among the 'natives'. This was an ascetic existence. The men rose at six and walked one and a half miles to the nearest Christian church. Breakfast was at nine and this was followed by mornings spent lecturing in colleges, teaching in schools and visits around the district. They broke at three for lunch and continued their missionary duties until eight in the evening. After all the frenzied rounds of socialising, Henrietta no doubt found this stay both humbling and spiritually refreshing.[42] Quite how the indigenous population responded to having both Christianity and Western values foisted upon them, however, is not recorded. From Delhi, the party travelled to Darjeeling, where they spent Christmas and New Year as guests of the president, Gerald Ritchie, his wife and their little daughter, Theo, who captivated Henrietta with her 'golden-haired, fairy-like' charms.[43] Their final destination in India was Ceylon, where they met up with Ernest and Alice Hart. But the highlight of this part of their tour for Henrietta was her reunion with one of the Haddon sisters, Charlotte. Charlotte had married a Mr Ferguson, editor of the *Colombo Gazette*. The couple had made their home in a cottage perched high on the mountains surrounding Ceylon. It would have been much cooler at this altitude and the scenery through which they travelled to meet the Fergusons was spectacular: 'an enchanting journey through inspiring lands'.[44]

The Harts were to accompany Henrietta, Samuel and Marion on the next stage of their tour. On 18 February 1901, they left India on the SS *Oriental*. Their destination was Penang in China, where they had intended to spend a few weeks visiting the various mission stations. However, in the event, they were only to stay for five days. Discovering that the 'plague was rampant' in Peking, they abandoned plans to visit this city and instead divided their time between Hong Kong and Canton.[45] Despite the brevity of their visit, Henrietta was, as always, acutely receptive to the cultural differences of this 'very foreign country'. They managed to cram in some 'fascinating experiences' and 'intoxicating' sights in between their visits to British missionaries. However, Henrietta remained sceptical about the extent to which the teaching of Christianity was being assimilated by the Chinese peoples.[46] As China had its own spiritual faiths in the forms of Buddhism, Taoism and Confucianism, this is hardly surprising. Given that the fundamental tenets of these faiths were benevolence, humanity and loyalty achieved through self-awareness and meditation, the hell, fire and brimstone preached from the Old Testament must have been hard to stomach. From Hong Kong, the travellers sailed to Japan across a tumultuous China sea. Poor Samuel spent much of the voyage in bed, but Henrietta was exhilarated by the intensity of the great waves relentlessly crashing against the sides of the SS *Acorna* as it heaved and swayed its way towards a 'cold and shivery' Nagasaki. They were to spend two months in Japan, which were to be the most pleasurable and stimulating part of their world trip. Ernest and Alice were fascinated by Japanese art, museums and technology, whilst Henrietta and Samuel were inspired by their visits to settlements, schools, mission stations, hospitals and prisons. There was also plenty of time to explore the richness and diversity of urban and rural Japan. Travelling in little wooden rickshaws, they were enthralled by the mountains, hot springs, emerald-green forests and immense rice lakes unfolding across the landscape. Particularly awesome for Henrietta was Japan's sacred mountain, Fuji Ama, which manifested itself as a 'vision of beauty', bathed in light 'from base to summit'.[47] Nearer the towns, they explored the shops, museums, temples and monasteries, 'revelling unstintingly' in the artefacts, architecture and history of this 'topsy-turvy land'.[48]

Whilst in Japan, Henrietta was invited by the Emperor to speak to 'the daughters of the nobles' about the work done by well-to-do English women for the urban poor. Once again, Henrietta was struck by the deference shown by these 'dainty maidens' coyly peeking from their 'bowed bodies' as they listened to the Emperor's exhortations to carry out similar work themselves. But Henrietta was certainly not prepared to 'kotow' to her hosts, no matter how socially elevated they were. Thus, instead of bowing deeply before the Princesses attending this occasion, Henrietta and Marion graced them with the 'court curtseys' customarily given to the English monarchy. Uncharacteristically, she makes no direct comment about the position held by women in upper-class Japanese society, but the implication remains that she was exasperated by what she perceived as their pathological acquiescence and passive acceptance of a largely ornamental role.[49] And as time passed, Henrietta became even more jaundiced about certain aspects of Japanese customs and culture:

> I have discovered the key to the Japanese character. Why they rise so early. Why they spend so much time in the city. Why they commit *hara-kiri*. All is because paper walls make a house so unendurable.[50]

She was also less than complimentary about the physical appearance of Japanese men, describing them as 'curiously dressed, shock-headed [and] flat-faced', conveniently overlooking how strange their English faces, with their pale skin, large noses and rounded eyes must have seemed to their hosts. Equally, Japanese women would no doubt have been perturbed by Henrietta's capacity for audacity and boldness, which, unusual enough in English women, was even rarer in Japanese circles. Henrietta did concede, however, that their Japanese hosts were unfailingly courteous, intelligent and remarkably well-informed. She was particularly impressed by one young graduate who was concerned about the political implications of the loss of W.R. Stead as the editor of the *Pall Mall Gazette*. As Henrietta observed, it was highly unlikely that even the most scholarly of British graduates would be similarly well-versed in the nuances of Japanese journalism.[51]

In April 1891, the Barnetts left Japan and sailed over the Pacific Ocean towards California. Once again, it was an icy-cold and turbulent crossing which left Samuel reeling with nausea for much of the time. They arrived in San Francisco on 7 May 1891, a few days after Henrietta's 40th birthday. After six months' experience of eastern values, culture and spirituality, this abrupt re-introduction to the brash, materialist and libertarian west was, to say the least, a culture shock. Categorically stating that they 'did not like San Francisco', Henrietta unleashed a sustained tirade against 'ungodly' Californian civilisation: its 'hideous towns, wasteful farming', the 'greedy spirit of Trades Unionists' and the 'sapping of home and family life' engendered by the ease with which divorce could be obtained. She was temporarily appeased by the Californian landscape: the snow-capped mountains, giant redwood forests and vast tracts of rose-strewn woodland but, as in India, her delight in these surroundings was diluted by her constant fear of coming across snakes basking in the sun-dappled paths on which they travelled. Nor was she impressed by the accommodation in the home of a Californian settler. Not only was the food 'rough and coarse', but the beds were dirty, washing facilities were sparse and the children were 'rude and unkempt'. Even the dogs were 'noisy'. What these Californians cherished as their 'liberty', Henrietta dismissed as 'lawlessness'.[52] Henrietta was also deeply troubled by the politics of capitalist greed in California. In particular, she blamed private sector associations such as the Pacific Railway for holding monopolies on life's necessities, thus 'keep[ing] down those who are down'. She also noted that the wealthier classes of America, unlike their European counterparts, had no aristocratic heritage and, therefore, no sense of *noblesse oblige*. In short, she implied that they were godless *parvenus*: *nouveau riche* tyrants with no social conscience whatsoever. As she opined, 'in India we met a nation of slaves, in California a nation of bullies'. However, as Lorraine Blair has pointed out, the Barnetts only visited Northern California, which did have long associations with capitalist ventures, notably gold-mining. Had they ventured further south, they would have witnessed Christian missions established by Spanish settlers that would have challenged their perceptions of California as 'godless'.[53]

Travelling north, Henrietta, Samuel and Marion moved on to Oregon, where they were refreshed by the 'Englishness' of its green, rolling hills and fresh air. Here, the fine stone buildings of Portland also met with Henrietta's approval. However, she thought that 'great greedy devil', Seattle, with its urban tangle of railway lines and its jumble of tall brick buildings, seemed like a grotesque octopus. Nonetheless, for all her criticism of American politics and profligacy, they were given unparalleled hospitality from acquaintances and strangers alike:

> We were welcomed, feted and feasted to an extent that greatly surprised us. Indeed, all the time we were in America, the appearance of our names in the papers as hotel guests immediately brought unknown friends, who either placed themselves or their carriages or their houses, or all three, at our disposal, and were determined to give us a 'good time'.[54]

Perhaps Henrietta's containing of the phrase 'good time' in inverted commas suggests her faint distaste for its implicit frivolity, but her mood improved as they travelled further north through British Columbia into Canada, taking in a view of the Rockies from the observation car window. Returning to the United States, she, Samuel and Marion went to visit Jane Addams at Hull House in Chicago. This was America's first settlement, which was established by Jane after she had been inspired by a visit to Toynbee Hall in 1887. Still only 30 years old, Jane shared many of the Barnetts' ideals and values, and dedicated her life to the securing of social justice in housing, factory reform and female suffrage. And as Henrietta soon discovered, Jane's methods of winning hearts and minds were very different from her own. During their visit, throughout which Jane was variously occupied with administrative tasks, household duties and the tending of sick babies, they were constantly interrupted by a posse of 'naughty boys' who would ring the front door bell and promptly run away. Nonetheless, Jane would answer each of these calls with tireless patience. Henrietta was incensed by these boys' behaviour and took it upon herself to intervene:

> Thinking to aid her, I waited in the side wing, and the next time that the little troop of little demons appeared I administered an argument which they *quite* understood. But on telling Miss Addams, her beautiful eyes filled with tears, and she said in her gentle, undulating American voice: 'You have put my work back, perhaps years. I was teaching them what is meant by "resist not evil." [55]

Such forbearance was quite beyond Henrietta's comprehension, but Jane's peaceable methods of dealing with these mischievous interruptions were to anticipate her subsequent work with the Women's International League for Peace. In 1931, her efforts were rewarded when she shared the Nobel Peace Prize with fellow pacifist Dr Nicholas Murray Butler.[56]

Following their visit to Chicago, the Barnett party retraced their steps to the Canadian/American border where they visited the Niagara Falls, a world-renowned tourist attraction since it was made accessible by rail in the early 19th century. Swathed in waterproof clothing, they sailed under the Falls on the *Maid of the Mist* and were spellbound by the 'broad mass of tumbled, leaping, messy waves' cascading all around them. For Henrietta, this 'emerald' and 'jade' grandeur seemed like an 'incantation of God himself': a manifestation of 'power, progress, patience and perpetuity'.[57] After this heady experience, the Barnetts spent the final weeks of their tour in New York City and Boston, New England. The ambience of Boston, already famed for its colleges, universities, elegant architecture and involvement with the Unitarian Church movement, would have appealed to Henrietta. It was in this city that the Barnett entourage received the ultimate in hospitality: the authorities of Boston put a carriage and guide at their disposal whilst the hotel owner insisted that their stay would incur no charge.[58] Henrietta was more ambivalent about New York. On the one hand, she cannot fail to have been inspired by the tangible sense of exuberance, optimism and self-belief epitomised by, for example, the construction of Brooklyn Bridge from Manhattan Island to New Jersey, a stunning and innovative feat of engineering completed just a few years before their arrival. But she was also left reeling by the pace of life in a city pulsating with a vibrant energy. For Henrietta, New York echoed with a cacophony of 'rush, rush, scream, hurry, hurry, get, get and get what?' As for the popular seaside attraction of Coney Island, Henrietta dismissed it as 'common and ugly' – the 'most damaging page America had yet given us to read about itself'.[59]

Coney Island, home of the 'hot dog' (invented in 1874), had been developed as a pleasure resort in the 1840s and, by 1891, its plethora of freak shows, carousels, entertainers, singers and hordes of boisterous holidaymakers carousing on the beach would have been anathema to Henrietta.

The Barnett party left New York on 8 July 1891 and arrived in Liverpool one week later. Many years later, Henrietta was still puzzling over how to disentangle the cultural contradictions embedded within America:

> We spent ten weeks in America, ten enriching but tiring weeks, resulting in a reverence for that great country and its great hodge-podge of peoples, a reverence not unmixed with fear. Will its great soul – for it has a great soul – burst its body? Or its spiritual force be crushed by its physical wealth? Much depends on its women, for they possess the responsibility of the consideration which in England has hitherto – 1916 – struggled and failed and agonised to obtain.[60]

Read post-9/11 Henrietta's words have a chillingly prophetic resonance. Her musings here also give clues into how she was formulating women's rights and their public role. On one level, she was clearly pro women's suffrage, achieved by her American sisters, but not to be granted in the UK until 1918, and then only for women over 30 – it was as late as 1929 before women over 21 were enfranchised. Her remarks about the weight of 'responsibility' carried by these enfranchised women, however, suggests that she still subscribed to the Victorian view that women alone were the nation's moral guardians.[61] As will be shown in a later chapter, such attitudes were becoming increasingly outmoded.

On a wider scale, Henrietta's ambivalence about American attitudes, values and beliefs was not untypical amongst the earnest English middle classes. Donald J. Olsen notes that for many late Victorians, these values were epitomised by American propensities towards the rapid consumption of food, pretentious demands for iced water and cocktails and loud complaints about the space and service provided in English hotels.[62] Even the popular fiction of the time was shot through with similar derision. For example, in George and Weedon Grossmith's *Diary of a Nobody* (1892), the 'grandiloquent', arrogant and successful American businessman, Mr Huttle, is set in unflattering opposition to the cautious, suburban and quintessentially English Charles Pooter.[63] Both the Grossmith brothers made clear their distaste for America and its people. According to Weedon, it was full of 'conceited asses', whilst for George the American lightweight suit represented a flaunting of traditional English masculine values.[64] Others, however, notably Ebenezer Howard, pioneer of the Garden City movement, were inspired by America's exuberance and optimism. In his early twenties, Howard had spent some time in first Nebraska and then Chicago. Whilst his business ventures were disastrous, he was highly impressed by the imaginative rebuilding of American communities after they were ravaged by 19th-century industrialisation. Meanwhile, American efforts to incorporate the best of urban and rural environments were to influence his own design for garden cities.[65] Henrietta was similarly taken with the open-plan gardens in American suburbs. For her, the lack of hedges and fences between properties suggested a communal spirit and a commonality of purpose which she was later to attempt to emulate in her planning of Hampstead Garden Suburb.[66]

On their return from this nine-month trip around the world, Henrietta declared them both to be 'greatly refreshed' and relieved to find their work in Whitechapel and Toynbee Hall in 'splendid order'. This, however, prompted Henrietta and Samuel to question whether or not their presence among this 'paraphernalia of a successful organisation' was still necessary. Indeed, whilst walking by a river near Nikko in Japan, the Barnetts had mooted the possibility of moving on from St Jude's and starting again in 'a new parish on different lines'. By this, they meant living side-by-side amongst the poor and under-privileged of even more squalid areas of the East End and, this time, without the material trappings they had acquired whilst in Whitechapel. Clearly influenced by the missionary workers they had met in India, they reasoned that this would be one way of maintaining closer contact with the spiritual and welfare needs of 'individual souls'. As things stood, they both felt that administrative and management duties prevented them from this more intimate association with their parishioners. So, Samuel requested an interview with the Bishop of London in order to put forward this proposal. To Henrietta's indignation and Samuel's pain, he completely rejected their offer, arguing that no much how they tried to distance themselves from their current achievements, people would follow them wherever they went. Deeply humiliated, Samuel was left with no choice but to continue in his roles in St Jude's and Toynbee Hall. However, to compensate, he determined that he would at least dedicate more time to the spiritual needs of East Enders who gathered in St Jude's Cottage and, 10 years later, in Erskine House in Hampstead.[67]

X

Wholesome Pleasures and Tawdry Delights

Class and Leisure in Victorian England

The Bishop of London's refusal of the Barnetts' offer to transfer their services to an even needier parish continued to irk them for some time. Perhaps he was more perceptive than they realised, however: by 1893, both Henrietta and Samuel were becoming less resilient to the incessant demands, frustrations and setbacks they had endured during almost twenty years in Whitechapel. In addition to her public responsibilities, Henrietta had also recently become the guardian of Dorothy Noel Woods, orphaned in 1891 after the deaths of her parents, both Toynbee volunteers and teachers. The Barnetts' friend, the Master of Balliol, was sufficiently astute to note the cracks produced by these public and private pressures and strongly recommended that they give up their efforts at St Jude's in order to channel their energies and qualities elsewhere. At first, Samuel refused, despite his friend's even deeper concerns about the extent of Henrietta's exhaustion. However, the Master of Balliol was nothing if not persistent in his determination to entice Samuel away from his mission in Whitechapel. It would appear that he had a timely word in the ear of Lord Herschell, then the Lord Chancellor, who subsequently offered Samuel the Canonry of Bristol. Samuel accepted, provided he did not have to relinquish his position as Warden of Toynbee Hall. This meant that the couple would divide their time between Clifton and London.[1] Henrietta was clearly invigorated by their new home. Along with Mary Moore, Dorothy, Marion Paterson, Phyllis Townsend and Mademoiselle Simers, Dorothy's governess, they moved into rooms at number 8, Royal Crescent, Clifton, the stylish and capacious home owned by their friend, Bishop Ellicott. It had spacious rooms, leaded windows, a garden and a balcony with glorious views over the River Avon and beyond to the emerald-green Cotswold hills. For the first time in 20 years, they were able to witness the unfurling and blossoming of an English country spring at first hand. In Whitechapel, only the temperature – and perhaps the variable rankness emanating from the streets – gave any indication of seasonal changes.[2]

Samuel spent 13 years as Canon and their time in Bristol was as pleasurable as it was purposeful. There were dinner parties, garden parties and ample opportunities to explore the surrounding Gloucester and Somerset countryside in their pony and trap or on bicycles. Henrietta revelled in entertaining an assortment of guests: Jane Addams, the founder of the Hull House settlement in Chicago, Sir Robert Hunter, who was later to be instrumental in helping Henrietta secure the land for the extension of Hampstead Heath, sundry dignitaries of Bristol and, most frequently of all, Toynbee residents eager for respite from their duties in Whitechapel. These guests would be treated to 'simple' food, plenty of rest and the 'simple' pleasures of cycling, picnicking and rambling through the woods on the banks of the Avon. Noting the decimation of these banks by years of 'ruthless' quarrying, Henrietta resolved to re-seed them. This operation involved collecting a variety of seeds from their gardens at Royal Crescent and Hampstead, mixing them with earth and then tying them into newspaper parcels about the size of a tennis ball. Armed with these missiles, Henrietta, Dorothy and Marion would hurl them down over the rocks. Despite many of these earth balls missing their targets, all were delighted when, a year or so later, the previously bare rocks yielded an eclectic medley of antirrhinum, valerians, alyssum, convolvulus and, most incongruous of all, Iceland poppies.[3]

As earlier chapters have shown, Henrietta's commitment to social and educational reform continued unabated throughout the 1890s. Her health continued to suffer, however, and her illnesses became more and more frequent. She had always been aware of the benefits of leisure and recreation for her overworked colleagues, but was not particularly adept at practising what she preached. As demonstrated in the previous chapter, even her holidays were hardly recreational. So it was perhaps fortuitous that her personal life was enriched by these new surroundings in Bristol as well as a new responsibility in her life: the guardianship of little Dorothy Noel Woods. Aged seven when she came to live with the Barnetts, Dorothy was a 'tiny' and 'fragile' waif who would have been grieving deeply for her parents, who had died within a year of one another. Nor was she particularly bright – indeed, as Henrietta put it, she was 'very backward – at seven, she looked like five'. But, perhaps recalling her own delicate childhood, Henrietta decided that Dorothy's schooling was to be postponed until 'riding, dancing, porridge, cream and Hampstead air had made her more robust'.[4] Both Samuel and Henrietta were enchanted by their little 'Dollums':

> To us both, my little ward was an uninterrupted joy, and she took a place in our lives as nothing else did before or since. Her pretty ways, her pale wavy hair, her large gentle eyes, the sweet modulation of her thin voice, drew us with strong cords to the Cottage [at Hampstead].[5]

Of course, Henrietta's work commitments meant that the responsibility for Dorothy's upbringing was shared with Marion and Mary Moore. Determined that Dorothy should not be subjected to the stultifying effects of a conventional education, the Barnetts hired a French governess, who taught lessons outside as much as possible. Given Henrietta's regrets concerning her own lack of formal education, it is perhaps surprising that she made this choice for Dorothy, but it is likely that her experiences on the School Boards during the 1880s and '90s had made her somewhat cynical about the benefits of classroom teaching. She had also become influenced by Fredrich Froebel's approach to education, which had been adopted by a few progressive educators, most notably Margaret McMillan, who opened kindergartens for slum children in London and, later, Bradford in the 1880s and '90s.[6] From a blend of Romanticism and Kantian philosophy, Froebel (1782-1852) had:

> evolved an education system for young children based on a notion of the human being as an organic unity, with the human mind as a spontaneously formative agency. The 'child-garden' [kindergarten] would allow the developing child to be active in a fitting way, and activity would permit the flowering of inborn capacities. But although space, clean air, brightness and movement were specified as absolute needs of children, Froebel's 'garden' of children was not necessarily either a physical space or an actual garden. Rather it was an organising metaphor for a particular

kind of relationship between the child and the universe.[7]

In spite of their best efforts, however, Dorothy did not warm to her lessons. Like the young Henrietta, she had no natural affinity for foreign languages, declaring that she could not imagine wanting to talk to 'any French person'. No doubt such a response caused Mademoiselle Simers to despair. Neither was Dorothy too keen on history, wishing that there were fewer nations so that there would be less to learn. Ever optimistic, the Barnetts encouraged her to take singing and piano lessons. These were not successful: little Dorothy merely managed to 'drone out her music to her own and everyone else's discomfort'. She did enjoy sewing and drawing but, most of all, she adored romping round their Hampstead garden, playing with

11   *Henrietta and Dorothy*

Henrietta's poodles and collies. Ever indulgent of her foster child, Henrietta hid any disappointment at her reluctance to learn, declaring that her sweetness of nature and generous disposition more than compensated for her 'lack of brain furniture'.[8] Perhaps most importantly, Dorothy reminded Henrietta and Samuel how to relax and revel in simple pleasures. Although they were still only in their forties, their preoccupation with their workload threatened to overwhelm them. As Samuel noted, the presence of this sunny-natured little girl was refreshing as well as rejuvenating. In a letter to Henrietta, he enthused about Dorothy's vivacity: her 'life ... originality and ... sweetness' as well as her ability to 'inherit qualities grown-ups learn by life and losses'.[9] Indeed, Samuel was Dorothy's adoring 'play-mate'. Together, they enlivened the quad at Toynbee Hall with their impromptu cricket matches and cajoled even the most earnest and learned of the Barnetts' colleagues into riotous games of 'Hide and Seek'.[10] Dorothy reserved her deepest affection and dependency for Henrietta – her beloved 'Guardey'. When ill, which she frequently was, Dorothy would be consoled by no one else. They also shared a mischievous sense of humour and a gift for mimicry: one which made Samuel helpless with laughter after they had all endured a particularly dire version of Shakespeare's *King John*.[11]

Dorothy must have also heightened the pleasures of life in Clifton. Whenever possible, they would take advantage of long and balmy summer evenings by cycling along the river banks, visiting tea gardens or picnicking in the nearby Leigh Woods and Nightingale Valley. Dorothy's favourite spot was an inn at the mouth of the River Avon where they would watch ships sail. These sights reminded Samuel of his grandfather's sailing days and he would launch into stories of hot climates and strange lands which never failed to delight Dorothy and her friend, Phyllis Townsend, who was a frequent visitor to Clifton and Hampstead. Sometimes, they would abandon their cycles by the side of the road and, scrambling over stiles, shamelessly trespass over private woodland in search of rare wild flowers and foliage. This ignited Dorothy's passion for botany, another interest she shared with Henrietta. As Dorothy grew a little older, the Barnetts added a large drawing room to St Jude's so that she could entertain her widening circle of friends. Here they would dance, sing, perform plays or simply giggle at the idiosyncrasies of adult life. Samuel's brother, Frank, his wife, Lou-Lou, and their children, Magnus, Samuel, Stephen and Mary, were more inclined to visit London now that the Barnetts had left Whitechapel. Samuel was especially fond of Magnus who, as a toddler, had lightened his gloom when coping with his cantankerous father during his final illness. For Henrietta, the presence of so much 'bright young life' was invigorating – especially after so many years working among the downtrodden and dispirited of Whitechapel and their 'neglected' offspring.[12] Indeed, their distance from the relentless grime of the East End made them appreciate how utterly depressing it was. As Samuel commented during a stay in Whitechapel in the summer of 1896:

> What a hot week! We have remembered Bristol as those in a hot and dry land remember fresh streams and cooling breezes.
> The streets have never looked more ugly or the state of the poor more trying. How they can endure the atmosphere, the heat, and the vermin of small, over-crowded rooms. What a lesson for them in patience, what for us in sympathy. [13]

Meanwhile, as Samuel had predicted in 1888, Henrietta was thriving in this new environment and its distance from Whitechapel. In addition to duties commensurate with her role as Canon's wife, such as opening sales of work, presenting prizes and giving speeches at women's meetings, she became increasingly involved with the Pupil-Teacher Association.[14] Of course, these new commitments ran in tandem with her existing projects: Barrack School reform, the Children's Holiday Cottage Fund, art exhibitions in Whitechapel, the Society for Befriending Young Servants and the training of servants at St Jude's Cottage to cite but a few. Most importantly, Henrietta was becoming increasingly convinced of the benefits to be gained from fresh air and country surroundings, especially for those incarcerated in industrial toil. An early manifestation of this awareness was her instigating of a campaign to preserve the Clifton gorge, which was under threat from years of indiscriminate quarrying. As far as Henrietta was concerned, these quarries should be closed down and replaced with the open-air museums and playgrounds she had noticed whilst travelling through Denmark in 1896:

> Cannot one picture the municipal trams laid all along that lovely river-bank, and Bristol's industrial toilers taking evening rides and for a few pennies reaching the tea-gardens and enjoying the zig-zag walks cut on the steep cliff sides? Has nothing been done to give to the majority of the rate-payers their share of their city's natural beauties?[15]

Despite her mobilising of support from worthies such as Sir Robert Hunt and Poor Law Commissioner, Lewis Fry, as well as the National Trust, the municipal councils of Bristol and Somerset remained indifferent to their demands. In the event, it wasn't until 1909 that a wealthy local resident, George Wills, purchased Henrietta's beloved Nightingale Valley and Leigh Woods in order to preserve them for the 'pleasure' of his 'fellow-citizens'.

On a wider level, Henrietta was becoming increasingly inspired by radical approaches to the creating of working-class communities. It is not known if she ever visited one of the earliest of these, the model village of Saltaire near Bradford, West Yorkshire, built between 1850 and 1873 by mill-owner, Sir Titus Salt, for his workers. But she did visit – and 'fall in love with' – George and Richard Cadbury's cocoa-works in Birmingham. Opened in 1897, this state-of-the-art factory was equipped with single-sex dressing rooms where the workers could change into freshly-laundered, snowy-white overalls as well as benefit from dining rooms, bathrooms and gardens between the workshops. Work areas were heated and well ventilated: a stark contrast to the sweltering, cramped and malodorous conditions endured by workers in the notorious industrial factories which had proliferated in the north of England. Best of all for Henrietta was the model village at Bourneville, which the Cadbury Brothers had constructed for their 2000 employees and their families. This comprised attractively-designed, well built cottages surrounded by trees, gardens and playgrounds 'within three minutes of every child'.[17] Each year, George Cadbury held a party for his employees at his 112-acre estate at The Manor, Northfield, just a few miles outside Birmingham.[18] Here, the guests would be treated to picnics, 'improving' games and, in accordance with the Cadbury brothers' Quaker beliefs, nothing more potent than strong tea.[19] Of course, there was a stern moral current underpinning the construction of these model communities. As Edward Akroyd, the Halifax wool manufacturer and founder of Akroydon, a purpose-built village for his employees, opined in his *On Improved Dwellings for the Working Class*:

> a clean, fresh, well-ordered house exercises on its inmates a moral no less than a physical influence, and has the direct tendency to make the members of a family sober, peaceable, and considerate of the feelings and happiness of others.[20]

George Cadbury also shared these beliefs. A lifelong observer of Temperance principles, he ensured that there were no licensed premises in Bourneville, and there were severe penalties for anyone found the worse for drink. Instead, he attempted to steer his employees towards more wholesome pursuits, such as concerts, lectures and gardening. From the latter, he maintained residents would gain 'physically, morally, and even spiritually' – as well as financially. Growing their own fruit and vegetables and selling the excess could, he believed, effectively reduce rents by up to two shillings per week.[21]

From a 21st-century standpoint, it is perhaps easy to be critical of these somewhat self-righteous attempts at social engineering, but Cadbury was more altruistic and tolerant than some of his mid-Victorian counterparts. For example, Titus Salt's rules for living in his model village were exacting, to say the least. 'Cleanliness, cheerfulness and order' were to 'reign supreme', inebriation would result in immediate eviction, under no circumstances was washing to be hung out behind or in front of properties and any person found lacking in personal hygiene would be fined three pence for each offence.[22] Cadbury was well aware of the debilitating effects of life in traditional industrial communities, where the overcrowded accommodation, coupled with the relentless toil of labour, left employees with lowered vitality, susceptibility to sickness and mental health problems, and disinclination to work. Little wonder then, he reasoned, that these 'jaded and spiritless' workers turned to gambling and drinking as means of distraction from these miseries.[23] The necessity for distraction as an antidote to the grind of everyday existence had long been a preoccupation of Henrietta, not just for herself and her colleagues, but also for those less privileged than themselves. She and Samuel were still able to take regular holidays at home and abroad but she did recognise that these were beyond the financial means of most. She was, however, becoming increasingly disturbed by the popularity of what she perceived as the unsavoury delights peddled by the fast-growing and increasingly commercialised entertainments industry. Since the 1870s, traditional working-class diversions such as cock-fighting, gin palaces, street-gambling, ratting and bear-baiting had all but disappeared, whilst pubs had had their licensing hours severely restricted. The great fairs of London formerly held at Southwark and St Bartholomew's had been abolished and, in their place, four regular bank holidays had been established, along with a rash of public museums, galleries, libraries, exhibitions and parks that were intended to encourage the working classes to make more purposeful use of their leisure time.[24] The working classes, however, proved resistant to these efforts to coerce them into conforming to middle-class norms. 'Penny-gaffs' and 'Judge and Jury' shows – bawdy and highly explicit theatrical entertainments – had ostensibly been banned, but they continued to flourish in London's murkier underworld.[25]

Similarly, betting and gambling may have been driven off the street, but the ever-resourceful punters soon found other means of indulging their passions via the 'bookie's runner' who had – unofficially – replaced the outlawed betting shops as well as the pubs, newsagents and tobacconists who had run books on the side.[26] As Charles Booth observed in his survey of London life:

> All must bet. Women as well as men. Bookies stand about and meet men as they come to and from their work. The police take no notice. See the sudden life in a street after a great race has been run and the newspaper is out: note the eagerness with which the paper is read. Boys on bicycles with reams of pink paper in a cloth bag on their back, scorching through the streets, tossing bundles to little boys waiting for them at street corners. Off rush the little boys, shouting at the tops of their voices, doors and factory gates open, men and boys tumble in their eagerness to read the latest 'speshul' and mark the winner.[27]

Indeed, by the 1890s, gambling had overtaken drink as the greatest 'vice'. Whilst the police turned a blind eye to the subculture of informal betting, attempts were made to raid and close down illegal gaming dens. These proved futile. The proprietor would simply pay the £5 fine imposed by the magistrates and immediately resume business, often on the same premises. The clergy were deeply disturbed by this new moral scourge, which was encouraged by 'newspapers, knowledge of arithmetic and more holidays'.[28] No doubt this was *not* what they had hoped would be the outcome of mass literacy. As far as Henrietta was concerned, with its potential to cause loss or pain, gambling 'sap[ped] the very foundations of honesty and integrity'.[29] Charles Booth was less censorious. Having personally visited gaming clubs – purely in the interests of sociological research – he concluded that they were much more innocuous than people imagined. No drinks were served at the gaming tables, stakes placed were modest and there were no overt displays of 'excitement' from the punters. Although the few women present were from the 'unfortunate' class, even they behaved 'very respectably'.[30]

Another popular form of entertainment for working-class Londoners was the 'freak' show, which gave spectators the chance to gawp and guffaw at such sights as the Fat Lady (in truth, an average-sized woman swathed in padding), the Pig-faced Woman (actually a performing bear with a partially-shaved face), the Cannibal Pygmies (in reality, two nine- and ten-year-old English children liberally daubed with feathers, beads and paint) or, even more bizarre, the Pipe-Smoking Oyster.[31] In fact, most of the so-called freaks of nature were elaborate illusions – as most people would have realised. But once again, Henrietta was appalled at what she imagined to be the sensationalism and cruelty inherent in such entertainment:

> Many of the shows at fairs ... should be avoided, for it must be pain for that fat woman to be kept so fat, and to the thin man to be half-starved, or for the poor crippled dwarf to have his deformity shown and criticised.[32]

What was most reprehensible for Henrietta was the lack of sympathy and fellow feeling in the crowds that gathered to mock and jeer at those unfortunates on display. Similarly, she condemned the bawdiness of certain theatrical acts in which humour was dependent upon the degradation or ridicule of others, and the raucousness of music hall acts. Nor did she approve of the 'selfishness' of those who stayed out late 'eating in the street, dropping litter' and, no doubt reliving the evening's entertainments, made far too much noise.[33]

Yet the Victorian working classes – as well as a sizeable middle-class and even aristocratic audience – adored the 'laughter', the 'blaze of light' and 'sham opulence' which radiated from music halls.[34] Music halls had evolved in the second half of the 19th century from an increasingly enterprising pub culture in which landlords would organise entertainments such as singers, acrobats and illusionists.[35] The reputation of the earliest halls was dubious, to say the least, but by the late 1880s, the increasing presence of women at these venues lent them a degree of respectability.[36] Stedman Jones argues that in working-class districts, where overcrowding, diversity of employment and impermanent accommodation made 'stable community life very difficult', the singing and the shared laughter fulfilled 'a craving for solidarity in facing the daily problems of poverty and family life'.[37] It also served as a means of countering middle-class evangelist or moral interference. The famous music-hall singer Marie Lloyd was well aware of her role in maintaining working-class esteem and morale:

> You take the pit [slang for music hall] on a Saturday night or a Bank Holiday. You don't suppose they want Sunday school stuff, do you? They want lively stuff with music that they can learn quickly. Why, if I was to try and sing highly moral songs they would fire ginger beer bottles and beer mugs at me. They don't pay their sixpences and shillings at Music Hall to hear the Salvation Army.[38]

So, music hall provided a ribald and entertaining diversion for its working-class audiences whilst staying grounded in the day-to-day realities of their lives. The comic realism of music-hall songs dealt with themes such as the ephemeral bliss of courtship, the trials and tribulations of marriage, and drudgery and exploitation at work. The popularity of music halls did not just perturb moral reformers like Henrietta. It also disturbed socialist activists who wanted to stir the working classes into rebellion against their oppression and exploitation. As far as these political reformers were concerned, by simply reflecting the injustices and iniquities of working-class lives back to them, rather than encouraging people to protest against them, the music hall merely served as a kind of 'opium for the masses': a means of anaesthetising them against the harsh realities they endured every day. Recent historians have argued that the music hall was also 'overwhelmingly a space in which popular militarism and Imperialism were propagated'.[39]

Yet the working class of London was not as brain-washed or as anaesthetised as these contemporary commentators and later historians have inferred. During the 1880s and

1890s, a new breed of young, relatively affluent working-class lads became increasingly notorious for 'toff-baiting'. As Rob Sindall notes, this reflected the determination of young 'roughs' to assert their difference from the gentility. Unsurprisingly, the respectable middle classes of London were incandescent with fury at this unprecedented impudence. In a letter to *The Times* one deeply affronted gentleman launched into a diatribe about such disrespectful youths jostling him in the street and deliberately knocking off his hat before proceeding to trample all over it. The assailants fled, but not before they 'felt the weight of [his] stick'. As well as suffering from wounded dignity, this gentleman was also appalled that 'such an outrage [could] be perpetuated, with probable impunity, in a broad and well-populated thoroughfare'. In other words, the working classes were now having the temerity to frequent the spacious and well tended streets of their middle-class counterparts. Another correspondent to *The Times* complained after he and his wife's attempt to ride their double tricycle along King's Road in Chelsea was impeded by a 'rough' who flung himself down and lay in their path. The violent braking which ensued nearly toppled the man and his wife from their seats. The young lad fell about laughing but, once threatened with the police, allegedly became violent and abusive before fleeing back into the labyrinthine squalor where he belonged.[40] Needless to say, the press thrived upon these stories of youthful working-class insurrection and seized every opportunity to distort, exaggerate and demonise their antics in order to create what the sociologist Stan Cohen was much later to identify as 'folk devils' and 'moral panics'.[41]

More insurrection was to follow. As John Springhall points out, young lads between the ages of 13 and 17 were increasingly likely to run wild or loaf around on street corners.[42] To Henrietta and Samuel's consternation, this trend was very much evident in Whitechapel. Their response – in common with strategic interventions from other like-minded Christian leaders – was to organise an assortment of clubs and activities underpinned by a rigorous religious ethos.[43] It was from such a standpoint that organisations such as the Boys' Brigade were founded. Springhall defines this as 'one of the primary instruments for the transmission of Christian manliness to the non-public schoolboy'.[44] By this, Springhall means that since the middle of the 19th century, Christianity was increasingly regarded as synonymous with emasculation. This image was not helped by a preponderance of well-meaning but ineffectual female Sunday School teachers who lacked the charisma and authority to hold the attention of older, streetwise boys. So, Christianity was re-branded and promoted as a 'muscular' religion intended to counter the idea that subscription to the Christian faith meant young men would be made 'soft, cowardly, effeminate and spiritless'. For William Smith, the founder of the Boys' Brigade, outdoor sports provided an ideal framework for the nurturing of courage, initiative and a team spirit in these volatile and unruly youths.[45] It hardly needs stating that there was much resistance to these wholesome interventions in working-class lives. And it wasn't just the 'feckless' working classes who ridiculed these objectives. Their 'respectable' neighbours also demonstrated their contempt at middle-class intervention by jeering and chanting as the hapless conscripts to the Boys' Brigade were paraded through the streets:

> 'Ere comes the Boys' Brigade
> Half-smovered in marmalade
> A two-penny 'apenny pill-box hat
> An 'alf a yard of braid.[46]

That was probably one of the tamer of the 'scurrilous' songs with which the Brigade was taunted; from the more hardened and cynical members of this resistance came more violent expressions of derision. Stones, bricks and bottles were hurled and this frequently culminated in fist fights between the rebels and the conformists, stung into defending their honour.

Springhall attributes the limited impact of Christian manliness on the working-class imagination to the considerable dichotomy between middle-class and proletarian perceptions of masculinity. If the middle-classes perceived the achievement of manliness as synonymous with bravery, independence and a sense of fair play, the working classes viewed it as an 'elongated rite of passage in which the manly was to be reached through swaggering, brawling and the oblivion introduced by either alcohol or violence'.[47] To some extent, that may have been the case. It is also worth noting, however, that middle-class men were equally capable of alcohol-soaked violence and abuse. The difference was that working-class shenanigans were much more likely to take place in the very public arena of the street or drinking den, whereas middle-class eruptions tended to take place in the privacy of the home or exclusive gentlemen's clubs. It could also be argued that they had a more legitimate outlet for aggression in the designated spaces of their various leisure activities: hunting, shooting and contact sports such as rugby. On another level, it is likely that the middle classes, with their stronger constitutions, were better able to deal with the effects of alcohol. Social commentator Robert Blatchford implied this with his belief that drunkenness among the poor was attributable to their enervated physical state rather than excessive consumption. As he put it, 'I have seen a journalist, and one very severe on the vices of the poor, drink eight shillings worth of whisky and soda in an evening, and do his work correctly … But the average poor labourer of the slums would be mad on a quarter of the liquor'.[48]

During the raucous celebrations of a hot and steamy August bank holiday in 1898, Henrietta's deepest misgivings about the working-class capacity for violence and insurrection were confirmed when a disproportionate number of revellers were arrested for drunkenness, fighting, assaults on police and street robbery. To make matters worse, this mutiny seemed much more organised than the random scraps and scuffles which had peppered East End life for decades. This gang violence was to bring the term 'hooliganism' into everyday conversation. The origins of the word are hazy. It was first popularised by a music-hall song containing the lyrics, 'Oh the Hooligans/Oh the Hooligans!/ Always on the riot/Cannot keep them quiet'. But many believe that 'Hooligan' is a corruption of the Irish name 'Houlighan'. Certainly, there was a gangster named Patrick Houlighan who was notorious throughout the capital for his daredevil lawlessness. He was sporadically employed as a chucker-out in the seediest pubs in London's Elephant and Castle district but spent more time banged up in jail. Indeed, he died in custody whilst awaiting trial for the manslaughter of a policeman.[49] The press were quick to milk this phenomenon of organised gang warfare for all its worth, and their responses ranged from the sanctimonious to the satirical. Predictably, there were outraged demands for sustained birching and severe custodial sentences, along with a manifesto from the South London Rate Payers Association exhorting members of the public to wield a 'discriminating application of the cat-o-nine-tails' in order to purge the streets of this 'reign of terror'.[50] Some journalists railed against the apparent apathy of the police; they may have had a point but, given their vulnerability to attacks by these gangs, it is perhaps hardly surprising that policemen kept as low a profile as possible. On one occasion, for example, a policeman attempted to arrest a one-legged recidivist for yet another instance of drunk and disorderly conduct. In the frenzied scuffle which ensued, the policeman was obliged to unscrew the miscreant's leg and use it as a truncheon as a means of subduing his kicking and cursing prisoner. A crowd soon gathered to witness this fracas and pelted the policeman and his colleagues with pepper. This created such chaos that no less than 12 police officers were needed to escort this 'wooden-legged ruffian' to the nearest police station. It was not uncommon for policemen to be seriously injured – or even killed – during these bouts of unrest.[51]

Yet while the majority of the press and the public responded with wholesale fear and loathing to this organised gang violence, others were more circumspect. In a sardonic retort to a pious editorial in *The Times* that drew a correlation between the quintessentially 'un-English' sweltering weather and equally alien street drunkenness and unrest, the *Daily Clarion* published a front-page poem offering an alternative view of why the working classes were driven to drink:

> Us chaps drink a lot
> When the weather is 'ot –
> That statement I will not deny it
> But it ought to be told
> That we drinks when it's cold
> An whene'er we can steal it or buy it
> We lives and we dies
> In foul dens and styes
> Without any fun or excitement
> Like sparrers in cages –
> Ard work and low wages
> Till we figgers within a hindictment.[52]

The radical and socialist press were not intending to condone the growing incidence of organised gang violence so much as point out that until this insurrection erupted, the vast majority of the privileged classes had been wilfully ignorant about the social and material privations endured by the poor and disaffected classes. Others implied that the moral panic generated by youthful insurgence was a convenient means of masking a more widespread concern of the summer of 1898 – the severe water shortage, which was partly attributable to the heat wave, but nonetheless hopelessly mismanaged by the East End Water Company. Urging for governmental intervention, *Reynold's Newspaper* were perhaps not entirely jesting when they suggested that if the hooligans were to target their lawlessness at certain members of the cabinet, then something would surely be done to address such flagrant inefficiency.[53]

There is, of course, an alternative interpretation to these unprecedented outbreaks of organised urban disorder. It would not have been so obvious to Victorian commentators but, from a 21st-century perspective in which youth sub-cultures are commonplace, it is easier to see how Victorian gangs like the Chelsea Boys, the Plaid Cap Brigade or Battersea's Velvet Cap Gang were rebelling against their material circumstances and defiantly asserting an identity rejecting both middle-class values and those of their parents' generation. The impression generated by both the reactionary and radical Victorian press was one which presupposed poverty and unemployment, but these young working-class men were likely to have been employed and to have a reasonable disposable income. Certainly, the propensity for bawdiness to erupt on bank holidays and at weekends suggests that many of them were working.[54] They also took a pride in their uniformity of appearance. Rather like the hoodies of the 21st century, or the punks of the late 1970s, the Victorian hooligans developed a specific dress code. As the *Daily Graphic* observed, far from looking scruffy and shabby, these young men were characterised by a 'cap set rakishly forward, well over the eyes' – presumably to avoid identification – tight, bell-bottomed trousers and a 'substantial leather belt heavily mounted with metal'. To the consternation of the middle classes, this latter accessory could also serve as an offensive weapon.[55] Tellingly, the Victorian gang members rejected wholesale any signifiers of middle-class respectability or working-class servility: the ubiquitous collars, ties, flat caps and hats donned (or doffed) by older men. So, by parodying the uniformity and militaristic strategies of their conformist counterparts in the Boys' Brigade, these young men made utterly clear their contempt for middle-class values and attempts to interfere in their lives and territory.

Henrietta and Samuel were certainly unsettled and saddened by the outbreaks of hooliganism, but characteristically avoided knee-jerk reactions. Samuel, no doubt remembering the high spirits of his brother, Frank, was especially sympathetic to the need for an outlet for youthful energy and frustrations. To this end, he supported the movement towards boys' clubs and organised sports and the religious ethos underpinning them. Attuned as he was to the hostile undercurrents which had pervaded Whitechapel for the past 30 years, he was sceptical of hyperbolic reactions to issues of hooliganism:

> There has been talk on Hooliganism almost as wild as the actions of the boys. There is nothing in the so-called outbreak to astonish people familiar with East or South London, and the one thing certain is that repression is not its cure ... Hooliganism is a revolt against authority, written in the coarse writing of a neglected neighbourhood. The spirit of revolt and the coarse writing will not be changed by hasty action, whether it be the use of the 'cat' or big clubs started in a hurry. The spirit of revolt will only be checked when an Authority is acknowledged 'Whose service is perfect freedom.'[56]

By 'Authority', Samuel was of course referring to the Christian ideals and principles that he believed had the capacity to defuse what he perceived as the desperation underpinning the misguided actions of the hooligan. He was also mindful of the extent to which large institutions had alienated the working-class residents of Whitechapel. In consequence, he advocated the provision of smaller, more intimate clubs catering for a diversity of interests including boxing, acting, billiards, music and dancing. However, he also warned that these clubs would only be successful in combating hooliganism if they were complemented by a sustained commitment to meaningful schooling, decent housing and, above all else, genuine Christian warmth and empathy between the classes.[57] Henrietta sympathised with Samuel's convictions but still maintained that the best results were to be achieved through the fostering of individual relationships between the classes:

> But when all these proposals are considered, the old doctrine remains true that good can only be done *one by one*. Unless the friendless are befriended, unless the boy is considered and put in circumstances fitted for his character ... he will hardly feel himself a member of society. Hooliganism is, indeed, the protest against treating the *poor as a lump*. The police may secure order in the streets, the

School Board may provide the means of education, the local Authority may secure
healthy homes, charitable people may learn how to give, but each individual has
his own needs which another individual can discover.[58]

Henrietta's emphasis on the need to feel a sense of belonging to rather than alienation
from society clearly influenced Samuel. In a radical break from traditional boys' clubs,
which were initiated and run by well-meaning middle class do-gooders, he was concerned
that the clubs should be run by the boys for the boys. Samuel justified this approach
by pointing out that the giving of charity in the forms of food and clothing along with
the obligatory moral-steeped lectures was patronising at best and, at worst, downright
disempowering. In place of such misguided intervention, Samuel suggested that by
enabling the boys to be instrumental in organising the clubs for themselves they would
develop the self-respect and independence necessary to become an autonomous member
of society.[59] Whilst Samuel no doubt had the best of intentions, such an ethos was
fraught with complexity. Despite his rejection of the austerity of the Charity Organisation
Society and his determination to give these East End lads what we would now call
'ownership' of their lives, there was still an overpowering sense that the hidden agenda
of these clubs was to dilute the chaotic vibrancy and excitement inherent in working-
class cultures with the imposition of more wholesome middle-class leisure pursuits. For
instance, gambling remained a constant problem in most clubs and the committees of
12 boys and – tellingly – three Toynbee Hall settlers would invariably deal severely with
those who perpetrated such an offence. Henrietta cites one example of a small boy
who was taught the error of his ways by the threat of expulsion from his club. He
did learn to toe the line but there must have been countless others who rejected these
attempts at social engineering. As Springhall's research reveals, these clubs' attempts
to attract the most feckless of working-class youths were, by and large, unsuccessful.[60]
Indeed, the majority of the members were recruited from the fast-growing group of
lower-middle-class suburban dwellers and the 'respectable' working classes, who were
beginning to aspire to a solidly middle-class lifestyle.[61]

For all Henrietta despaired at the intransigent nature of this working-class penchant
for bawdy, belligerent and frivolous entertainment, she did not entirely shield Dorothy
from this culture. She and Samuel would take their little 'Dollums' to Whitechapel,
where she would play games such as cricket and hide-and-seek with the men at Toynbee
Hall. Enchanted by her 'delicate manners' and the 'twinkle of her petticoats', the
settlers were no doubt glad of this distraction from the gloom and grind of social
reform.[62] Similarly, Dorothy was closely involved with the Whitechapel women and
girls who came to stay at St Jude's Cottage: those rescued by Henrietta from what she
termed as the 'rubbish heaps of humanity' in the Whitechapel Workhouse. No doubt,
however, these women were carefully vetted before their admittance to St Jude's. They
may well have had chequered – if not colourful – pasts, but poverty, debt, hunger and
drink had variously ground most of them down into servile and pathetic gratitude for
Henrietta's imperious benevolence. One woman, a widow and 70 years old, had lived
in the workhouse for 16 years. She had given birth to seven children, five of whom
died in infancy. The remaining two, Eliza and Fred, had survived into adulthood, but
Eliza died in childbirth and Fred had been fatally afflicted with heatstroke whilst serving
with the British Army in India. Finally, her husband had died from respiratory failure
at the age of sixty-six. Penniless, she had no alternative but to pawn her furniture,

give up her home and go to 'the 'Ouse'. Another had endured married life with a feckless, philandering and drunken husband who eventually – and much to her relief – left her for another woman. She managed to eke out a living for herself and her son, Billy, by a debilitating grind of cleaning, factory work and tailoring. This arduous labour was to leave her crippled by arthritis and no longer able to work. Meanwhile, Billy had married at the age of 20 and his family responsibilities meant that he was unable to support his mother. So, she had also become incarcerated in the dullness and monotony of the workhouse. Some, however, were more spirited. One drunken old reprobate charmed Henrietta with her irrepressible sense of fun and sharp eye for a bargain. She also persuaded her hostess that she had relinquished for once and for all 'the drink that done [her] in', but the temptation of a night on the town with a 'young Don Quixote' had proved too much to resist. This alcohol-fuelled lapse from grace cost this woman her place at St Jude's and simultaneously left Samuel out of pocket. He had to fork out eight shillings to pay off the hansom cab driver who had escorted her home from central London.[63]

Perhaps Henrietta was hoping that exposure to these deprived – or depraved – residents of Whitechapel would kindle a social conscience in Dorothy so that when she was older, she could make an active contribution to the Barnetts' efforts at reform. No doubt with this in mind, Samuel and Henrietta made arrangements for the now 16-year-old Dorothy to have some formal education through attendance at a girls' boarding school. According to Samuel, she took a great delight in her new status as a pupil and chattered brightly about her form, her schoolmistresses and her fellow students. To his chagrin, however, her butterfly mentality meant that she showed no signs of wanting to settle to her lessons and instead, much preferred the more frivolous pursuits of dancing and acting. Henrietta would have attributed this to her want of intellect, but it is also conceivable that over-indulgence from her doting guardians discouraged Dorothy from developing any sense of motivation or responsibility. In the event, Dorothy was only to spend one term at school. She had always suffered from uncertain health and Samuel's letters make frequent references his concerns about the various illnesses which blighted her childhood and adolescence. These ranged from rheumatic fever and tonsillitis to kidney problems, heart murmurs and raging temperatures. By the age of 16 she seemed to have 'outgrown' her weaknesses and according to Henrietta, had blossomed into a 'tall, erect, intelligent [and] stable' beauty.[64] However, Henrietta's optimism was premature. In the sweltering summer of 1900, Dorothy contracted diphtheria and became dangerously ill. Because of immunisation since the mid-20th century, diphtheria is currently very rare but at the end of the 19th century, it snuffed out the lives of many. It manifests itself as a virulent infection of the throat and larynx which produces considerable swelling of the respiratory tract. In consequence, Dorothy teetered on the brink of death for many weeks but, largely thanks to the unwavering ministrations of Henrietta and Marion, she gradually rallied from the worst of the infection. However, toxins released by the diphtheria bacteria affected her heart, already inflamed by the rheumatic fever she had suffered in infancy. So, by October 1900, poor Dorothy was in a piteous state: listless, fragile and pathetically dependent on the constant presence of her beloved 'Guardey', Henrietta. She lingered on for five more months until 8 March 1901, when she slipped away aged only seventeen.[65]

Henrietta and Samuel were inconsolable. For 10 years, Dorothy had been the 'treasure' who had lightened their lives in so many ways. Her death left Henrietta emotionally and physically exhausted. Throughout her illness, Dorothy had made 'incessant' demands on her 'beloved Guardey' which had meant that Henrietta's work had been neglected for all of that year. Also, Samuel's commitments in Bristol meant that they had to spend much time apart from each other. Not surprisingly, this solitary burden caused Henrietta to plunge into a prolonged period of illness herself. In Samuel's biography, Henrietta underplays the profound desolation which she was enduring, but his letters leave no doubt about the severity of her delayed reaction to her intense desolation. Henrietta's first impulse was to immerse herself in her work: by June 1902, she had produced a proposal for her book on the beginnings of Toynbee Hall, was 'breathing life' into the Pupil Teachers' Organisation and organising countless classes, parties and committee meetings. Such a spiral of activity may well have enabled her to repress the pain of her loss but the subsequent illness of her sister Fanny was to push even Henrietta beyond the limits of resilience.[66] Along with the ever-loyal Marion and two nurses, Henrietta nurtured Fanny back to health. But as soon as Fanny had recovered, Henrietta succumbed to a profound depression which lingered for months. In a letter to his sister-in-law, LouLou, Samuel fretted over her listless state:

> Thank you for your letter with its loving sympathy. I know all we can do is wait, but it is sad that Yetta makes so little progress. I doubt if she is really one bit better. The last two days she has been at her worst. She lies in the big room by the open window, reads simple books, and feels very poorly. If we talk telling her things she becomes too interested, if we don't she gets dull … I am trying to get on with work but it is hard to do things without her in which she has so large a part. It is hard to make things go anyhow. I puzzle and puzzle over the signs of the times.[67]

By May 1902, Henrietta was beginning to rally. In a letter to Frank, Samuel reported that she was busying herself by taking the girls from Erskine House on a trip to the zoo, visiting art galleries and, as discussed above, continuing her campaign against the destruction of the banks of the River Avon.

However, she was also about to embark on her most ambitious and radical project so far: the creation of a Garden Suburb at Hampstead in which 'all classes would live together in right conditions of beauty and space'.[68] Mervyn Miller, historian of Hampstead Garden Suburb, has suggested that Henrietta's 'beautiful green-golden scheme' was a means of displacing the grief generated by Dorothy's death.[69] He may well have a point, but it is also likely that witnessing the tiny and fragile Dorothy blossom into a tall, beautiful young woman had convinced her of the benefits not only of a loving home but also of a rural environment. Of course, she would have witnessed similar benefits of Hampstead for the careworn and defeated refugees from Whitechapel. Throughout her time in the East End she had perceived an inevitable link between the squalid living conditions and the disaffection of the working-class residents. So, to Henrietta, the solution was obvious. What was needed was a rural community for all, regardless of class, gender or ability. This, she reasoned, would be far more effective than what she had for many years privately regarded as the 'artificial machinery' of Toynbee Hall: temporary and inadequate substitutes for 'relationships naturally born of neighbourliness'.[70]

XI

—❦—

Suburban Chic

Planning and Developing Hampstead Garden Suburb

Seven years after moving from the squalor of Whitechapel to their Hampstead retreat, Henrietta and Samuel were en route to Russia, where they met an American traveller who informed them of plans to extend the Northern Line of the Underground from Central London to Hampstead and Golders Green. Henrietta was – to say the least – horrified, because the implications of this scheme were all too obvious:

> If this were to be so, it would result in the ruin of that most sylvan restfulness of the most beautiful open space near London. The trains would also bring the builder and it required no imagination to see the rows of ugly villas such as disfigure Willesden and most of the suburbs of London, in the foreground of that far-reaching and far-famed view. Therefore there was nothing to do but enlarge the Heath.[1]

It is perhaps hard to empathise with what seems to be a knee-jerk response to the threat of change to a rural setting that shows snobbish disdain for suburban development, but in the late 19th and early 20th centuries, middle-class contempt for lower-middle-class suburban housing and, more particularly, their inhabitants (modestly-paid, white-collar workers and their families) was almost universal. In short, the alleged uniformity, mediocrity and insularity of these housing developments were held to be synonymous with the insipid values and pale aspirations of their inhabitants.[2] Historians have lost no time in highlighting Henrietta's less than altruistic motives (initially, at least) for extending the Heath. The architectural critic and historian W.A. Eden is overtly cynical here, asserting that were it not for the threat to the tranquillity of her country retreat, it would never have occurred to Henrietta to realise the potential of her rather 'literal' aspirations of Hampstead Heath's 'green pastures'.[3] Likewise, the Hampstead Garden Suburb historian C.W. Ikin makes caustic references to the Barnett's country home and implies that for Henrietta, it provided a rural idyll in which she could 'rear poodles' and indulge the whims of her foster daughter.[4] No doubt similar reservations were held – and privately expressed – by many of Henrietta's contemporaries. It cannot be denied that a certain amount of self-interest may have prompted Henrietta's actions, but she can hardly be blamed for wanting to preserve some sanctuary from the constant violence, grime and grind of Whitechapel. Whatever her motives, Henrietta responded swiftly to this proposed extension of the London Underground. Within a few months, she had mobilised a Heath Extension Council to prevent this potential disfigurement of Hampstead Heath. Her initial proposal involved the raising of funds to buy 80 acres of Heath land owned by the Eton College trustees. Subsequently, this land would be given over to London County Council 'to be kept for an open space at all times'. Despite the 'difficult, drawn-out and discouraging' tasks involved in haranguing local authorities, City companies and private donors to subscribe to her scheme, Henrietta and her fellow workers eventually secured the £22,000 necessary to fund the Heath extension.

As Henrietta made clear, the process of raising this amount of money was tedious in the extreme, but it was while she was engaged in these 'very dull, arduous and continuous duties' that the idea of creating a Garden Suburb first occurred to her. This suggests an impulse, but it could also be argued that while immersed in the monotony of 'addressing envelopes, folding circulars [and] stamping letters', Henrietta was able to weave together fragments of ideals, ideas and observations she had accumulated from decades of experience into an innovative scheme for social integration.[5] For many years she had been frustrated by the social class system of England, in which the more favourable areas were colonised by the rich and privileged whilst the poor were herded into malodorous, crowded and dingy slums. One outcome of this was mutual antipathy between the classes and Henrietta resolved to challenge this by dissolving the topographical class divisions which, to her mind, were among the 'deepest' social iniquities.[6] No doubt mindful of the recent instances of organised street violence, the danger she and other social reformers most feared was likely to have been that of an anarchic revolt from an increasingly vociferous and volatile working class.

Of course, Henrietta was the first to admit that her vision of a Garden Suburb was by no means original, and she freely acknowledged her debt to factory owners such as George Cadbury, Lord Leverhulme and Joseph Rowntree. As discussed earlier, both these men had provided attractive, well-built housing in semi-rural settings for their factory workers in the suburbs of Birmingham, Liverpool and York respectively. In addition, she cannot fail to have been influenced by Ebenezer Howard, the pioneer of the Garden City movement in England, whose ideals were fundamental to all environmental and housing reform in the early 20th century.[7] Underpinning his vision was his desire to combine the best of the urban and the rural – the 'beauty of nature', 'social opportunity' and 'bright homes and gardens' in his 'Town-Country' blueprint for a Garden City.[8] Eventually, the fruitions of his aspirations were to materialise in the architecturally acclaimed developments at Letchworth and Welwyn Garden City in the south of England. Thus inspired to create such an environment herself, Henrietta set about securing the remaining 250 acres belonging to the Eton College Trust. This was a considerable undertaking for a woman already in middle age, which would demand substantial amounts of effort and energy. Yet it also provided Henrietta with an invigorating opportunity to challenge the conventions of suburban development along with the class divisions which it perpetuated. Contrasting the 'beautiful homes' of the rich with the 'small villas' and carefully-cherished gardens of the lower middle classes, she proceeded to stir the consciences of the rich:

> Must we be content, now that education is bringing all sorts of people nearer together in sympathy, to have classes topographically divided by an arbitrary division depending upon their rate-paying powers? Is it a natural sequence that hundreds of people with multi-form possibilities and varied tastes should be obliged to live in houses exactly alike, so close that there is not room to develop their tastes, or opportunity of turning buried potential into facts?[9]

Clearly, Henrietta was sufficiently independent to reject her contemporaries' dismissal of suburban dreariness, trivia and mediocrity. Instead, she recognised that behind the identical facades of suburban homes lay a diversity of hopes, attitudes and aspirations that often remained stifled by lack of funds and opportunities. But above all else, she railed against the iniquities endured by the working classes and exacerbated by their 'mean streets' and 'closely-built gardenless boxes' which – to her mind – completely snuffed out any human potential.[10]

In order to realise her vision of a socially integrated suburban community with 'pleasant houses and gardens', along with 'educational, social and recreational facilities', Henrietta had numerous obstacles to negotiate. Not least of these was a scathing eruption from the Leeds-born journalist and most vituperative critic of suburbia, Thomas Crosland. No doubt in ferocious denial of his own lower-middle class-upbringing in the less than salubrious district of Beeston, South Leeds, Crosland denounced her scheme as a 'specious, vulgar and undesirable'.[11] Henrietta would have brushed aside such irascible contempt, but negotiations with Samuel were more delicate. He was deeply disturbed by the idea of Henrietta undertaking such a vast project – not least because of her frequently occurring bouts of poor health and depression. In a rare moment of self-assertion he declared his intention to share neither the work nor the responsibility involved in the creating of the Suburb. But the ever-resourceful Henrietta was not to be thwarted. By exploiting Samuel's tendency to privilege the spiritual over the material, she contrived to gain his moral support by convincing him that her project was a *divine* rather than a *worldly* mission. Perhaps she was even secretly relieved that Samuel didn't volunteer any practical assistance. After all, the Garden Suburb project was a perfect opportunity to apply her ideals without having to subordinate these to Samuel's spiritual values. Equally, by gaining his moral support, Henrietta was able to avoid compromising social expectations regarding a wife's obedience to her husband.[12]

Henrietta used similar guile in her dealings with the Eton College Trustees. She would have been apoplectic with indignation when her initial request to purchase the land was refused because she was 'only a woman' and therefore deemed incapable of running such a large estate. However, the trustees were prepared to reconsider if she had a 'few men' behind her. So, channelling her indignation into resolve, Henrietta promptly assembled 'a veritable showman's 'happy family' of earls, lawyers and churchmen.[13] These were all high-profile worthies who would have been heavily preoccupied with their own professional commitments, and so they would have been precluded from becoming too involved with the practicalities of developing the Suburb. Once this apparently male-dominated trust was established, the Eton College Trustees were quite content to grant the option of purchase. By contriving to gain nominal rather than practical support from these men, Henrietta ensured that she was able to pursue her scheme without having her ideas compromised by their interventions. No doubt plenty would interpret Henrietta's contrivances as evidence of her capacity for guile and the beginning of her tendencies towards autocracy. However, the tensions between her fervent commitment to social reform and her subordinate status as a middle-class, middle-aged wife left her with no alternative but to realise her vision via shrewd and manipulative tactics. Defending her friend against accusations of a dictatorial streak, Marion Paterson recalls that despite Henrietta's 'energy of will' and 'strongly-expressed opinions '... is she never seemed to desire to control'.[14] Beatrice Webb also affirmed

Henrietta's 'masculine-minded' business acumen, which was enlivened by her sense of humour. According to Webb this was also 'masculine in its broadness [and] offensive to the fastidious [but] invigorating to those who enjoyed laughing at the absurdities of human nature'.[15] Certainly, it seems that when it suited her purpose, Henrietta deliberately adopted traditionally masculine attributes of forthrightness, courage and broad humour. In part, this was a ploy to gain the attention and respect of influential men. Of course, it also gave her a means of achieving a voice in the male-dominated world of environmental planning.

Whilst Henrietta would have approved of the principles underpinning Ebenezer Howard's model for a Garden City, she – like many of his contemporaries – would have less than impressed with what Robert Fishman called his 'rationalistic, geometric methods of town planning'.[16] However, she was much more receptive to the socialist and aesthetic ideals of Raymond Unwin, the Arts and Crafts architect commissioned to build the first Garden City at Letchworth. As Fishman points out, Unwin's designs 'bore little resemblance to Howard's plan for geometric boulevards and iron-and-steel Crystal Palaces'.[17] Instead, Unwin and his partner, Barry Parker, transposed their model of a medieval village onto Howard's original plan:

> In the context of [Unwin's and Parker's] time, their designs for Letchworth stood for cleanliness, simplicity, and the honest use of materials – qualities the Arts and Crafts movement associated with the 14th century and hoped to revive in the 20th ...
>
> For Unwin, the beautiful old English villages had the appearance of being an organic whole [in which all the residents] were personally in touch with each other, consciously and frankly accepting their relations.[18]

In other words, Unwin believed that the medieval village provided a community where people of all classes could live together in harmony. He was one of the few architects of his time who was not entirely hostile to the suburban environment. This doesn't mean that he condoned speculative suburban development, but he did recognise the benefits of living in the suburbs, such as proximity to work and distance from urban congestion. So, it seems that his adaptation of Ebenezer Howard's 'Town-Country' model at Letchworth caused him to speculate about how it could be applied to suburban development. Also, instead of drizzling contempt on suburban dwellers, he clearly had much sympathy for those incarcerated in 'squalid ugliness ... unrelieved by a scrap of green'.[19] According to Unwin, suburban housing should be:

> satisfactory from the point of view of health and economy, and at the same time afford some opportunity for the gradual development of a simple dignity and beauty in the cottage, which assuredly is necessary, not only to the proper growth of the gentler and finer instincts of men, but to the producing of that indefinable something which makes the difference between a mere shelter and a home.[20]

As Mervyn Miller observes, the ideas expressed in Henrietta's article outlining her proposals for the Garden Suburb at Hampstead bear more than a passing resemblance to those advocated by Unwin in his 1902 tract on housing reform, *Cottage Homes and Common Sense*.[21] Having seen the fruition of Unwin's ideas at Letchworth, Henrietta became convinced that he was the man for her 'beautiful green-golden scheme',[22] so she lost no time in persuading him to be the chief architect for her Garden Suburb. She also cajoled him into accompanying her on her lecture and lantern slide tours promoting the Suburb.[23] As far as Henrietta was concerned, Unwin was nothing less than inspirational. Not only did she revere him for his 'fertility of imagination' but also his ability to sense the 'power for growth' in the most 'tiresome' and 'insignificant' of people. Between them, they produced the most seductive means of promoting the Suburb: a stylised plan drawn by Unwin and endorsed with Henrietta's handwritten comments.[24]

For Henrietta, the 250 acres surrounding the Heath extension represented a clear space on which she could inscribe her ideal community: an antithesis of the social segregation and dearth of architectural charms which characterised most suburban development in London. Her first priority was to preserve the rural ambience of the Heath – its harebell-strewn meadows, verdant hedgerows, grazing lambs and woodland birdsong – and make it accessible to all, regardless of circumstances.[25] So, she and Unwin used the stylised plan of the Suburb to illustrate how they proposed to integrate homes for all classes amongst the Heath's undulating contours. This would provide harmony between landscape and architecture, which Unwin believed was essential to successful housing development.[26]

Unwin's illustrations are clearly intended to evoke images of rural England and medieval villages. His proposed roads are gently curved and, apart from their width – stipulated by Henrietta to be not less than 40 feet – are reminiscent of meandering country lanes. Such a layout would provide a complete contrast to the brutalising 'mean streets' of working-class districts as well as the uniform monotony of suburban roads. Similarly, the cul-de-sac arrangements of the artisans' cottages in the lower-right-hand corner of the plan are evocative of the random grouping of houses of medieval hamlets. For Unwin, this type of layout embodied a spirit of social harmony along with a mutual respect for privacy. The chequer-board grouping of some properties and the unconventional terracing of others reflected Unwin's belief that the 'privacy', 'shelter' and 'comfort' provided by a home should not be at the expense of either fresh air and sunlight or social interaction.[27]

In her written prospectus for the Suburb, Henrietta states that all the houses in her scheme, regardless of size, will be 'picturesque' and constructed in a way which ensured they did not 'spoil each other's outlook'.[28] As Unwin's plan reveals, many of the smaller dwellings overlook the Heath extension, the most attractive part of the proposed Suburb. Likewise, the houses intended for the industrial classes are mingled among 70 acres of fertile meadowland on the northern edge of the Health. For Henrietta, an environment of this type had radical potential for alleviating the social squalor and moral degradation emanating from urban squalor. In the earliest paper produced by the Garden Suburb Trust, she asserts:

> We already have evidence that … in cleaner air, with open space near to their doors, with gardens where family labour would produce vegetables, fruit, and flowers, the people would develop a sense of home life and an interest in nature which form the best security against temptations.[29]

On Unwin's plan, however, Henrietta's handwritten comments are not so persuasive about the physical and moral benefits of such a community so much as contrived to beguile more affluent clients with the beauty of its setting. She draws attention to the 'high ridge' to the west of the Heath extension 'from whence some of the most distant views are obtained' and on which some of the larger homes will be constructed. However, what she does *not* emphasise in the plan is her intention that these views and spaces should be made available to all Suburb residents, rich or poor. Perhaps recalling her own rural childhood, she uses the plan to appeal to the growing number of 'child-centred' families.[30] She highlights the tree-shaded park with its play area and pond for paddling, skating, sailing toy boats or taking dogs for a swim. In her article promoting the Suburb, however, Henrietta is much less idealistic about childish pleasures and gives assurance that their 'noise … shall be locally limited'.[31] That said, whilst she had always found the antics of children irksome, her previous experiences of the brutal means used to exert control over them in Barrack schools made her resolve to incorporate small cottage homes for orphaned children in the Suburb.[32] Yet no reference is made to these intentions in Unwin's drawing; nor did it mention her plan to include accommodation for people with physical or learning disabilities. Even in her written proposal for the Suburb, she only hints at these intentions by alluding to the residents' responsibility to 'bear the needy and handicapped in *daily* mind'.[33] By 'daily', Henrietta meant everyday proximity. In other words, she was determined that the less fortunate should live in the 'very midst' of the privileged.[34] She was also sufficiently shrewd to realise that overt insistence on such altruism, especially towards the noisy and quarrelsome refugees from Barrack schools, would alienate those residents upon whose presence and affluence she was relying in order to create her socially-integrated Garden Suburb.

This aspect of Henrietta's scheme echoes Ebenezer Howard's humanitarian concerns in town planning. Howard had also recognised the extent to which decent quality of life was denied not only to the urban and rural poor but also those with physical and learning disabilities. So, in his model for town-country development, he incorporated asylums for deaf and blind people, farms for those with epilepsy and cottage homes for orphans. However, Howard's diagram of his town-country model indicates that such accommodation would be segregated from the remainder of the community.[35] In contrast, it was Henrietta's intention to integrate all residents of the Suburb, regardless of their abilities. Unlike most community planners, Henrietta and Unwin recognised that not everybody lived in a traditional family unit, so the plan and proposal for Hampstead Garden Suburb included quadrangle-type developments for widows, single working women, working lads and retired residents. Both Henrietta and Unwin deplored the cheap, self-contained tenements provided for single people on a limited budget and proposed instead the building of affordable accommodation incorporating large and airy common rooms with shared cooking facilities and communal gardens. As well as the financial benefits of shared amenities, these living arrangements could also help to alleviate the social isolation of single people. As Kathleen Slack points out, Henrietta was particularly sympathetic to the plight of single, self-supporting women and their 'frequently unsatisfactory living conditions'.[36] Certainly, Henrietta's first-hand observations of women's physical vulnerability in urban areas prompted her to prioritise their needs within the Suburb. Such awareness was also to prompt her to situate this accommodation near to streets as well-lit and spacious as those in the most affluent areas of London.[37] Recognising that some women may prefer self-contained housing, she proposed the construction of semi-detached housing in which the ground floor would be occupied by a traditional working-class family with the upper floor rented to a single woman. Henrietta believed this would be mutually beneficial. The single woman would bestow a 'refining influence' on her neighbour's children whilst simultaneously 'taking delight' in the gardens tended by the family downstairs.[38]

On Unwin's plan, these mutual benefits are the only hints of reciprocity and proximity between the classes. As Henrietta's handwritten comments make clear, the areas set aside for lower-middle-class clerks and their families are separated from 'richer homes' by wide, tree-lined roads. Likewise, extensive woodland appears to shield the homes proposed for the working-classes from their more affluent counterparts. Only the quadrangle developments designed for communal living appear at random on the plan – except for their conspicuous absence from the working-class quarter. Perhaps Henrietta's intention here was to ensure that the affluent were in daily contact with the less fortunate and that single people were in no way made to feel ostracised. Given her contempt for frivolous and extravagant pursuits, it's hardly surprising that she wanted to instil more social responsibility in those she believed were governed by the 'ethics of luxury'. On the other hand, however, her motives in segregating the working-class homes from both those of the affluent and the disabled are more complex. In fact, it could be argued that she was creating a working-class ghetto which replicated the social divisions found in conventional suburban development. However, it is also likely that Henrietta took into account the extent to which mixing larger homes with modest cottages may generate envy and resentment among the less well off. Her experiences of Whitechapel were also likely to have made her aware of the penchant of those living in reduced circumstances to debase and deride those weaker than themselves: the disabled, the orphaned and the ill who were at the forefront of Henrietta's concerns.

Other concerns which informed Henrietta's scheme for the Suburb related to the recreational and cultural lives of the residents. So, on Unwin's drawing, she indicated the five acres set aside to meet the residents' spiritual and intellectual needs: land for a church, chapel, library and a social club. Here, she hoped all residents would be drawn together by common interests.[40] Indeed, her determination to place this meeting ground was made manifest even before she had gained the option to purchase the land for the Suburb:

> Lord Crewe [her fellow Garden Suburb Trust member] and I walked across the fields, climbed the hedges, and toiled through stubbly grass until we reached what is now Central Square. 'This is the highest place, and as is fitting, we will have the houses for worship and for learning,' I said, and there they now stand.[41]

This positioning of what were to become St Jude's Church and the Suburb Institute is another deviation from Ebenezer Howard's model Garden City. The space at the centre of his diagram incorporates a large, glass-covered shopping area surrounded by parks, recreation areas, cafés, museums and libraries: an eclectic medley of education, entertainment and consumerism. But in Unwin's plan for Hampstead Garden Suburb, the amenities provided for consumerism and recreation are clearly segregated from religious and educational activities. There are three compact shopping parades positioned on the outer eastern edge of the Suburb, convenient for some of the quadrangle developments and cottage homes, but at a considerable distance from the proposed

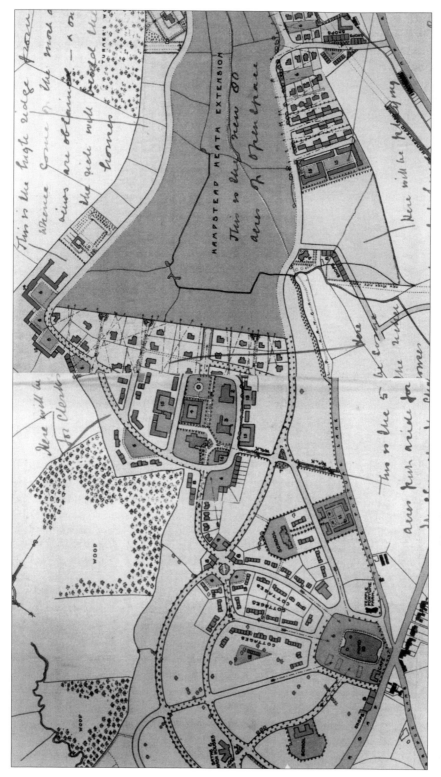

12 *Detail from Unwin's proposed Garden Suburb at Hampstead*

working-class homes. And recreation is – at this stage – limited to the provision of tea-rooms, shaded arbours and garden allotments.

W.A. Eden has pointed out that by literally and metaphorically elevating religious and educational institutions, Henrietta and Unwin were neglecting to consider the 'pull' of Howard's social magnet: the eclectic mix of amenities which attracted and encouraged a diversity of social interaction. At the same time, he argues that the positioning of the church and the educational institute represent a reaction against the integration of the secular and the religious which characterised the Barnetts' efforts at Toynbee Hall.[42] Certainly, both the church and the institute are a considerable distance from the shops and their position at the top of a steep hill may well have deterred some residents from taking advantage of their facilities. However, it's doubtful that Henrietta would have regarded the separation of the secular and the religious as a retrograde step. To say the least, she was privately increasingly ambivalent about the redemptive powers of religion and had much more faith in the potential for education to have a greater impact on social and moral reform. As Marion Paterson put it, Henrietta saw education as a life-long process and one which she 'valued as much as anything'.[43] However, Henrietta's frequent references to the substantial benefits of education suggest that she valued it *more* than anything else.[44] While her status as a clergyman's wife may well have prevented her from outwardly expressing her preferences, she did at least ensure that the church and the educational institute shared the same site and occupied equivalent areas of space. This at least implies equality between the secular and the religious. By physically separating these two buildings, Henrietta could leave spiritual matters to her husband while creating a space for herself to develop social, cultural and educational activities in the Suburb.

Henrietta's critics also note how her ideals and Unwin's plan imply a nostalgic yearning for the values and architecture of a long-gone past. Certainly, Unwin was an idealist rather than a pragmatist. As Robert Fishman puts it, Unwin's recuperation of a medieval past was more 'reactionary' than 'radical': a naive attempt to infuse modern society with the imagined 'stability' and 'unity' of feudal class systems.[45] Even more apparent is Unwin's distaste for the industrialisation and the 'debilitating influence of the machine age on art'.[46] As Walter L. Creese notes, the mechanical processes of mass production jarred his aesthetic sensibilities to such an extent that he was blinded to any potential technology promised for progress and reform.[47] Such attitudes were – and are – not uncommon amongst 19th-century social commentators and 20th-century proponents of Green politics. As Sean Ledwith observes:

> The technological achievements of the last two centuries are perceived largely as a kind of spiritual collapse in which an organic bond between man and nature was brutally severed. Modern society is likewise seen as having abandoned the values which kept earlier societies in harmony with their environment.[48]

Once again, Unwin's deep misgivings about technological progress indicate a significant deviation from Ebenezer Howard's attitudes towards town planning. In fact, Howard's own debilitating experiences of urban and rural poverty left him with absolutely no illusions about an idyllic past along with an unwavering faith in progress.[49] Nor was Henrietta quite as avowedly anti-progress as Unwin. Whilst she was also enchanted by the appearance of picturesque country villages, her desire to create a community where a social mix of residents may 'work, wash and garden' suggests that she wanted to instil a pragmatic rather than a romantic spirit of harmony popularly – if inaccurately – associated with rural life.[50] Clearly, this desire has its origins in the extremes between the regions of which Henrietta had direct experience: the Sussex countryside of her childhood and the two decades she spent among the poverty of Whitechapel. Not only did she realise how these were riven by antipathy between different social classes but also how the 'ribald gaiety' of the urban poor was comparable with the complacent 'pleasure-seeking' of the rural rich.[51] So, it is hardly surprising that Henrietta looked neither to town nor country as a model for a community intended to foster mutual respect between its residents. Instead, she sought to adapt, rather than adopt, a pre-industrial model which she associated with a practical sense of purposefulness and co-operation she believed to be the result of class divisions within society.

By March 1906, the Hampstead Garden Suburb Trust Company was formed and the land purchased. This was in spite of the numerous obstacles and objections which had dogged Henrietta's pursuit of her vision for the Suburb. Some argued that the scheme was not financially viable; others grumbled that the working classes could not be trusted to tend their gardens; a sizeable number doubted whether different classes could co-exist in harmony. Samuel despaired at such cynicism:

> The Garden Suburb is still a great anxiety. The Board wants to go to allotment on Tuesday but £10,000 is still wanting. People shrink from a sort of business philanthropy. Their ideal is a giver of money who receives thanks and an approving conscience. The ideal of a business man all of whose investments increase the well-being of his fellows is not in their minds. But my wife will not be beaten![52]

Certainly, Henrietta refused to be defeated. It is a measure of her tenacity and self-belief that her 'many talks, frequent lectures, much display of imaginary plans' and what she freely admits were 'castles in the air' resulted in so many people being cajoled or coerced into investing in the Suburb. Some were motivated by the prospect of preserving the beauty of the Heath and others were eager to engage in a 'social experiment'.[53] Henrietta clearly wished to do both but the somewhat mechanistic connotations of the term 'social experiment' obscure the personal creativity and passion which fuelled her vision of a community both 'productive and pleasurable'.[54] It is not difficult to imagine the sense of triumph she felt when her vision materialised:

> It is an interesting and significant coincidence that the last time [the Heath land] changed hands it was under the signature of Henricus Octavus – Henry VIII – a king who bought it with royal gold for his pleasure. The next time it changed hands the deeds were signed by Henrietta Octavia, a woman who bought it on behalf of a public company , with the people's money to buy the people's homes.[55]

According to Marion Paterson, Henrietta's main objective in the creating of the Suburb was the 'making of a bit of God's earth beautiful for generations ahead'.[56] For Henrietta, however, the possibilities of a sensitively landscaped environment and gardened cottages extended well beyond the picturesque. In her prospectus for the Suburb, she emphasised the practical benefits of setting aside potential building land for gardens. In order to reinforce her argument, she was shrewd enough to cite the financial success of George Cadbury's incorporation of gardens in his development at Bournville.[57] Clearly, she thought such pragmatic observations from such an influential man would persuade potential male investors of the financial viability of her scheme. At the same time, Henrietta's prospectus is tinged with romantic pastoral imagery: 'the beautiful open space' of the 'common sward' and the 'creeper-draped balcony' infused with the 'magic of prosperity which turns sand into gold'.[58] In another article charting the progress of the Suburb, she eulogised 'the sloping orchards of apple orchards' over which 'the sky flames forth its uninterrupted glory'.[59] Similarly, whilst engaged in the planning of the Suburb institute, Henrietta dreamily mused over 'art students under rose pergolas' alongside others resting behind 'flower-covered windscreens'.[60] Henrietta's penchant for pastoral imagery has provoked some to question the depth of her aesthetic sensibilities.[61] As Raymond Unwin was later to comment, Henrietta's high principles were 'more influenced by picturesque ideals than by … sound aesthetic judgement'.[62] Most blunt of all was Edwin Lutyens, the distinguished architect commissioned to plan the Suburb's Central Square. No doubt stung by Henrietta's initial objections to his church designs, he grumbled that she was a 'nice woman … but proud of being a philistine [who] had no idea beyond a window box full of geraniums, calceolarias and lobelias, over which you can see a goose on the green'.[63]

Here, Lutyens is echoing the cacophony of disdain for suburban gardens from critics such as T.W.H. Crosland, who dismissed them as repositories for 'pathetic primeval desires'.[64] Lutyens' sardonic reference to geraniums, lobelias and calceolarias suggests a profusion of colour which Crosland would have perceived as the epitome of vulgarity. His remark also suggests that Henrietta had been seduced by the shallow pleasures of 'instant' gardening: a practice deplored by Lutyens' friend, the eminent horticulturalist, Gertrude Jekyll.[65] So, in other words, the overriding implication of Lutyens' statement is that Henrietta's passion for gardening and landscaping amounted to little more than a self-indulgent affection for the superficially picturesque. Certainly, Henrietta's garlanding of her articles with floral imagery tends towards the overblown, but her purpose here may have been less ingenuous than it appeared. Whilst she was shrewd enough to use pragmatic means of persuasion in order to engage the minds of her investors, she was simultaneously captivating their hearts by appealing to people's needs for recreation and recuperation which were symbolised by the regenerative properties of gardening. Once the Suburb was established, it could be argued that Henrietta deliberately fostered working-class interest in gardening in order to counter what she condemned as the 'vulgar stupidities' of traditional working-class recreation.[66] Yet she also believed that the pleasures and purposeful outcomes of gardening would generate a bond between the residents and their community. As she put it, the cultivation of a garden gives ' the purest, deepest and most re-creative of pleasures' through which all may be able to 'feel in themselves the joy of being creators'.[67] So, in a sense, the making of the Suburb was analogous for her with the nurturing of a garden in which different shrubs, trees and flowers not only serve as attractive foils for each other, but also make a variety of contributions to mutual vigour and vitality. From her own experiences of gardening, Henrietta would have realised that plants grown in isolation fail to thrive as well as those grouped together. This may have caused her to make similar assumptions about the mixing of social groups. Similarly, she would have noted the deleterious effects of planting in poor soil with inadequate air, light and space. Even Samuel suggested a connection between plants grown in such conditions and people stunted by their environment in his observations about the 'disease' afflicting the 'fertile soil' of children growing up in Whitechapel.[68]

Whilst visiting America in 1891, Henrietta had been inspired by the implications of their wall-less gardens and shared open spaces. For her, these represented mutual trust, interdependence and a capacity to give a sense of unity within a community.[69] It was her intention to replicate this design in the Suburb, but this met with much resistance from fellow trustees, who did not share her enthusiasm for blurring the boundaries between the more affluent homes. So she compromised by agreeing to the delineation of property by hedges. She did, however, insist on the setting aside of one acre of land for the growing of hedge plants. These were not to be the ubiquitous privets of traditional Victorian and Edwardian suburbs but those which evoked a pastoral idyll such as sweet briar, holly, yew and wild rose.[70] She did not have to compromise her ideals in the homes for less affluent residents. Both communal and single-unit family homes were grouped around public unwalled gardens. No doubt bearing in mind George Cadbury's experiences of his residents' indifference to gardening, Henrietta deemed the letting companies responsible for the general maintenance of the shared open spaces. Their expenses were to be covered by the rents for these properties.[71]

Henrietta cut the first sod on the land of Hampstead Garden Suburb on 2 May 1907, just a few days short of her 56th birthday. She referred to this symbolic act as a 'privilege', but she must have been euphoric. Meanwhile, Samuel – despite his continued determination not to become directly involved with the Suburb – was awestruck by her achievements. He declared that whenever he saw the developing Suburb he 'burst with pride that Yetta should have created such a place'.[72] Nor was he alone in this admiration – both for the ambience of the Suburb and Henrietta's resourcefulness, energy, imagination and sheer tenacity. In 1909, following their visit to the Suburb, Lucy Masterman, wife of the Liberal MP Charles Masterman, enthused about:

> the dear little clean houses in gardens with splendid sweeps of country all round under snow. We saw a little quadrangle for maiden ladies and the nicest street was one called Asmuns Place, up a slope, with two big trees in front of it ... Charles was fascinated and agreed that it made one nearly cry to think that Camberwell and West Ham and Peckham might all have been like that if people had only taken thought and looked after them.[73]

Similarly, the Bishop of London declared himself 'privileged' to share Henrietta's 'vision' of the Suburb, which was an 'exact contrast and antidote of all she had seen and known in Whitechapel'. He also recognised that her achievement was all the more remarkable because she was a woman. As he put it, 'few women have lived to see their dream come so beautifully true'.[74] But Henrietta's cutting of the first sod was only the beginning of many arduous tasks and frustrating setbacks. In Samuel's biography, she underplayed these adversities, instead emphasising the triumphs and highlights of the Suburb's first decade. Marion Paterson did likewise: she recorded one of the earliest resident's memories of this sod-cutting ceremony and her subsequent choosing of a plot of land:

> We were told we could build a house. It was very exciting and we chose a plot in Temple Fortune. This was the first house – at least, the first group of houses to be built and many a time people would ask if they could come over and see over it. To Dame Henrietta, our family owe a huge debt; in fact she changed the whole of our existence. Without this suburb we should have had to live in a pokey house in a suburban suburb – this place provided an escape. We breathed mentally and expanded.[75]

Meanwhile, Henrietta took great pride in asserting how her 'ambitious and portentous list' of aspirations for the Garden Suburb had materialised. By 1918, it boasted three places of worship, the Institute, which incorporated a range of educational activities for all ages, clubs for single women, a hospital for survivors of the First World War, a council school, homes for war widows and their children as well as cottage homes and retirement flats. Of course, there were also houses of diverse sizes and designs, all surrounded by their own gardens, flowers, fresh air and space. As Samuel was to comment in 1912:

> The Suburb is a perpetual joy. The houses increase, and the Central Square, with its fine building, its promenade in the wind and sky, and its flowers, refreshes our hearts. Yesterday, a party of children were acting a history play for a roomful of colonial visitors. The estate looked unsurpassingly fair. The children are coming here on Thursday to act for a party of Erskine old convalescents.[76]

Henrietta also went to great lengths to emphasise how the Suburb had achieved international acclaim. She quoted a letter from Raymond Unwin in which he described the preaching of the 'Garden Suburb gospel' to an audience in Chicago, who subsequently deemed Hampstead Garden Suburb to be the 'most poetical side of city planning' which was 'prized as an example by all those who are working for civic betterment' in the USA. The greatest glory for Henrietta must have been when Queen Mary came to view her accomplishments in the Suburb on bright cold morning in February 1918. After a guided tour in which she inspected the Institute, the chauffeurs' flats, the ladies' hostel, the woodland and homes for the wealthy, Her Majesty graciously acquiesced to drinking coffee in Henrietta's dining-room before posing for a photograph in front of the Canon Barnett Memorial Homestead.[77]

As the numerous histories of the planning and development of Hampstead Garden Suburb will testify, however, it did not evolve as smoothly – or as single-handedly – as Henrietta implied.[78] Apart from numerous wrangles with planning applications, internal disagreements amongst trustees and frequently strained relations between Henrietta and the Suburb architects, the residents themselves were to prove much more vociferous and much less acquiescent than she had anticipated. There was even insurrection from the workmen employed by contractors to build the houses. This was hardly surprising: not only were they excluded from using the Suburb's refreshment rooms, they were also expected to sleep with the horses.[79] Henrietta was outraged to learn about this and immediately ordered the contractors to provide more suitable sleeping and refreshment facilities. Despite all these obstacles, Henrietta clearly maintained her steadfast belief that the ethos of Hampstead Garden Suburb had the potential to counter the class divide which she regarded as 'one of the deepest social wrongs and one of the gravest of national dangers':

> The Garden Suburb has at least led the way in showing how thousands of people of all classes of society, of all sorts of opinions, of all standards of income, can live in helpful neighbourliness; and that at the Institute people of every shade of thought can unite to exchange ideas, and by their care for literature, art, music, history, or nature obliterate class barriers. The scheme is founded on an ethical basis, and has as its aim the development of human understanding, whereby spiritual forces are given freedom.[80]

13   *Henrietta and Samuel share a joke with Herbert Asquith on the presentation of their portrait by Sir Hubert von Herkomer, 1908*

So, once Henrietta had transposed her ideals onto the physical environment of the Suburb, her next mission was its 'cultural' landscaping: the recreational, educational and social activities intended to promote wholesome pleasures and harmony for all, including the 'young, the weak, the ill [and] the ignorant' for whom she had cared throughout her working life.[81]

XII

Cultural Landscaping

Shaping Leisure and Pleasure in Hampstead Garden Suburb

Once the building of the Suburb was expanding and the first residents were moving in, Henrietta began to wield her 'affectionate' and 'cunning plan' to promote gardening as a wholesome form of recreation.[1] In May 1909, she formed the Hampstead Garden Suburb Horticultural Society in order to encourage an interest in gardening amongst all classes of the Suburb residents. By 1911, its membership stood at two hundred. For the writer of an article in the local magazine, the *Town Crier*, this number signalled a lingering apathy among the majority of the Suburb residents. Clearly intending to prick their consciences, the article asserts:

> On the estate, there are now some 750 houses, and every householder is supposed to take an interest in his garden. We hope before the end of this season at least to double the number of subscribers ... The chief aim of the Society is to inculcate a pride in the cultivation of plants, trees and flowers, both beautiful and useful; and by inciting the members to a spirit of friendly rivalry to raise the standard of horticulture to a higher point as can be attained in suburban gardens.[2]

The writer of this article may be anonymous but the persistence and values enmeshed within it are undoubtedly those of Henrietta. In a further attempt to stir residents from their torpor, the Horticultural Society organised annual competitions and an August Bank Holiday Flower Show. The prize for the former was what Stuart Gray described – somewhat bluntly (if accurately) – a 'hideous copper pot' donated by Henrietta.[3] Rules were little less than draconian: judges were to make random inspections to ensure that 'no outside assistance' enabled any unfair advantage.[4] Not surprisingly, such exhortations have been seen as evidence of Henrietta's increasingly despotic tendencies.[5] Yet they were also underpinned by her passionate belief in the redemptive potential of gardening as well as its capacity to unite people from a diversity of backgrounds:

> We shall enjoy seeing ... Shakespeare devotees at work with the plants he cared for; people of any age learning about vegetable gardening and young folk vieing [sic] with each other on the appearance of their plots ... We shall see two outdoor gymnasiums in full use, properly equipped for little folk as well as for full-grown men and we shall see the old, the hard-worked and the tired sitting at ease ... as people of every age and degree enjoy quiet games on the lawn.[6]

Certainly, the attendance record at the horticultural classes indicates that many of the Suburb's residents shared Henrietta's enthusiasm for gardening. These classes were by far the most popular, attracting an average of 105 students compared with, for example, the 21 tempted by the poetry classes or the six wanting to learn First Aid.[7]

So, unlike many of her contemporaries, Henrietta did at least take seriously suburban dwellers' interest in gardening. She also recognised the expense involved in such a pastime and, with this in mind, arranged for tools to be loaned to those who could not afford to buy their own.[8] The residents' burgeoning passion for gardening did not always create the hoped-for spirit of harmony or even 'friendly rivalry', however. As complaints submitted to the Suburb Trust reveal, the self-regulation which Henrietta had implicitly encouraged among the residents generated more than a degree of hostility.[9] The produce of these gardens was not always welcomed either. Eileen Elias' childhood visits to Hampstead Garden Suburb in the early 20th century were blighted by mounds of 'hideous tight-looking Brussels sprouts, sickly pale cauliflower, mushy cabbage and even mushier carrots, turnips and Swedes' which appeared on her plate every lunchtime.[10] Other residents used their gardens to keep pet dogs and, inevitably, this provoked gripes from their neighbours. On 25 April 1913, a Suburb resident wrote to the *Hendon and Finchley Times* grumbling about the noise of these pets and their owners' inability to control them. The implication of this and similar complaints was that these miscreants were too steeped in their East End ways to assimilate rural codes of conduct. The working-class residents were also irritated by the eccentricities of their upper-class neighbours. For instance, the interminable squawking of a peacock kept in one of the larger gardens often disturbed the sleep of those already exhausted by the long hours worked during the day.[11]

As well as fostering an interest in gardening, Henrietta was also keen to encourage the Suburb residents to participate in a variety of sports. Her underlying purpose here was to provide a wholesome outlet for energies which might otherwise be expended upon aimless horseplay or indiscriminate 'sex-romping'.[12] To this end, the Suburb Club House provided a range of facilities including tennis, cricket, bowls, croquet, cycling and billiards. As this Club House was primarily intended to channel the physical energies of the working-class residents, all membership applications and activities had to be vetted by Club Committee members.[13] Conspicuous by its absence was a football pitch, despite the game's immense popularity among the youthful members of the working classes. Whilst Henrietta had never shown any personal interest in competitive games, she did recognise the degree of skill inherent in some of these. However, she regarded football as the epitome of brutal conflict – not least because of her witnessing the eruptions of violence which had punctuated the impromptu matches in the back streets and alleyways of Whitechapel.[14] As far as spectator sports were concerned, she would have agreed with Lord Baden-Powell, founder of the Boy Scouts, who frequently castigated the 'narrow-chested, hunched-up, miserable specimens' learning to be a 'nation of wasters' on Edwardian football terraces.[15]

Given Henrietta's denunciation of drunkenness among the feckless working – and upper – classes, it is hardly surprising that the selling of alcohol was not permitted within the boundaries of the Suburb. The *Royal Oak Hotel*, perilously close to its northern edge, was handed over to the Public Houses Trust in 1907 – a transfer which the Suburb Trust viewed with 'great satisfaction'.[16] This enabled the Suburb to incorporate the 'purest principles of Temperance Reform' by ensuring that on no part of its 'beautiful estate' could any brewer or distiller sell the 'deleterious stuff that incubated in the vat'.[17] Instead, tea rooms were dotted around the Suburb, but only after Henrietta had sought assurance from the Church of England Temperance Society that they would not at any time be granted licences to sell alcohol on their premises.[18] Whilst Henrietta's attitudes to drinking may seem overbearing, they need not necessarily have had much impact on the Suburb residents. After all, both the *Royal Oak* and the *Old Bull and Bush* at Golders Green were within a reasonable walking distance. It is also highly unlikely that anyone seeking the bawdy pleasures of the pub, music hall or football match would have moved out to Hampstead Garden Suburb in the first place.

Having attended to the residents' needs for recreation and refreshment, Henrietta took it upon herself to address their intellectual needs through the provision of educational activities at the Suburb Institute. These included home-centred topics such as dressmaking, cookery and home nursing, as well as academic subjects such as French, English Literature and Art History. Meanwhile, residents lacking vocational qualifications were exhorted to improve their career prospects by enrolling on courses in book-keeping, shorthand and business arithmetic.[19] As the President of the Institute, Henrietta took a passionate and active interest in the students' progress. She clearly had much respect for teachers with professional integrity, but she was also quick to discern any shortcomings among her staff. Upon hearing of an impending visit from His Majesty's Inspector of Schools, she decided to conduct a pre-inspection assessment herself. Her ensuing report noted that whilst a handful of teachers were 'very capable' others variously lacked 'inspiration' or 'initiative', were 'dull and dour without human qualities' or 'wanting in tact in their handling of students'.[20] No doubt Henrietta's interventions here coupled with her somewhat acerbic tones could be held as giving further evidence of her despotic tendencies. More than anything else, however, she was determined to ensure that the Institute students were not alienated by unimaginative teachers and their joyless means of imparting knowledge. As far as Henrietta was concerned, this type of instruction merely 'fed the mind' without 'stirring' the emotions.[21] Conversely, she believed that teaching should be provocative rather than informative: an interactive process which ignites curiosity and instils the desire to learn more.

Once established, however, the classes deemed necessary to address the basic needs of the Suburb residents prompted little interest. For instance, Henrietta had secured the services of a Mrs Crump who had volunteered to run a course on 'The Training of Moral Habits in Young Children'. However, the complete lack of response to this suggests that parents felt sufficiently competent to forego her offer.[22] As Lori Loeb points out, the advertising and magazines of the Edwardian period had already done much to promote the health and welfare of children.[23] And, of course, the shift towards smaller families facilitated greater attention to children's individual needs. Moreover, the Wesleyan austerity implicit in Mrs Crump's proposed class would hardly endear an increasingly child-centred Edwardian public. Nor did classes in Home Hygiene attract many students.[24] Once again, this suggests that Henrietta may have underestimated the existing knowledge and expertise of the working and lower middle classes. Indeed, the Victorian and Edwardian obsession with scrubbing, cleaning, polishing and scraping in all but the most feckless of households has been well documented.[25] Meanwhile, vocational classes in basic literacy and numeracy were organised for the working-class residents of the Suburb. Once again, these failed to captivate their target group – if indeed it existed at all. The cheaper housing on the northern edge of the Suburb had attracted artisans and the lower middle classes – butchers, bakers, clerks, nurses, cabinet-makers and post office employees – rather than the unskilled labouring classes.[26]

It is unlikely that skilled employees such as these would have required much in the way of remedial education. Their indifference to courses such as Business Routine and Arithmetic indicates that these white-collar workers and small business owners considered that their practical experience was sufficient.[27] Even they did have any lingering doubts about gaps in their education, there was a plethora of study and self-improvement guides available from the end of the 19th century onwards. These covered a diversity of topics ranging from literature, art and poetry to medicine, sports and commerce. Book reviews in newspapers and periodicals such as *TitBits* also helped to broaden public tastes.[28] The literary establishment would no doubt have sneered at these lower-middle-class pretensions to culture, but the popularity of such articles indicates that the working and lower middle classes were eager to take responsibility for their own education. Indeed, this shift towards self-education also implies that they were seeking to tailor their own blend of practical and academic knowledge which was relevant to their personal and professional lives.

After only one year, the basic and vocational courses at the Institute were replaced by academic subjects such as French, Philosophy, Literature and History, and recreational activities such as lace-making, outdoor sketching, photography and a rambling club. Henrietta also proposed the introduction of inter-class activities: for example, a trip to Stratford would appeal to literature students as well as those in the rambling club. Here, it seems that Henrietta was responding to comments by the HMI report on the Institute. He had praised Henrietta's 'desire to bring together people of different classes' but recommended that she should promote more equality between students and tutors through study groups rather than perpetuate the tutor/student hierarchy.[29] From the changes in the content and the delivery of the Institute curriculum, it is clear that Henrietta was willing to learn from the HMI's recommendations. It is also intriguing, however, to note the extent to which this new curriculum was designed – wittingly or otherwise – to appeal to an already well-educated middle-class. This suggests that whilst Henrietta could envisage a breaking down of the hierarchy between tutors and middle-class students, she was unwilling to extend such magnanimity to their less affluent counterparts.

Henrietta's attempts to refine and educate the working and lower middle classes were largely met with resistance. Nor did these people seem particularly keen to attend the public lectures at the Institute. Some of these would have been downright intimidating: the arts and literature conversations chaired by Henrietta, for example, would hardly have appealed to those doubting their intellectual capacities. From a more practical point of view, the demands of the working day would probably have left them too exhausted to contemplate climbing the hill to the Institute. Yet Henrietta persisted in her efforts to address moral issues affecting the lives of the Suburb residents. In 1913, lectures were held at the Institute and the Free Church on the tensions between women's economic independence and their parental responsibilities. It is not clear who attended these lectures but their tone indicates that they were intended to install moral panics concerning women's increasingly vociferous demands for political and financial emancipation. The first of these amounted to little more than a sustained rant on the deleterious effects of women's economic independence on the moral and physical welfare of the family. The second was more specific. It advocated training for motherhood and castigated the 'evil effects' of 'improper marriages': liaisons between those deemed ignorant, immature or both. It also embodied stern warnings against any budding feminist impulses amongst the Suburb's women.[30] Clearly, these impulses were regarded as an even greater threat to social stability than the ignorance or immaturity associated with working-class families. The extent to which these lectures echoed Henrietta's views can only be speculated, but it is highly likely that she was instrumental in commissioning the speakers. Of course, she did have feminist tendencies herself, but these were rooted in the 19th-century women's purist movement which held male sexuality as responsible for many of society's problems. As far as the purist feminists were concerned it was a woman's mission to refine these men and encourage them to curb their sexual impulses.[31] Henrietta would therefore have been disturbed by this shift towards more militant feminism because she would have regarded it as an appropriation of the 'male roughnesses that women ought to temper.[32] Equally, she may also have feared that women's preoccupation with their political rights may cause them to neglect their maternal responsibilities.

No matter how justified Henrietta felt in her views, they were becoming increasingly outmoded. For whilst there were a few arson attacks which were attributed to Suffragette activists, the majority of the Suburb's women only supported peaceful campaigns for enfranchisement.[33] Also, many of the feminist campaigns of the early 20th century related to the welfare of mothers and children.[34] As far as women's economic independence was concerned, financial circumstances often left mothers with no choice but to seek paid employment out of the home. For some women, this caused a significant shift in their attitudes to child-rearing. One working mother doubted that the children of her 'gushing' and 'coddling' non-working counterparts would be as 'affectionate and independent' as her own offspring.[35] This suggests that far from her economic independence adversely affecting her children, she was providing them with a positive adult female role model.

On another level, residents were also growing increasingly resentful of Henrietta's determination to shape the culture as well as the landscape of the Suburb. As early as 1909, Edwin Lutyens was relaying details of Henrietta's 'preposterous cheek' in a letter to his wife, Emily. He grumbled that 'she gets panics and won't let anybody do anything but herself and I believe that the bottom of it is that a Ratepayers' Association has been formed against *her*'.[36] Of course, Lutyens' mischievous glee at this insurrection would have been enhanced by his own resentment of the control which Henrietta had wielded over his plans for Central Square. Yet his letters reveal the extent to which Henrietta was becoming increasingly subject to betrayal by her fellow Trust members. Indeed, Henrietta regarded Alfred Lyttelton, the Chair of the Trust, as an 'old friend' with a 'deep and living commitment to the ethos of the Suburb.[37] Similarly, she assumed that she shared a friendship with Lutyens that 'storms could not shatter'.[38] In private conversation with Lutyens, however, Lyttelton had referred to Barnett as a 'dangerous woman' who was responsible for all the unpopular decisions made by the Trust.[39] However, close attention to the manoeuvres of male members of the Trust reveals that they were equally keen to discourage residents' interventions in the administration of the Suburb. In fact, Christopher Ikin remains inclined to 'blame Mrs Barnett' for refusing to negotiate with those wishing to form a Residents' Association, even though it was Alfred Lyttelton who informed their deputation that 'it was not advisable to proceed further with their requests'.[40] So it is likely that Henrietta's 'panics' were generated not just by rebellion from the residents but also by her (well-founded) suspicion that she was being used as a scapegoat by other Trust members.

The residents were not to be deterred, however, and nor were their requests unreasonable. They pointed out that the 'patriarchal government' of the Suburb was inappropriate in an active community and suggested that a delegation of residents could help to dispel the 'certain degree of friction' evident within the community.[41] Through their persistence, the Suburb's Residents' Association was officially founded in October 1911. By the following month, Henrietta's displeasure was made abundantly clear. In the November 1911 edition of the *Town Crier* she asserted that whilst the Trust 'welcomed every courteous communication from any organisation [they did] not wish the inhabitants of the Estate to feel bound to communicate with them through an Association'.[42] Henrietta did at least have the courage to claim ownership of such acerbic views. Nonetheless, her reprimand to those she regarded as sufficiently ungracious to gripe about the ethos underlying their Suburb must have been profoundly irritating to residents increasingly stifled by the Trust's parental clasp. As well as resenting the dissent amongst the Suburb's residents, Henrietta must have been perplexed by their apparent ingratitude. This suggests that she simply had not anticipated the expectations of the less affluent tenants and owner-occupiers of the Suburb. Nor did she anticipate the capacity of what she imagined as the industrial classes to articulate these expectations. After all, Henrietta's experiences of *all* classes had been somewhat limited. She had witnessed extremes of poverty in London's East End at first hand and, at the other end of the social spectrum, had mixed with the upper-class intelligentsia as well as their more hedonistic peers. However, the attitudes, values and aspirations of the 'respectable' working and lower middle classes were outside her experiences and observations. They were neither the deserving poor nor the degenerate rich. Rather, they formed a social group incorporating many diversities yet demonstrating a strong sense of identity and self-confidence. Hampstead Garden Suburb, with its sensitive design, clean air and proximity to the centre of London, would have provided them with an attractive alternative to conventional suburban housing developments. However, whilst Henrietta may well have gleaned their 'multiform possibilities', her overriding desire to create a socially mixed utopia caused her to overlook their already existing sense of autonomy and social responsibility. In other words, despite Alfred Lyttelton's associating of the Suburb with a medieval village, these people did not see themselves as humble serfs, pathetically grateful for the crumbs of largesse cast by a benevolent feudal system. Rather, they saw themselves as responsible and resourceful adults wanting a stake in their community.

As well as begrudging the paternalistic interventions of the Suburb Trust, the working- and lower-middle-class residents would soon have discovered that the practicalities of life in the Suburb were less idyllic than they had imagined. Artisans and clerical workers would have earned a weekly wage between 30s. and £2 10s. [43] Rents for the more modest homes were in the region of 8s. per week and tube fares into London were 4d. each day.[44] Rents and travelling costs were not, therefore, excessive – but heating, furnishing and lighting expenses were still to be considered. Most of the houses were open-plan, and Raymond Unwin's sketch for an 'artizan's living room' incorporates built-in furniture designed to be aesthetically pleasing as well as functional. Both Unwin and his partner, Barry Parker, believed that furniture designs and fittings should harmonise with their surroundings.[45] It is doubtful, however, whether the more modestly paid residents would have been in a position to replace their existing furniture with these individually-crafted fittings. They would have had to manoeuvre their Victorian

14   *A group of children in Asmun's Place*

sideboards, tables, chairs and sofas from their former parlours and dining rooms around the recesses, inglenooks and alcoves of a single, open-plan room. This furniture would have been mass-produced and of the ornate and cumbersome style much derided by Arts and Crafts architects.[46] Not only would it have stood uneasily amongst the rustic simplicity of such an interior, but the height and volume of this furniture would also have negated the light-giving properties of the white-washed walls (the Arts and Crafts movement was against the convoluted intricacies of Victorian wallpaper design). This lack of natural light would have been compounded by the small-paned windows of the cottages. These may well have provided an attractive alternative to what T.W.H. Crosland castigated as the 'glassy-eyed' windows of conventional suburban housing, but they would also have necessitated much reliance on artificial lighting.[47]

All the houses in Hampstead Garden Suburb were equipped with gas lighting, but this was by no means economical.[48] Nor was it particularly efficient: not only did it create dirt but it also tended to give off as much heat as light.[49] Residents would have needed to supplement their household lighting with oil lamps and candles: more hidden costs arising from Arts-and-Crafts-style living. Meanwhile, the material realities of heating these homes on a modest income after a full day's work and trudge uphill from Golders Green tube station would have been far removed from the merry rustic glow emanating from Unwin's sketch. All the rooms had coal-fires, with the one in the living room incorporating a cooking range. For cosmetic rather than practical reasons, coal bunkers were installed next to the outdoor lavatories at the bottom of the garden. The process of bringing in coal was therefore arduous – and treacherous on wet nights, when rotting vegetation made paths slimy.[50] The open-plan design of these cottages would also have meant that much of the heat from the fire would have drifted upstairs. This heat loss would have been compounded by the draughty realities of Unwin's insistence on the health-giving properties of well-ventilated spaces.[51] In fact, it appears that his eulogising of open space, fresh air and sunshine left him oblivious to the frequently leaden gloom of the English climate. Cottage residents would have spent many an evening sharing their firesides with still-damp laundry or coaxing the range to defy the caprices of the draughts encircling their all-purpose domestic space. The cleaning of all Victorian and Edwardian suburban housing was irksome for those unable to afford domestic help. For all their whimsical charms, the Garden Suburb cottages were much more troublesome to clean than conventional suburban homes. What Unwin called the 'simple dignity and beauty' of the wooden beams and open staircases must have been compromised by their propensity to harbour dust and cobwebs.[52] The negotiating of rustic nooks and sloping recesses with a scrubbing brush, mop and bucket would have been as gruelling as it was frustrating. The whitewashed walls would soon become smudged by gas lighting and smoke from the fires. Heavily ornate, mass-produced Victorian wallpaper may well have caused elitist lips to curl, but it was at least effective at absorbing the inevitable grime of everyday life.

To a great extent, the practicalities of living in and maintaining a cottage-style home on a modest budget expose the tensions between the socialist and aesthetic principles underpinning the Arts and Crafts movement. There is no doubt that Unwin was driven by an abiding 'sympathy for the underdog' as well as a strong commitment to the social responsibilities of the architect and town planner.[53] He was equally bound, however, by the aesthetic ideals which he believed would enhance the built environment as well as enrich the lives of its inhabitants:

> It is that which is provided over and above the bare house and street which really counts. It is just that little margin of imaginative treatment which transforms our work from the building of clean stables for animals into the building of homes for human beings, which is of value; for it is just this which … influences the inner heart of man.[54]

Unwin's intention was to refine people he regarded as stunted by the mechanism and mass-production of an industrial age. This, he reasoned, would instil in them an acknowledgment of the beauty in the simplicity of his architectural designs. In turn, he believed that this would encourage them to reject the vulgar ornamentation which characterised mass-produced goods. The sheer effort of servicing his cottages, however, may well have hampered their occupants' appreciation of 'the subtle colouring of the play of sunlight or firelight on a whitewashed wall'.[55] Neither were his initial proposals cheap. So, no matter how well-intentioned his motives, the proposed costs of his housing would have been significantly beyond the means of lower-paid workers.[56] Henrietta was not prepared to stand for this and insisted that Unwin should compromise on his more exacting (and expensive) standards in order to make the Suburb housing accessible to the working classes. This profoundly irritated Unwin who, nearly 30 years later, harboured an abiding resentment of Henrietta's 'severe sense of economy'.[57] This was with some justification. In the event, Henrietta's determination to make housing on the Suburb available to all social groups resulted in more attention being given to the facades of the small cottages than their inner construction. In consequence, these properties were afflicted with a chronic dampness which ultimately increased their maintenance costs.[58]

These material shortcomings and instances of dissent have been systematically airbrushed from Henrietta's version of the Suburb's history. For all its flaws, the Suburb also offered many benefits – for families as well as single, self-supporting women and men of all ages and classes. Public attention had been drawn to the plight of young male clerks forced to leave home and find lodgings in central London a decade earlier by journalist Robert Wright. Condemning the exploitation of these young men by the 'subtle ingenuity' of unscrupulous landladies, he argued that these 'notoriously over-worked and underpaid' workers had a 'first claim on the social reformer and philanthropist':

> Go into the cheap coffee-houses in the City and its environs and note the appearance of the young men who patronise them. The sort of life they are forced to live is proclaimed in the shiny black coat, the frayed collar, the shabby cuffs, and above all, in the pale, haggard, 'washed-out' look on their faces … The perpetual struggle to make ends meet and to reconcile poverty with gentility is heartbreaking.[59]

Of course, these young men's pallor could also be attributed to what White terms the 'doubtful distractions' of their night life rather than the nasty food dished up among the dirt and squalor of their lodgings. In order to address these issues, White proposed the establishment of low-cost communal dwellings for these young men. Amenities would include clean single rooms, cooked meals, a laundry service, ample hot and cold water and shared recreational areas. He made it clear that this accommodation should be made sufficiently comfortable to acknowledge the difference between these clerks' class position and that of the lower-class 'dossers' for whom rather more basic communal accommodation already existed. White also had a not-so-hidden agenda: he proposed that rules regarding curfew hours and behaviour should be carefully constructed and rigidly enforced. So, underlying his emotive plea for these young clerks to be saved from the 'fangs' of capitalist 'bloodsuckers' is his anxiety that they were vulnerable to corruption by those parasitic by-products of capitalism: young people's gambling, drinking and carousing dens, which began to proliferate throughout London from the late 19th century onwards.[60] Such an agenda also underpinned Henrietta's provision of communal dwellings for single, self-supporting young men and women. In 1910, Waterlow Court was built for middle-class 'ladies' and Queen's Court for lower-class 'working women'.[61] Similarly, the Suburb eventually incorporated 'residences' for young, middle-class men and 'hostels' for their working-class counterparts.[62] These were also governed by stringent rules and regulations, particularly concerning visits from members of the opposite sex.[63] No doubt these young men and women were expected to comply with conditions similar to those imposed on older residents in their communal accommodation. Some of these related to the regular sweeping of balconies, restrictions on the drying of washing and the maintenance of standards of cleanliness inside the flats. The keeping of pets was also strictly forbidden.[64]

There are very few oral or written accounts of how the Suburb was experienced by its first residents. But Jean Franklin Grant's handwritten account of her parents' experiences gives some insights into life in the early years of the Suburb.[65] Her father, Andrew Moffatt, was one of the first residents of the Suburb. He had moved into Wordsworth Walk with his first wife and their young son in 1907. Three years later, his wife died and Andrew moved to another house in the Suburb on Hogarth Hill. At that time, the houses on Wordsworth Walk were intended to accommodate the lower middle classes, whilst those on Hogarth Hill were slightly more substantial. Indeed, Andrew's relocation may have coincided with his promotion to head drapery cutter and designer at Maple and Co. department store in London.

Andrew's second wife, Jean's mother, was Laura Franklin, who moved to the Suburb in 1907. She did not rent her home but stayed with friends who lived in the area. Laura worked as a French translator and a saleswoman at Peter Robinson's department store. She was 31 when she moved to Hampstead Garden Suburb and would have been precisely the calibre of single, respectable and educated woman that Henrietta wanted so as to refine her community. Laura moved in just six weeks after the Northern line to London opened. This suggests that, as Henrietta had predicted, ease of access to central London would encourage those on modest incomes to move out to the Suburb. But it is interesting that Laura chose to stay with friends rather than rent the self-contained accommodation on the first floor of family homes intended for single women like herself. As the cost would not have been prohibitive, it is likely that Laura did not want to compromise her independence by taking on moral responsibility for the family downstairs. After all, single woman in the Edwardian area were far removed from the pitiful or ridiculed spinster figure of the 19th century. Rather, they were spirited, sexually and financially independent 'New Women'.[66] Although Henrietta cannot have failed to be aware of these radical new models of femininity, she effectively sidestepped her by prioritising the needs of acquiescent, rather than assertive, self-supporting women.

Laura's particular circumstances suggest that she was neither a needy spinster nor an anarchic New Woman. She may well have had no intention of taking on the role of moral guardian, but she obviously enjoyed many of the Suburb's leisure opportunities. She met her husband-to-be through their involvement with St Jude's Church choir and subsequently joined in many of the Institute activities, through which she became very friendly with Henrietta. Laura and Andrew married in 1914 when they were aged 38 and 48 respectively. However, marriage did not cause Laura to give up her independence. She continued to stand on a crowded tube to her job in London until only six weeks before Jean was born in 1917. Whether or not she returned to work after the birth is unclear but within five years, Laura and Andrew had started their own retail business. Even by the time she moved to the Suburb, therefore, Laura would have had a firm sense of her adult identity as well as pride in her work and independence. Whilst she may well have enjoyed the Suburb's cultural and religious activities, it is likely that her spiritual values and tastes were formed well before she moved there. In other words, like many of the early residents, she needed neither the protection nor guidance implicit in Henrietta's efforts at the cultural shaping of the Suburb. Rather, Laura's involvement in the church and Institute activities suggests that she was keen to have her stake in the community and, in turn, have some influence on its development.

Henrietta may well have underestimated the resourcefulness and independence of some of the Suburb's residents. Yet others would have been attracted to Hampstead Garden Suburb because of the principles underlying its picturesque housing and setting. Amongst papers found at number 14, Asmun's Place, the former home of Alice Haws and her son, Arthur, are various documents including National Health Insurance cards, Post Office savings books and the death certificate of Alice's husband, also Arthur, who died aged 39 in February 1901.[67] These fragments give clues as to why, despite significant disadvantages, the Suburb environment continued to appeal to

15 *An Artizan's Living Room from Parker and Unwin,* The Art of Building a Home *(London: Longman and Green, 1901)*

those on modest incomes. Alice and Arthur moved to Hampstead Garden Suburb from Kensington in 1909. In order to maintain their two-bedroomed home, Alice worked as a waitress in London while Arthur was employed as a book-keeper for a group of City accountants. Arthur would have earned between 30s. and £2 per week and his mother between £1 and 30s.[68] For Alice, one of the attractions of the Suburb would have been in its ethos of Christian values, sobriety and self improvement: amongst her papers are a Church of England Temperance Society pledge signed by Arthur senior and pamphlets addressing the 'formidable facts of temptation and sin' endorsed by the Purity Department of the National British Women's Temperance Society. As a single parent, Alice probably intended these to instil a sense of morality in her adolescent son. Another attraction of the Suburb would have been its safety. Whilst younger self-supporting women may well have been revelling in their independence, it is doubtful whether Alice, significantly older, would have shared their confidence. As widowhood would have made it necessary for her to work, neither her single nor employed status were determined by personal choice. Also, like Henrietta, Alice would have been old enough to remember the times when urban spaces were associated with menace, violence and immorality.[69] So, it is likely that Alice was haunted by memories of these as she walked through the streets of London. However, Henrietta's influence on the design of the Suburb ensured the physical safety of women by providing well-lit, open streets as opposed to the shadowy back streets characteristic of conventional urban and suburban development. While Raymond Unwin was more concerned about the unprepossessing appearances of these spaces, Henrietta clearly associated them with the urban depravity and danger she had witnessed during her years amongst the labyrinthine alleys of Whitechapel.[70]

   Also, despite the practical shortcomings of life in Hampstead Garden Suburb, for
women in Alice's position, it offered an environment in which they could develop a
sense of identity and self-worth. For example, paternalist developments such as Lord
Leverhulme's Port Sunlight were founded on the assumption that woman's primary
role would be that of full-time mother and homemaker.[71] Whilst Henrietta recognised
women's domestic roles, she also acknowledged that many women were single and
self-supporting. Not only did she arrange for adequate domestic support to be available
for these women, but she also ensured that they were provided with a range of safe
and stimulating recreational activities ranging from literary visits to lace-making.[72] Of
course, other suburban communities also incorporated a variety of leisure activities,
but these tended to be geared towards couples or families. As a result, single or
childless people may have felt excluded from the social life of the community. At least
the activities in Hampstead Garden Suburb did have the potential to encourage the
mixing of all its residents, regardless of age, class, gender or marital status. One of
the most enduring criticisms of Henrietta's scheme for social integration is that she
failed to provide the employment which had forged the identities of the communities
on which she had based Hampstead Garden Suburb. So, residents were drawn away
from the heart of the Suburb – the Institute and the churches in Central Square
– to the tube station and the shops on the Suburb boundaries.[73] Indirectly, however,
the creation of the Suburb *did* generate employment – particularly for women. As
advertisements in the local papers demonstrate, there were opportunities for paid
work in teaching, retail, catering and nursing in the numerous enterprises established
in the early years of the Suburb.[74] Of course, the larger houses in the Suburb would
also have created employment for an array of housekeepers, cooks, parlour maids,
nannies and gardeners.
   If there was one main flaw in Henrietta's design and development of Hampstead
Garden Suburb, it was her unyielding belief in environmental determinism: the notion
that people are inevitably shaped by their cultural and physical surroundings. In the
end, the tenacity with which she clung to this belief drove her to over-determine the
vision which she had nurtured throughout her life. So whilst she may have been able
to circumvent opposition from powerful and influential men, it was local resentment
of her relentless interventions which ultimately coerced her into a somewhat grudging
capitulation to the residents' demands. It was also through her founding and developing
of Hampstead Garden Suburb that the enduring image of Henrietta was forged: that of
an impatient, dictatorial, and manipulative tyrant who would variously bulldoze, coerce
or beleaguer until she achieved her ends. Whilst Henrietta's despotic streak should not
go unrecorded, however, it should not be allowed to overshadow her tenacity, vision,
energy and fervent commitment to social and housing reform – which culminated
in what remains one of the most imaginative and innovative housing developments
ever created.

XIII

A Benevolent Tyrant

Life Beyond the Suburb

By the time Henrietta had cut the first sod of Hampstead Garden Suburb, she and Samuel had already decided to sever their ties with Toynbee Hall and Whitechapel. This must have been a painful decision – not least because of all the time, energy and, of course, memories embedded within their 30 years of service and achievement among their people. Henrietta already had another project in which to channel her still formidable energies and, meanwhile, Samuel had also been offered another position: this time, the opportunity to become Canon of Westminster Abbey. Despite increasingly poor health, he was considerably invigorated by this offer, as he felt it would be the ideal platform to convince rich and influential people of the need to continue the fight against poverty and deprivation in the East End of London. Needless to say, these people were convinced. Hundreds of letters of support and congratulations flooded in and the ever-conscientious Samuel insisted on replying to them all personally. Not surprisingly, this had a detrimental effect on his already fragile health. So, what should have been his monumental inauguration on 9 August 1906 was marred by the exhaustion betrayed by Samuel's faltering delivery of what Henrietta described as the 'interminable Latin document' inflicted on a largely uncomprehending audience.[1]

Nor was their move from Bristol to 3, Little Cloisters, Westminster the liberating experience they had expected. It was too cramped, dark and dingy to accommodate Samuel's considerable book collection, let alone the numerous members of the Barnett household and staff. Henrietta immediately set about organising builders and decorators and within three months they had moved into their newly renovated home. Samuel, however, still regarded it as a 'wretched place' and continued to yearn for the intellectual stimulation and earnest sense of purpose which permeated the Toynbee Hall settlement.[2] Yet there was no shortage of visitors to their new home. As Henrietta observed, their move to the centre of London resulted in an influx of country friends and acquaintances who suddenly seemed to develop the need for frequent business trips to the City. This exasperated Henrietta – and Samuel – although he was characteristically rather more forbearing about this social whirl than his wife. Both found the constant round of parties, receptions and home entertaining a shallow distraction from issues which still clamoured for their attention: the poverty, unemployment and continuing class divisions epitomised for Samuel by the 'superior existence of flowers which waved in dignity and beauty over the heads over struggling and sweating humans' at some particularly meaningless function at the Foreign Office. The sheer tedium, extravagance and futility of this event left them both questioning the point of such gatherings to the government of the country.[3]

There were compensations. Henrietta and Samuel both took immense pride in showing friends from the East End around Westminster Abbey. Ever keen to instil structure and purpose, Henrietta deemed that these tours were best conducted and used a thematic approach. Visitors chose between guided historical, biographical, philosophical or architectural walks around the Abbey. When a more enlightened Department of Education allowed school trips to be included in timetabled hours, Samuel took over from hapless teachers attempting to engage bewildered children with the majesty of the Abbey by transforming their 'vacant strolls' and vague 'mooning' into living history lessons.[4] Also, pre-empting the heritage industry of the later 20th century, Henrietta discerned the profits that could be made from the wealthy tourists from America and Europe who gathered in throngs in and around the Abbey during the summer months. She proposed the opening of a gift shop inside the Abbey where visitors could buy 'well-chosen literature, postcards and tasteful reproductions' superior to the indignity of those peddled by street traders who loitered outside the north door of the building. Henrietta almost succeeded in this venture but was overruled by a somewhat cautious Dean who feared that it would set a sacrilegious precedent that would be exploited by those less scrupulous than the Barnetts.[5]

A few months after moving in to The Cloisters, Mary Moore, Henrietta's cherished nurse from her childhood days, became progressively frail and faltering. At first, Henrietta and Samuel hoped that this was merely symptomatic of Mary's age. She had just had her 81st birthday, but was still insisting on fulfilling her daily round of duties. By March 1907, however, they could no longer dismiss her worsening condition and a doctor was summoned to the Barnett household. After examining his patient, he confided to Henrietta and Samuel that Mary was suffering from terminal cancer. Both were distraught by both this unwelcome news and also the idea that someone as sweet, gentle and selfless as Mary should be sentenced to such a painful end to her life. Samuel in particular was very anxious to protect Mary from the harsh realities of her illness. In a letter to Frank, he implored him not to make any reference to her condition as he didn't want her to hear so much as an 'echo' of how ill she was. Henrietta was rather more pragmatic. She had no intention of telling Mary how seriously ill she was but also realised that her nurse was astute enough to discern the truth for herself.[6] The next six months were harrowing in the extreme for Henrietta. She and Samuel had hired a nurse to help care for Mary, but when the old lady was racked with pain through the long, humid summer nights of 1907 only her treasured Yetta could bring her any solace. Henrietta herself could not bear to be away from her bedside. What really tore Henrietta apart was the bravery, patience and uncomplaining good humour with which Mary endured the agonies and indignities of her final illness. Supremely resilient and courageous herself, Henrietta certainly did not let Mary witness the profound sadness she was experiencing, but when her nurse lapsed into brief and fitful sleep, she would sob inconsolably for much of the night. By October, Samuel, ever attuned to Henrietta's emotional turmoil, became increasingly concerned for her health, but was equally awed by the enduring mutual love, consideration and respect between the two women:

> I am anxious about my wife. She is sorely tried as day by day and night by night she watches, expecting the last hour of one who has loved and is loved so much. There is great beauty in such a death-bed. Nurse on her side hides her pain lest her child should suffer, and [Henrietta] hides her grief lest Nurse should suffer

16   *No. 3, Little Cloisters from the windows of No. 4, Little Cloisters*

... It is inexpressibly sad ... 'Where pain ends gain ends,' and pain certainly does bring out love.[7]

Mary finally died on 30 November 1907. Right until the end, she remained loving, lucid and thoughtful – especially towards Henrietta, for whom she had spent almost a lifetime caring. For Henrietta, this loss must have represented the severance of one of the final links to her childhood, when she had endeared herself to and exasperated the long-suffering and infinitely patient Mary in equal measures. In 1929, the 79-year-old Henrietta recalled how inspired she had been by this selfless, gentle and wise woman who had 'taught her to sew, speak the truth, fear nothing except sin and snakes; and to consider the poor'. No doubt Mary, a spirited if somewhat more self-effacing woman herself, was intensely proud of Henrietta's fearless determination, which had culminated in so many achievements – particularly since the pathetic little scrap of humanity she had been hired to nurse 56 years earlier had not been expected to survive beyond a few months. Samuel, too, was deeply affected by Mary's death. Meandering through the grounds of Exeter College, Oxford a week or so before she died, he was struck by the melancholy mistiness of its autumnal hues and – with Mary in mind – mused on how 'the way beauty waits for death' was immensely touching. Yet he also missed Henrietta dreadfully when these work commitments meant he had to leave her alone with Mary. As he wrote to her one lonely night:

It is a grand position to be able to talk to people on their highest interests, but all kinds of doubts and hopes haunt one to make one depressed. I can no more tell them what I want to tell them than I can tell you how I love you. I wonder what you would be saying if you were here now. The hour is one in which I want loving, the pores of one's being get opened and anything but love hurts.[9]

To all but those closest to her – Samuel, Marion and Alice – Henrietta concealed her profound sadness about Mary's death, and channelled her energies into cajoling and coercing co-operation from those instrumental in helping her develop Hampstead Garden Suburb. Only a few months later, however, the Barnett household was left reeling from another – wholly unexpected – loss. Frank, Samuel's fun-loving, irrepressible and mischievous brother, was playing a round of golf on his favourite course when he collapsed and died from a heart attack. Henrietta and Samuel were utterly stunned by this news, especially as Frank had only just returned home after spending a few days with them – apparently in excellent health and exuberant spirits. Samuel was numb with grief and disbelief: Frank was 63 years old but had always seemed much younger. Underlying his youthful ebullience and optimism lay a warm sensitivity which had made him Samuel's trusted confidante since early adulthood. Apart from Henrietta, Frank was one of the few who really understood the intense frustrations and energies burning beneath Samuel's mild and courteous outer demeanour. As Samuel put it, Frank 'filled the biggest place in our life's joy and now there is a great void'.[10] For Samuel, that void was never to be filled. Rather, his misery was accentuated by his inheritance of the family business and all its concomitant responsibilities and concerns. Here he was supported by his nephew, Samuel – known as Uely – who joined Henrietta and Samuel at Cloisters after his father's death. Lasting affection and respect were to blossom between them all.

The death of Frank triggered a noticeable decline in Samuel's health. He had been suffering from debilitating headaches for several years and these were becoming much more frequent. Numerous remedies were prescribed and tried, including frequent sojourns to friends' country houses, where it was hoped that he would rally to the allegedly magical properties of fresh air and sunshine. Despite the best efforts and 'tender solicitude' of their many friends, however, Samuel's relief from these bouts of pain was temporary at best, so his doctor advised a complete rest from all work commitment and responsibility. Samuel duly obeyed, but to little avail. Only a few days after heeding this advice, he lost consciousness for several hours in which he was believed to be hovering towards death. Subsequently, he was to spend 15 weeks resting in his bedroom at St Jude's Cottage. At first, this made him agitated and anxious – not least because he felt he was failing in his duties to others.[11] He was also racked with guilt for burdening Henrietta with extra work. By February 1910 he was feeling a little stronger, and was no doubt energised by Henrietta, who was still in a frenzy of activity at Hampstead Garden Suburb.[12] What Samuel did not know was that his doctor had recently warned Henrietta that Samuel's condition meant that he was unlikely to survive more than a few years. Henrietta kept this devastating news entirely to herself. This must have demanded profound self-control – especially considering the vituperative criticism and hostility she was enduring from Suburb architects, residents and Trust members during this period. No matter how much these dissidents were increasingly dismissing her as a stubborn, irascible and unreasonable woman, Henrietta was still capable of deep feeling. As she recalled a few years later, her awareness of the severity of Samuel's illness meant that:

> Each day was treasured more, each pregnant suggestion remembered, every gay glad incident enfolded deep. For 40 years we had doubled our joys and halved our sorrows by sharing them, and yet now the most holy of anticipated events had to be kept secret. It is hard to write of such pain.[13]

It must have been even harder to endure. Samuel's respite from his poor health was only fleeting and by 1911 he was confined to bed after another series of violent heart attacks. What was especially frustrating was that his mind was as nimble and as questioning as it had ever been, but his body – as he himself realised – was no longer fit for use. Indeed, he still burned inwardly at the apathy and injustice which continued to plague society:

> Quietness makes me impatient. I should like to curse Parliament which goes on playing with words. I should like to rouse workmen to clear out the MPs as Cromwell did. I should like to tell the workmen the danger they are in from their own narrowness. I should like to tell the parsons to make themselves clear and no longer halt between peace and truth. I should like to disestablish the clergy. I should like to say with Danton, dare, dare and again dare. This, you see is the mind which grows in idleness.[14]

In many respects, Samuel's physical decline enabled this outpouring of intense intellectual activity. Perhaps this enforced inertia enabled him to clarify thoughts and ideas which had hovered at the edge of his consciousness for all his adult life. He also read voraciously, and the time he had available for reflecting on the insights of others meant that he was able to articulate and assert his beliefs with much less diffidence and circumspection than previously. He also revelled in the time and space spent with close friends or taking drives in the countryside (Henrietta had finally persuaded him to buy the motor car she had coveted ever since she had thrilled at breaking the speed limit of 12mph in their friend's Mercedes back in their Bristol days). Needless to say, Samuel had not approved of such lawless frivolity, so Henrietta and her friends had to reserve their daredevil 30mph antics for when Samuel was safely occupied in worthier pursuits.[15] As well as motoring though nearby Richmond and Kingston upon Thames, they also travelled along Henrietta's beloved south coast and the Sussex Downs which had enchanted her since childhood. Despite the marked decline in his health and virtual absence from public life, Samuel continued to be held in the highest of esteem among his ecclesiastical and academic colleagues. In 1912, he was awarded a DCL degree by Oxford University. He was delighted for two reasons. Firstly, he saw it as a vindication of and approbation for his life's struggles and achievements. Secondly, his greatest sense of pride was ignited when the conferring of his degree was greeted by a spontaneous outburst of applause from the graduates in the audience: all ordinary working men for whom a university education would have been a pipe dream just a generation earlier.[16]

Samuel had also been enlivened by their move from the claustrophobic chambers of number 3, Little Cloisters to the much more spacious and luxurious accommodation next door. This had been vacated by their neighbour, Canon Beeching, who had been promoted to the position of Dean of Norwich Cathedral. His health caused him some reservations about the move but the elegant and historic charms of the house, along with its sunny aspect and large, flower-strewn gardens soon allayed these misgivings.[17] Henrietta had already determined that they should have a retreat from London and the inevitable accompanying whirl of visitors, which may well have stimulated Samuel but also sapped his rapidly depleting energies. A few months earlier, she had found the perfect escape from the demands of their public life: an imposing house in King's Esplanade, Hove which was just a few metres from the seafront. This would have provided a welcome distance from the hostility of the Hampstead Garden Suburb dissidents as well as the draining sycophancy of followers constantly clamouring for snippets of Henrietta and Samuel's remnants of precious time together. Indeed, the fact that they had to sell St Jude's Cottage to fund this purchase is a measure of how much Henrietta was re-thinking her priorities. She was still brimming over with energy and enthusiasm for her Hampstead Garden Suburb project, but obviously realised that physical distance from it would be beneficial to her health as well as Samuel's. Samuel greatly appreciated this investment in 'sky and air' and looked forward to spending the summer of 1913 reading, relaxing and reflecting in their new home.[18]

This was never to happen. In April 1913, just after Samuel had been appointed as Sub-Dean of Westminster Abbey, his health worsened considerably. He was expected to die within days, but he lingered for two more months, tortured by pain, breathlessness and agonised thoughts racing through his constantly active and questioning mind. Occasionally, the cocktail of drugs prescribed to relieve his intractable pain would cloud his thinking and he would wrestle with unsolved dilemmas from many years previously. As lucidity returned, he would implore Henrietta over and over again to impress upon the Church that the progress of the world was dependent on how Christianity was presented to the Chinese nation. He also fretted over other unfinished business in his life: the future of Toynbee Hall, the progress of the WEA and ongoing projects at Westminster Abbey as well as social insurrection: notably, the industrial unrest of 1912-3 and the women's suffrage movement.[19] Most of all, he needed Henrietta's

17   *No 4, Little Cloisters and the Abbey Towers*

constant presence. She often asked him if he would like to see any of the friends, relatives and neighbours who were united in their concern for this gentle, unassuming, but infinitely wise man who had touched and inspired so many lives in so many different ways. He always replied, 'Until I am better I want only you.' Henrietta was utterly crushed by her witnessing of this suffering endured by the person who had loved, cherished and supported her throughout all her youthful petulance, mood swings, contrariness and ferocious determination to challenge the iniquities of society. Thus engulfed in despair she was impervious to all kindly meant expressions of sympathy but one. Standing by the garden gate at their house in Hove awaiting the daily visit of the fish-hawker, Henrietta was accosted by a ragged and unkempt woman intent on scrounging a few coppers. Under normal circumstances, Henrietta would most certainly have sent her packing but such was her misery that she automatically handed over the sum demanded. Probably no stranger to strife herself, the woman sensed Henrietta's sorrow and asked her why she was so unhappy. Henrietta blurted out that the person she loved best in the whole world was about to leave her. With a candour that Henrietta would have appreciated, the woman looked at her and asked, 'Is he with yer or 'ave they took him away?' Henrietta replied that he was still at home to which the woman responded, 'Oh, be thankful then, be thankful that you've got him to do for. 'Tis awful to 'ave to put 'em away when they're ill and wants yer most and you know all their little ways. That's what I 'ave 'ad to do before now.' This silenced Henrietta and set her musing:

> As she spoke I seemed to see, beyond the room facing the sunny sea where my dear one lay, the long drear wards with rows of beds filled with 'cases', the efficient official nurses whose motive was duty not love; the patients and their weary, fretful, hopeless desire to die at home with those they cared for; and to realise the pity, the pathos of such separations.[20]

Promising to pray for them both, but not without remonstrating with Henrietta for her lack of the Catholic faith which would have comforted her, the tender-hearted tramp headed off down the Esplanade, never to be seen again. But Henrietta never forgot this timely reminder of how human pain could be exacerbated by poverty and deprivation. And probably for the first time in her life, she fully appreciated how the unwashed and unkempt were just as capable of feeling profound sorrow as their more educated and affluent counterparts.

Samuel died on 17 June 1913. Almost immediately, the authorities at the Abbey began mobilising arrangements for a grand funeral service befitting such an illustrious member of their fellowship. Samuel, however, had pre-empted this and countered such pomp and ceremony by expressing his wishes that, first, he wanted his funeral to take place in St Jude's Church, and, second, that the service should be as simple and cheap as possible. Nor did he want flowers wasting over his dead body. Rather, he wanted them to bring 'joy and comfort to living people'.[21] So, in accordance with his wishes, Samuel was cremated following a simple funeral in Whitechapel attended by family, friends and local residents who had never forgotten the infinite patience and wisdom of their former vicar. Subsequently, Samuel's ashes were buried in the graveyard of St Helen's, Hangleton, near Hove, a tiny 12th-century church nestling at the foot of the Sussex Downs. In the days following his death, more than 1,100 letters of condolence arrived at their Westminster home. Henrietta included a selection from these in the biography of Samuel which she began writing shortly after his death. All paid tribute to his modesty, vision, inspiration and unending empathy with the outcasts of society. A few also recognised the deep significance of Henrietta's influence in Samuel's work. As Luke Paget, the Bishop of Stepney was to comment:

> One feels that the whole East End ought in some way to express to you, dear Mrs Barnett, what it feels when it knows of Canon Barnett's death! It needs many voices to do this, and pray let mine be one of them. He and you have stood side by side in it all, and all that is felt for him is felt for you. Your wise and tender love for the poor; your confidence in them and faith in their best; your work and your power of inspiring them have made all the difference. The best that is being done now is very largely the immediate result of your labours, and the good that shall be done will bear the constant impression of your touch.[22]

Newspapers and journals were also fulsome in their praise and respect for the life and work of Samuel. Wiped out with emotional exhaustion and crushed with grief, Henrietta was beyond responding to all these tributes personally. Instead, she sent each correspondent a copy of a passage from one of their favourite poets, Robert Browning, which encapsulated her feelings for Samuel: 'Through such souls alone/God stooping shows sufficient of his light/For us in the dark to rise by. And I rise.'[23]

No doubt Henrietta gained some solace from the sympathies of those also mourning for Samuel, but her most cherished letter must have been the very last one he was ever to write to her whilst she was suffering from influenza during the cold, damp months of February 1913. Because Samuel's health was too delicate to risk succumbing to a similar infection himself, he and Henrietta were forced to spend a few weeks apart. As always, Samuel yearned to be with her but took the opportunity to reflect on their long partnership:

Wife of my young days, wife of my old days, always inspiring, always protecting, God bless you and give you a restful day … There is a delightful hush about today. It is a day for peaceful thinking, a day for turning over old photos and living again in old times. Bless you, is the chief word of your old lover. Oh, how I miss you, how I shall miss you when the lights come and there is no-one to read to … Oh, my dear one, as you lie still let the memories of what have been revive, comfort and strengthen you. All we endure is just meant to teach us how to love, and the lesson is infinite.

Get well soon,

Yours and yours and yours, Samuel[24]

The extent of Henrietta's sense of loneliness and isolation after Samuel's death can only be imagined. She was far too proud and self-contained to allow anyone even the merest glimpse into the vulnerability carefully masked by her outer resilience. Perhaps only Marion Paterson would have witnessed her grief at the loss of the only person who loved her unconditionally and whom she loved and respected in return. Of course, Marion was devoted to Henrietta but, whilst Henrietta was clearly very fond of Marion, it is likely that her slavish loyalty did not inspire the esteem in which Henrietta held Samuel. So, in the months following Samuel's death, Henrietta sublimated her grief and despair into organising a series of memorials to his life, work and faith. These included a marble tablet in Westminster Abbey inscribed with the words, 'Fear Not to Sow Because of the Birds', sentiments which for Henrietta, summed up Samuel's unwavering courage and faith, a silver lamp in St Jude's On the Hill, Hampstead, and the establishing of trust funds for numerous educational and social projects. Of these, the closest to Henrietta's heart was her long-held dream to found a girls' secondary school at Hampstead Garden Suburb. By 1918 this was – in part – realised, when Queen Mary laid the foundation stone of what was to become the Suburb High School in the south part of the Institute building. A few years later, it was re-named The Henrietta Barnett School in honour of its namesake, who had recently been awarded a DBE in recognition of her public achievements. Henrietta also busied herself not only in writing Samuel's two-volume biography but also completing, editing and publishing his frenetic efforts at scribbling down his last thoughts on the state of the nation. [25]

It has been commented that after Samuel died, Henrietta became noticeably more stubborn, dictatorial and arrogant. Indeed, by the age of 70, what Beatrice Webb had identified many years earlier as self-confidence bordering on conceit had transmogrified into what Henrietta's fellow Trust Board member, Captain H.L. Reiss, termed a 'despotic masterfulness'. Others have confirmed her propensity for vituperative criticism and even violent abuse, whilst some Suburb residents recall childhood memories of 'scuttling in fright' at the sight of Henrietta's chauffeur-driven Rolls forging an imperious path towards her house in South Square, bought with part of the proceeds from the Hove house she had briefly shared with Samuel.[26] Quite why Henrietta decided to sell the house in Hove is not clear, but her intention to continue with her various public roles was soon made manifest. Her new house on South Square overlooked the churchyard and was large enough to warrant the employment of a cook, parlourmaid, chauffeur and a boot-boy.[27] Of course, it was also the perfect base from which to supervise the continued development of the Suburb. This could account for the increased resentment of her undeniably tyrannical streak: prior to this, other commitments had prevented extensive involvement – or, as the Trust Board saw it – unwarranted interference in Suburb affairs. Equally it should be remembered that, in early 20th-century society, what would now be interpreted as feistiness, resolve and self-assertion would have been regarded as Henrietta's 'unfeminine' arrogance and aggression.

Just a year after Henrietta moved back to Hampstead Garden Suburb, the First World War broke out. This was to change the nature of society – and the Suburb – for ever. The first noticeable impact in the Suburb was the dearth of domestic servants: women went to work in previously male-dominated industries or munitions factories where they earned more pay and enjoyed greater camaraderie, whilst the men – no doubt encouraged by the ubiquitous exhortations on Lord Kitchener's posters – signed up for the armed services. Prior to 1914, the demand for nannies, cooks, cleaners, maids and gardeners had been so great that a Suburb Employment Bureau had been formed. This had resulted in an influx of young girls moving to the Suburb, some no more than 13 or 14 years old, in search of work in an area perceived by their families as a 'healthy and wholesome' alternative to life in the north of England or Wales. Many of these girls, however, were desperately lonely, and ill-suited to domestic service in an environment very different from their homes.[28] Wages were low, hours were excessive and the cost of public transport would have meant that visits home would have been out of the question. It is also likely that they would have been stifled by the lack of vitality and companionship in the Suburb. It is therefore unsurprising that many of them drifted to London, where – as a *Church Gazette* article darkly implied – they would descend into seedier employment such as bar work or even prostitution.[29] The war was also to impact on the social life of the Suburb. In 1909, the Suburb Club House had opened. Henrietta had great hopes for this venture, which she believed would provide a space where 'fellowship of common ideals and aspirations could find expression both to stimulate and restrain'. It comprised tennis courts, a croquet lawn, a bowling green, billiard tables and a reading room piled stacked with books, periodicals and daily newspapers. After 1914, however, it was used as a hospital to tend the wounded and shell-shocked casualties of the carnage in Europe. Although the Club was re-opened after the war ended, it would have signalled the end of the innocent idealism which had suffused the earliest years of the Suburb's development. According to the residents of that time, there really had been a sense of community in which class distinctions were overcome, and all had taken part in pageants, masques, fêtes and galas.[30] After 1918, increases in the cost of living meant that fewer working-class people were attracted to the area and even some of the more established and affluent Suburb dwellers, disillusioned by the lack of domestic servants, sold their large, high-maintenance homes or let them out as apartments. Of course, many of the younger male residents of the Suburb would have perished in the war: records show that Alice Haws, the resident mentioned in the previous chapter, was still living in the Suburb in 1919 but, ominously, there is no further trace of her son, who would have been in his early thirties by that time.[31]

During the First World War, Hampstead Garden Suburb residents were encouraged to provide accommodation for a number of Belgian refugees fleeing the German occupation of their country. Indeed, they were congratulated upon their readiness to offer hospitality to their 'unfortunate friends from Belgium'. Henrietta was among the first to set an example by furnishing and appointing the house next door to her own for this purpose. The reality was somewhat different: when the refugees duly arrived Henrietta was appalled by their 'greedy, quarrelsome and dirty' habits. Only when they began to pay rent did she change her attitude and reconstruct them as 'honourable sufferers whose pitiable circumstances call for abundant help'. The other residents were not overly gracious either. Some resented the fact that young, healthy Belgian men were safely ensconced in the Suburb whilst countless numbers of their British counterparts were being slaughtered in unimaginable conditions on Europe's battlefields. Meanwhile, Belgian children were taunted and pelted with stones by the Suburb's children.[32] A consequence of the First World War was that an unprecedented number of women with young children were widowed and experienced huge hardship, both financially and emotionally. Henrietta, always sympathetic to the plight of single, unsupported women, organised the building of flats on the Suburb to house them. The construction of this development was funded by Sir Alfred Yarrow and, in another memorial to Samuel, was named the Canon Barnett Homestead. Once they were no longer needed for the accommodation of war widows, they were let out to elderly tenants at low rates. These older women were grateful for this attractive accommodation, but did have some reservations. As one old lady commented, 'I like it all, and my little garden too, except the window, but Mrs Barnett is such a draughty lady.'[33] No doubt the war widows were similarly grateful for somewhere to live – initially at least. However, as Henrietta was later to discover, war pensions eventually gave some of these women unprecedented economic freedom. Indeed, as one young woman told her, 'I'm only 26, I've worked hard ever since I left school and never earned so much as they give me now for doing nothing'. Needless to say, Henrietta disapproved of what she saw as undeserved handouts which would inevitably lead to 'mischief' and 'character deterioration'.[34]

Henrietta may well have been censorious about such indiscriminate charity but she also boiled with indignation about post-war reconstruction of a 'Land fit for Heroes':

> The evidence of progress in a nation is the beauty of a citizen's public places and the simplicity of their private houses. If this is true, then our nation is not progressing, for we see jewels of fabulous value on the necks of old and ugly women, and houses erected by the nation as 'Homes for Heroes' which are mean, and dull, and blots on our fair countryside. We see huge parks and wonderful motors, and extravagant clothing, and the streets denuded of everything that can please or uplift or feed the thoughts of the great mass of people.[35]

In particular, Henrietta singled out the post-war housing development at Dagenham in Essex as exemplifying the 'huge, dreary and annoying monotony' of modern building. She also despised the new and cost-effective trend of high-rise building: the 'streets in the sky' which continue to dominate urban development in the 21st century. As far as Henrietta was concerned, their flat lines, drab bricks and uniformity of shape and design were infinitely depressing.[36] The paucity of progress in England was accentuated when she and Marion made a return trip to America in 1920. No doubt haunted by uncomfortable memories of the treatment meted out to the Belgian refugees during the war, she was struck by the sympathy and support offered to 'bewildered' immigrants pursuing the American Dream but utterly disorientated by the noise, bustle, cultural differences and 'thousand and one things that are forbidden in a highly civilised state'. She also noted the marked improvements in American health, education, wealth and

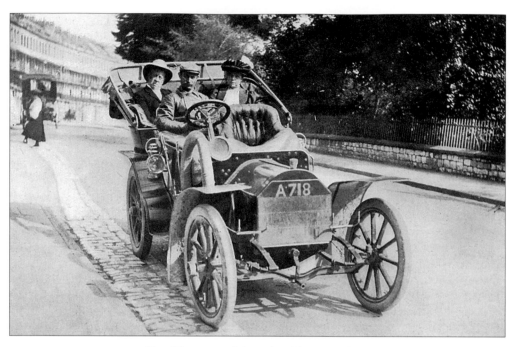

18   *Henrietta and Samuel in Henry Ward's car*

happiness. For Henrietta this was evidence of progress almost entirely absent back in England.[37]

Given Henrietta's negative views on American manners and mores expressed following her visit almost 30 years previously, it is perhaps surprising that she was so willing to reconsider her former impressions. It is to her credit that, at the age of almost seventy, she was still so engaged with societal injustices and so receptive to, and inspired by, new ideas and progress. Indeed, as she asserted just before she returned to America, 'I am not at all fond of driving in the middle of the road – I like pioneering'.[38] So, Henrietta was particularly impressed with the ambience of 'safe gaiety' in Chicago: its imaginative housing, beautifully landscaped public parks with an assortment of free entertainments, theatres, museums, lecture halls and children's playgrounds. However, New York was a different matter entirely. In contrast to Chicago, there were no play areas or places of wholesome entertainment, just 'hideous and vicious abnormalities' emanating from dance halls, cabarets, music theatres, casinos and that most decadent symbol of 20th-century popular culture, the cinema, with its peddling of silver-screen dreams. What really horrified Henrietta was the fact that in many of these low haunts, admission to young women was free. The ulterior motive of this, she opined, was the promotion of 'vice and iniquitous pleasures'. Nor was she fooled by the Prohibition laws. Like every other visitor to New York, Henrietta soon heard countless tales of the subterfuge adopted to procure illicit liquor.[39] Needless to say, there was a considerable demand for hip-flasks. Indeed, Henrietta witnessed one hapless drunkard clutching one of these who, on tumbling down some steps, felt something trickling down his leg. 'O Gawd,' he gasped in horror. 'Gawd grant that it may be my blood'.[40] Street crime was also rife in New York City. On the orders of

Henrietta, a policeman arrested a 'dirty, ragged, sullen and disreputable' lad who was menacing passers-by with his lawless antics. This incident did make her concede that free movies at the City cinemas did at least keep such troublemakers off the streets. She also had to admit that since the end of the First World War, the behaviour of boys in England had become increasingly troublesome. But nothing had prepared her for what she witnessed in the New York Women's Courts. This motley crew comprised 'young, sly, rebellious and giddy girls, whose only God was pleasure', an assortment of older women who had been arrested for backstreet abortion rackets and – revealing Henrietta's deeply entrenched racism – the 'repulsive' bunch of 'black and half-caste' offenders who, to her mind, were the most degraded, hardened and mendacious of this collection of female miscreants.[41]

Touring through the outer, leafier suburbs of New York, Henrietta was somewhat placated by more encouraging signs of modernity and progress. Here, mass production meant that ordinary families could afford what in England would still have been a luxury available only to the extremely wealthy: the motor-car. So, Henrietta was heartened by the sight of Model T Fords packed with parents and children driving out into the country for 'delightful family picnics'.[42] What she clearly did not grasp, however, was the politics of envy generated by these class and wealth divisions in New York City. Although the Great Depression was still 10 years away, there was already much disillusionment among young native and immigrant blue-collar workers, who perceived themselves as disenfranchised from the American Dream enjoyed by their wealthier counterparts. Their envy can only have been exacerbated by the relentless images of opulence and plenty projected onto cinema screens throughout the state. Three years later, Henrietta was interviewed by an American journalist about her impressions of New York and Chicago. Having had time to reflect, she was rather more diplomatic about its shortcomings. She praised the humanity of the children's courts, the 'wonderful care and patience' shown to the 'unfortunate women' in the New York courts and the Prohibition laws which, she opined, would be welcomed in England where people were 'drinking themselves to death'. Despite her distaste for high-rise development in England, she even declared that she found the spectacular skyscrapers of New York and Chicago inspiring and exciting. However, she did make some constructive suggestions. One aspect of American life which really disturbed her was the tendency to 'ghettoise' the immigrant populations. This segregation of nationalities, she asserted, was wrong. Either they should stop immigration altogether or 'put an end to the home in the pig-sty'. Other suggestions she made included moving factories out to rural America, providing housing schemes for workers like the ones at Bourneville, New Earswick and Port Sunlight and implementing a cheaper transport system. She also castigated the dubious sanitary arrangements in Chicago and New York tenements, arguing that 'we do not mind spending money on war, why should we dislike spending it on a fight to remove dirt, disease and unhappiness?'.[43]

Social reformers in America were so impressed with the 71-year-old Henrietta's clear-sighted vision for the future that she was offered an 'attractive salary' to implement these schemes.[44] No doubt she was immensely flattered by this offer but declined because she still had numerous public commitments in England. In particular, she continued with her fervent commitment to the State Children's Association, through which she railed against the fact that fundamental rights that 'every child should be treated as an individual with potentialities, with the right to be loved, and taught how to love' were not yet fully met. Following a premature report of her death in 1929, she retorted that she had no intention of 'taking that interesting step' before those rights were fulfilled.[45] Certainly, despite years of campaigning, some state nurseries and orphanages remained depressing, austere places. After visiting one of these in the late 1920s, Henrietta despaired at the paucity of amusement and stimulation, the inadequate diet of boiled mince, potatoes and watery rice pudding, and the quality of the 'dull-witted' staff. One was a 'roughish' middle-aged woman, deemed 'hardly fit for responsibility' and another was a laundress who allowed her charges to crawl off to the 'care' of her 'disagreeable looking partner'. The children were uniformly bored, ill-kept and neglected, all cast-offs from 'immoral, whining, colourless' parents too drunk and irresponsible to care for their offspring themselves. Henrietta saw the recently introduced foster parent scheme as a more humane alternative to this institutionalised lifestyle but pointed out that the benefits paid to foster carers – between 4s. and 5s. – were inadequate and exploitative.[46] It was, however, a tremendous comfort to her that the children – even those in the orphanages – in Hampstead Garden Suburb were 'taller, heavier and broader' than children in the surrounding neighbourhood. Declaring this at a State Children's Association meeting, she stated that although it may 'sound like boasting' it was 'just gratitude' that her 'grandmotherly heart' was able 'to beam over these lovely children'.[47]

Although Henrietta was a lifelong champion for children's rights, she was not in the slightest bit sentimental. This led to her generating of another controversy when, at the age of 70, she wrote an article bemoaning modern parenting styles and, more particularly, their attitudes to learning. This was no doubt in response to what she saw as evidence of the over-indulgence of children whose 'greed, cruelty and untruthfulness' were placidly tolerated in the fond hope that 'growth would eradicate them'. As far as Henrietta was concerned, the popularity of toy soldiers, gun and tanks exacerbated the pugilistic streak in little boys and deplored that these 'reminders of hate and enmity' privileged competitive, over co-operative, games. As for nursery rhymes, Henrietta regarded these as 'utter nonsense' which neither developed sympathy, stimulated imagination nor nourished a sense of human responsibility. The fashion for comics and films also dismayed her. Films, she asserted, were an 'unwholesome influence' in which sensationalist plots such as 'kidnapping, murder, and thefts of pearl necklaces' made 'wrong-doings attractive' and in turn, encouraged delinquent behaviour.[48] Not surprisingly, Henrietta's somewhat joyless views on popular culture provoked wry amusement in the press. As she recorded, cartoons depicted her as a 'grim, bony and austere' harridan, stretching out a 'claw-like hand to grab the joy from babies'. Another writer attributed her alleged bitterness to the fact that Henrietta was 'probably smarting from the annoyances of supertax and the upkeep of her six-cylinder motor-car'.[49] She did attempt to defend her views. To her mind, fairy tales, Easter eggs and all the make-believe of childhood merely served to exclude children from the adult world they were desperately trying to understand. She could still remember – more than sixty years later – how frustrated she had been as a child by the ways adults avoided giving her endless questions serious attention. Nor did she disapprove of all childhood playthings. Dolls, Henrietta believed, were instrumental in nurturing the maternal instinct, whilst toys like bricks, jigsaws, arts and crafts materials and carpentry tools developed logic as well as creativity. And even Henrietta recognised that a particularly evangelical little girl was taking Christian values to extremes when she punished her doll collection for the perpetration of sins including adultery, blasphemy and hypocrisy.[50]

Until 1931, Henrietta remained publicly active and continued her prolific output of writing and – after 1924 – broadcasting. By then, she had been made a Dame of the British Empire in recognition of her lifetime service to housing and social reform. Henrietta was enchanted by the 'marvellous' new medium of radio and its potential to reach an unprecedented audience. Her debut broadcast was on the BBC on 26 October 1924, when she was invited to speak on child welfare. By then, she was dividing her time between Hampstead and Hove. After returning from America, she had invested some of the proceeds from a property in Bristol in a 'tiny little house' in the seaside place she and Samuel had hoped to share their final years. The house, number 12, Wish Road, Hove, was an attractive Edwardian semi-detached villa just a few hundred yards from the seafront as well as a short car journey from Samuel's grave and her beloved Sussex Downs. It was also, of course, only a couple of miles from Brighton, where she had spent idyllic summers romping on the beach with her brothers, sisters and an assortment of dogs and ponies. Henrietta's last interviews were held to celebrate her 80th birthday in the *Daily Mail*, the *Nursing Times* and, finally, the *Edinburgh Evening News*. In the *Mail* interview, she was invited to reflect on series of questions. In this, she maintained that the most detestable human quality was 'lying' whilst 'honesty' was the greatest virtue. Asked which 'living celebrity' she admired the most, she named her cleaner, Mrs Baker, and Jane Addams, her long-standing friend who was to receive the Nobel Prize in 1931 for her settlement work in Chicago. She also revealed that if she could begin her life again, she would 'study science, preferably astronomy and teaching it'.[51] In the *Nursing Times*, she asserted that the 'first duty of an old woman is to be beautiful',[52] something on which she expanded in the *Edinburgh Evening News*:

> I think the primary duty of the aged is to be happy, lively, gay, glad, and by being all this she will create an atmosphere of peace, goodwill, and contentment. Experience will have taught her that troubles are often transitory, that the solace of sorrows is their power of producing kindnesses, that most clouds have silver linings and sometimes even golden ones.[53]

Such mellow homilies must have provoked snorts of derision amongst those who knew Henrietta well – especially those on the Suburb Trust Board, whom she continued to harangue on a regular basis.[54] Certainly, Henrietta did not radiate an atmosphere of serenity when she attended the annual Henrietta Barnett School prize-giving. Driven by Palmer, her 'shrivelled' chauffeur in an 'ancient Rolls', she would sweep out of the car, forge a formidable path into the school hall and take her place centre-stage. Miss Hutchings, the headteacher, was – to the delight of the ranks of white-dressed, black-stockinged girls – unfailingly reduced to a flustered and blushing bundle of nerves by this imperious presence, for Henrietta always took mischievous glee in making some outrageous statement at these gatherings – usually at the expense of the hapless Miss Hutchings.[55]

Henrietta must have really relished these opportunities for irreverence. For so many years in her public life, she had been obliged to repress her sharp wit and caustic sense of absurdity. One of her greatest regrets was the dry earnestness which she felt had characterised much of her writing and speeches. In her introduction to the collection of these, she made the wistful observation that:

Personally I dislike my past utterances – they either bore me or arouse my fiercest criticism. I wish that more jokes could have been included. My frivolous mind delights in odd, quaint tales but perhaps they are only permissible when they can be punctuated with laughter, and that is not possible in a book; so, shorn of ephemeral humour, these speeches are now issued with apologies.[56]

Henrietta's articles may not have been infused with wit and humour, but whilst she may have variously exasperated, intimidated, bulldozed and shamed many into action she also inspired, invigorated and emboldened plenty more. Back in 1909 the journalist and social activist W.R. Stead had marvelled that she had not 'worn out the physical vehicle which has had to carry for so long her eager and impetuous self'.[57] It was this 'divine discontent' which kept her burning intellectually and spiritually for many years to come. In 1930, John Northcote, extolling her 'unflagging initiative, energy and genius for cooperation and fellowship', perhaps best encapsulated Henrietta's enduring spirit by marvelling how, despite the plethora of frustrations, setbacks, oppositions, personal sorrows and public defeats which had often peppered her life and work, 'she never failed to hitch her wagon to a star'.[58]

After 1931, however, Henrietta began to fade from public life. The emotional and physical ill health with which she had struggled throughout her life could no longer be defeated. From her bed at number 1, South Square, she continued to maintain a grasp on her financial affairs but, by her own admission, was becoming increasingly tired. By 1932, she was suffering from frequent bouts of pneumonia and an enlarged heart which caused breathlessness and fatigue following the slightest exertion. She wanted to see no one except Marion and, indeed, wished to say 'nothing to nobody'. All she craved was to be 'let alone and in quiet'. There are only fragments remaining about her final, lonely years, all lovingly collected and archived by Marion, herself then in her seventies, but still devoted to caring for the woman with whom she had shared her life since the age of nineteen. These include letters, innumerable lists and a touching collection of photos of cats and kittens carefully cut out from Christmas cards and calendars, all inscribed with Henrietta's comments. One, a photo of a tabby cat, possibly a gift to Marion, reads:

Pussy is still thinking of all to be done ... she sits and thinks – has an inspiration and looks up – follows it with energetic anxiety ... then watches its flight away into the distance.[59]

The extent to which this wistful musing encapsulated Henrietta's persistent yearning for the former vitality, skirmishes and activity which had enlivened all her working life can only be imagined.

On 10 June 1936, Henrietta died peacefully with Marion at her side. Marion was overwhelmed with despair. Her reply to a letter from Uely, Henrietta's nephew and co-trustee of her will, reveals the extent of her loss:

I thank you for your sympathy. I need it for one of the severest blows of my life. I look back on 59 years of unblemished friendship and I realise afresh as I have done so often before how much I owe them both. What would my life have been without them? I cannot write more today but I shall hope to hear from you and to know all you can tell me. I had never thought she would go before me – but she has gone and I shall see her no more. I suppose you had expected this but I had not and I feel scarcely able to bear it. No one can know what it is to me.

I do not feel as if I could go among strangers. Hard as it is, I would rather be alone at all events until I have ceased to live in the past.[60]

Marion, a slight, retiring and forlorn figure clad in the deepest of black, did summon up the strength to attend Henrietta's funeral five days later. The service was conducted by Cosmo Lang, Archbishop of Canterbury, at Westminster Abbey. She was subsequently buried at Samuel's side in the graveyard set at the foot of the Sussex Downs which had delighted, inspired and sustained her since childhood. Lang's funeral address – rather like her obituary in the *Daily Herald* – acknowledged the extent of Henrietta's work in housing and social reform but simultaneously diminished her achievements by subordinating the 'ideals and plans which had glowed in her fervent imagination' to their subsequent 'clarifying, defining and disciplining' by the mind of her husband.[61] However, Lang later admitted in private that Samuel 'was but the mouthpiece of Henrietta and her opinions'.[62] Although personal letters of condolence sent to Marion variously acknowledge Henrietta's 'remarkable personality', 'passionate rebellion', 'charming vivacity', 'deep sincerity', 'provocative courage' and 'moving spirit', Marion's efforts to represent her friend thus have subsequently been marginalised by the rather less sympathetic and enduring images that this book has attempted to challenge.[63] For even the crown-like public memorial to Henrietta in Hampstead Garden Suburb, designed by the playful and irreverent Edwin Lutyens, could be interpreted as a sardonic comment on Henrietta's imperiousness and magisterial inclinations.

However, Henrietta Barnett, Dame of the British Empire, social and housing reformer, campaigner, writer and broadcaster, as well as loving wife of Samuel, ferociously loyal friend of many and a thorn in the flesh of plenty more, had once been asked to write an obituary for Octavia Hill following her death in August 1912. The piece that she produced could equally serve as a vindication of her own fascinating and contradictory qualities. It is appropriate that, since she has been silenced for so long, the final words in this book should belong to Henrietta:

When I read [Octavia's] obituary notices, crediting her with commonplace virtues of kindness and unselfishness and gentleness, it annoyed me because those were not her virtues, and enumerating them gave the wrong impression of her character. She was strong-willed – some thought self-willed – but the strong will was never used for self. She was impatient in little things, persistent with long-suffering in big ones; often dictatorial in manner but humble to self-effacement before those she loved or admired. She had high standards for everyone, for herself, ruthlessly exalted ones, and she dealt out disapprobation and often scorn to those who fell below her standards for them, but she sometimes erred in sympathy by urging them to attain her standards for them, instead of their own for themselves.[64]

Notes

Introduction
1. Barnett, Henrietta, *Canon Barnett, His Life, Work and Friends*, Vol. 2 (1918b), p.313.
2. Grossmith, George and Grossmith, Weedon, *Diary of a Nobody* (1892).
3. Interview with Judy Charlton, Hampstead Garden Suburb (January 2003) and correspondence from Jo Velleman (5 November 2002).
4. Crosland, T.W.H., *The Suburbans* (1905), p.199.
5. For example, W.A. Eden, 'Hampstead Garden Suburb, 1907-1957' in *Journal of the Royal Institute of British Architects*, October (1957), pp.489-95; Brigid Grafton Green, *Hampstead Garden Suburb, 1907-1977: A History* (London: Hampstead Garden Suburb Residents' Association); C.K. Ikin, *Hampstead Garden Suburb: Dreams and Realities* (New Hampstead Garden Suburb Trust, 1990); Mervyn Miller and A. Stuart Gray, *Hampstead Garden Suburb: A History* (Phillimore, 1992); Kathleen M. Slack, *Henrietta's Dream: A Chronicle of the Hampstead Garden Suburb* (Hampstead Garden Suburb Archive Trust, 1997).
6. Behlmer, George, *Friends of the Family: The English Home and its Guardians, 1850-1940* (1998), p.46.
7. Peterson, M. Jeanne, *Family, Love and Work in the Lives of Victorian Gentlewomen* (1989), p.23; Walkowitz, Judith, *City of Dreadful Delights: Narratives of Sexual Danger in Late-Victorian London* (1994), p.59.
8. Watkins, Micky, *Henrietta Barnett in Whitechapel: Her First Fifty Years* (2005).

Chapter One
1. Mayhew, Henry, *London Labour and London Poor* (1851).
2. Disraeli, Benjamin, *Sybil, Or the Two Nations* (1845).
3. Gaskell, Elizabeth, *Mary Barton* (1848).
4. Brontë, Charlotte, *Shirley* (1849).
5. Stedman Jones, Gareth, 'Working-class culture and working-class politics in London, 1870-1900' (1973) in Bernard Waites, Tony Bennett and Graham Martin (eds), *Popular Culture: Past and Present* (1989), p.92.
6. Behlmer, George, *Friends of the Family: The English Home and its Guardians, 1850-1940* (1998), p.23.
7. Shonfield, Zuzanna, *The Precariously Privileged: A Professional Family in Victorian England* (1987) p.v.
8. Dickens, Charles, *Dombey and Son* (1848).
9. Briggs, Asa, *Victorian Things* (1988), pp.53-6; Auerbach, Jeffrey A., *The Great Exhibition of 1851: A Nation on Display* (1999), pp.2-11; McLeod, John, *Beginning Postcolonialism* (2000), p.7.
10. Watkins, Micky, *Henrietta Barnett in Whitechapel: Her First Fifty Years* (2005), p.9.

11. Advertisement in Humphrey, Mrs, *Manners for Men* (1897).
12. Interview with John Coulter, librarian at Lewisham Local Studies Library, 18 February 2003.
13. Paterson, Marion, Unpublished biography of Henrietta Barnett (Undated, *c*.1936), p.3.
14. Phillips, Jane and Peter, *Victorians Home and Away* (1978), p.24.
15. Paterson, p.5.
16. Coulter, John, *Lewisham History and Guide* (1990), p.7.
17. Coulter (1990), pp.11-12.
18. Coulter, John, *Sydenham and Forest Hill Past* (1999), p.55.
19. 1851 Census, Lewisham Local History Archives.
20. Coulter (1999), p.64.
21. Coulter (1999), p.66.
22. Cited in Coulter (1999), p.67.
23. Barnett, Henrietta, *The Making of the Body* (1901), p.215.
24. Poovey, Mary, *Uneven Developments: The Ideological Work of Gender in Mid-Victorian England* (1989), p.130.
25. Barnett (1901), pp.110-1.
26. Paterson, p.2.
27. Paterson, p.4.
28. Barnett (1901), p.200.
29. Poovey (1989), p.130.
30. Barnett, Henrietta, *Matters that Matter* (1930), p.247.
31. Barnett (1930), pp.247-8.
32. Barrett Browning, Elizabeth, *Aurora Leigh and Other Poems* (1857).
33. Paterson, p.31.
34. Jordan, Thomas E., *Victorian Childhood: Themes and Variations* (1987), pp.155.
35. Barnett (1930), p.10.
36. Brontë, (1839) quoted in Jordan, pp.156-7.
37. Paterson, p.4.
38. Purvis, June, 'Social class, education and ideals of femininity' in Madeleine Arnot and Gaby Weiner (eds), *Gender and the Politics of Schooling* (1987).
39. Ruskin, John, *Sesame and Lilies* (1865).
40. *Clapham Gazette and Local Advertiser*, 2 February 1854, p.1.
41. Brontë, (1849).
42. Shonfield (1987), p.17.
43. Dickens, *Hard Times* (1854/1985), p.48.
44. Collins, Philip, *Dickens and Education* (1963), pp.38-9.
45. H.M. Inspector's Report quoted in Collins, p.151.
46. *Clapham Gazette and Local Advertiser*, 2 February 1854, p.1.
47. Paterson, p.17.
48. Collins, p.151.

49. Paterson, p.2.
50. Barnett (1930), p.10.
51. Paterson, p.2.
52. Paterson, p.11.
53. Barnett (1930), p.246.
54. Jordan, p.157.
55. Walvin, James, *A Child's World: A Social History of English Childhood, 1800-1914* (1982), pp.30-3.
56. Walvin, p.50.
57. Paterson.
58. Barnett (1901), pp.20-1.
59. Paterson, p.3.
60. Paterson, p.4-5.
61. Paterson, p.5.
62. Paterson, pp.5-6.
63. Creedon, Alison, 'A Benevolent Tyrant? The Principles and Practices of Henrietta Barnett (1851-1936), Social Reformer and Founder of Hampstead Garden Suburb' in *Women's History Review*,Volume 11, No.2 (2002), p.242.
64. Barnett, *Canon Barnett, His Life, Work and Friends,* Vol.1 (1918a), p.38.
65. Walton, James, 'Residential amenity, respectable morality and the rise of the entertainment industry' in Waites *et al* (eds), (1989), p.133.
66. Coulter (1999), p.106.
67. Creedon, Alison, 'Representations of Suburban Culture, 1890-1914' (2001), p.3. Unpublished PhD thesis. University of Leeds 2001.
68. Malchow, H., *Gentlemen Capitalists* (1991), p.167.
69. *Sydenham Times,* 4 February 1862, p.1.
70. Paterson, p.3.
71. Tosh, John, *A Man's Place: Masculinity and the Middle-Class Home* (1999), p.33.
72. Barnett (1918a), p.38.
73. Barnett (1930), p.10.
74. Barnett (1930), p.222.
75. Paterson, p.3.
76. Koven, Seth, 'Henrietta Barnett (1851-1936): the auto/biography of a late-Victorian marriage' in Susan Pederson and Peter Mandler (eds), *After the Victorians: Private Conscience and Public Duty* (1994), pp.40-1.
77. Paterson, p.14.

Chapter Two
1. www.dovermuseum.co.uk accessed 21 May 2003.
2. *Dover Express,* 4 January 1867, p.3.
3. Barnett, Henrietta, *Canon Barnett: His Life, Work and Friends,* Vol. 2 (1918b), p.51.
4. Paterson, Marion, Unpublished biography of Henrietta Barnett (Undated, *c.*1936), p.9.
5. Collins, Phillip, *Dickens and Education* (1963), p.89.
6. Paterson, p.9.
7. Paterson, pp.8-9.
8. Vicinus, Martha, *Independent Women: Work and Community for Single Women, 1850-1920* (1985), p.188.
9. Paterson, p.11.
10. Paterson, p.8.
11. Paterson, p.11; p.7.
12. Watkins, Micky, 'Henrietta Barnett before the Suburb' in *Hampstead Garden Suburb News,* May 2001.
13. Koven, Seth, 'Henrietta Barnett (1851-1936): the auto/biography of a late-Victorian marriage' in Susan Pederson and Peter Mandler (eds), *After the Victorians: Private Conscience and Public Duty in Modern Britain* (1994), p.34.
14. Vicinus, p.290.
15. Walkowitz, Judith, *City of Dreadful Delights:*

Narratives of Sexual Danger in Late- Victorian London (1994), p.140; Koven, Seth, *Slumming: Sexual and Social Politics in Victorian London* (2004), pp.16-17.
16. Koven (1994), p.34; Koven (2004), p.301-2.
17. Jordan, Thomas E., *Victorian Childhood: Themes and Variations* (1987), pp.168-9.
18. Collins (1963), p.91.
19. Charles Dickens cited in Collins (1963), p.87.
20. Steedman, Carolyn, *Strange Dislocations: Childhood and the Idea of Human Interiority* (1995), p.113.
21. Steedman, p.5.
22. Collins, pp.88-9.
23. Paterson, p.19.
24. Koven, (1994), p.34.
25. Paterson, p.27.
26. Paterson, pp.8-9.
27. Paterson, p.8.
28. Brontë, Charlotte, *Jane Eyre* (1847/1987), p.51.
29. Brontë, p.73.
30. Brontë, p.85.
31. Paterson, p.8.
32. Paterson, p.7.
33. Barnett, Henrietta, *Matters that Matter* (1930), p.343.
34. Brontë, p.73; p.78.
35. Paterson, p.8.
36. Edmond, Rob, *Affairs of the Hearth: Victorian Poetry and Domestic Narrative* (1988), p.186.
37. Brontë, p.78.
38. Vicinus, p.165.
39. Webb, Beatrice, *My Apprenticeship* (1926), pp.221-2.
40. Barnett, Henrietta, 'Principles of Recreation' in Samuel Barnett and Mrs S.A. Barnett, *Towards Social Reform* (1909), p.293.
41. Briggs, Asa, *Victorian Things* (1988), p.26.
42. Paterson, p.12.
43. Purvis, June, 'Social class, education and ideals of femininity' in Madeleine Arnot and Gaby Weiner (eds), *Gender and the Politics of Schooling* (1987), p.254.
44. Purvis, p.254-5.
45. Carey, John, *The Intellectuals and the Masses: Pride and Prejudice among the Literary Intelligentsia* (1992), p.100.
46. Carey, p.99.
47. Ehrenrich, Barbara and English, Deirdre, *For Her Own Good: 150 Years of the Experts' Advice to Women* (1979), p.23; Ussher, Jane, *Women's Madness: Misogyny or Mental Illness?* (1991), p.65.
48. Nead, Lynda, *Myths of Sexuality: Representations of Women in Victorian Britain* (1988).
49. Tennyson, Alfred Lord, 'The Princess' (1847).
50. Collins, Wilkie, *The Woman in White* (Originally published in 1860, 1985 edition cited), p.80.
51. Ashton, Rosemary, *George Eliot: A Life* (1996), p.377.
52. Carey, p.100.
53. Barnett, Henrietta, *The Making of the Home* (1875), pp.149 and 176-7.
54. Barnett, (1875), p.7.
55. Barnett, (1875), p.206.

Chapter Three
1. Paterson, Marion, Unpublished biography of Henrietta Barnett (Undated, *c.*1936), p.122.
2. Watkins, Micky, 'Henrietta Barnett before the Suburb' in *Hampstead Garden Suburb News* (May 2001), p.20.
3. Paterson, p.12.
4. Watkins, Micky, *Henrietta Barnett in Whitechapel: Her First Fifty Years* (2005), p.20.
5. Olsen, Donald J., *The Growth of Victorian London*

(London: Batsford, 1976), p.162.
6. Olsen, p.168.
7. Article in *Building News* (1863) cited in Olsen, p.223.
8. Paterson, p.12.
9. Barnett, Henrietta, *The Making of the Home* (1875), pp.161-2.
10. Paterson, p.12.
11. Barnett, Henrietta, *Canon Barnett: His Life, Work and Friends*, Vol. 1 (1918a), p.35.
12. Ross, Ellen, *Motherhood in Outcast London, 1870-1914* (1993), p.16.
13. Jordan, Thomas E., *Victorian Childhood: Themes and Variations* (1987), p.248.
14. Darley, Gillian, *Octavia Hill: A Life* (1990), pp.115-16.
15. Darley, p.116.
16. Darley, p.117.
17. Henrietta Barnett quoted in Darley, p.123.
18. Darley, p.122.
19. Darley, p.98.
20. Darley, p.122.
21. Darley, p.113.
22. Octavia Hill quoted in Barnett (1918a), pp.29-30.
23. Barnett, (1918a), p.29.
24. James Greenwood (1869) quoted in Jordan, p.248.
25. Ross, pp.18-19.
26. Hughes, Kathryn, 'How to be Good' in *Sunday Times Culture* (9 March 2003), p.41.
27. Jordan, p.250.
28. Ross, pp.18-19.
29. Ross, pp.19-20.
30. Barnett, (1875), p.107.
31. Luckin, Bill, 'Evaluating the Sanitary Revolution: Typhus and Typhoid in London, 1851-1900' in Robert Woods and John Woodward (eds), *Urban Disease and Mortality in Nineteenth-Century London* (1984), p.115.
32. Barnett, (1875), p.107.
33. Ross, p.32.
34. Ross, p.41.
35. Barnett, (1875), pp.116 23.
36. Barnett, (1875), p.67.
37. Luckin, (1984), pp.112-13.
38. Behlmer, George, *Friends of the Family: The English Home and its Guardians, 1850-1940* (1998), p.15.
39. Barnett, (1875), p.67.
40. Barnett, (1875), p.109.
41. Steedman, Carolyn, *Strange Dislocations: Childhood and the Idea of Human Interiority* (1995), p.115.
42. Barnett, (1918a), p.30.
43. Octavia Hill (1870) quoted in Barnett (1918a), p.30.
44. Barnett, (1918a), p.31.
45. Webb, Beatrice, *My Apprenticeship* (1926), p.221.
46. Paterson, p.13.
47. Walter Webb quoted in Paterson, p.16.
48. Paterson, pp.13-14.
49. The Franco-Prussian War (1870-1) was caused by Bismarck's desire for German expansion and unification. A key disputed area between France and Germany was Alsace-Lorraine and negotiations broke down in the summer of 1870. Prussian victory was secured at Sedan in September 1870, when Louis Napoleon was deposed. Subsequently, between March and May 1871, the Paris Commune was suppressed by the new regime. As Micky Watkins notes, Henrietta's German maternal lineage would have prompted her loyalties to lie with the Prussians. However, these connections were possibly suppressed in *Canon Barnett* as

Henrietta was writing this during World War One when anti-German feeling was particularly high (Watkins [2005], p.31). Nonetheless, as mentioned in the following chapter, Henrietta was clearly moved by the extent of the carnage suffered by the French.
50. Paterson,), p.14.
51. Paterson, pp.14-15.
52. Paterson, p.15.
53. Paterson, pp.15-16.
54. Darley, p.14.
55. Barnett, (1918a), pp.34-5.
56. Barnett, (1918a), p.13.
57. Barnett, (1918a), p.25.
58. Barnett, (1918a), p.35.
59. Letter from Samuel to Henrietta (31 December 1871) in Barnett (1918a), pp.35-6.
60. Barnett, (1918a), p.37.
61. Paterson, p.15.
62. Barnett, (1918a), pp.38-9.
63. Barnett, (1918a), pp.37-8.
64. Barnett, (1918a), p.38.
65. Barnett, (1918a), p.47.
66. Letter from Samuel to Henrietta (30 March 1872) in Barnett (1918a), p.39.
67. Ehrenrich, Barbara and English, Deirdre, *For Her Own Good: 150 Years of Experts' Advice to Women* (1979), p.23; Vicinus, Martha, *Independent Women: Work and Community for Single Women, 1850-1920* (1985), p.20.
68. Letter from Samuel to Henrietta (8 May 1872) in Barnett (1918a), p.47.
69. Barnett, (1918a), p.42.
70. Barnett, (1918a), p.49.
71. Barnett, (1918a), p.45.
72. Paterson, p.17.
73. Barnett, (1918a), p.45.
74. Letter from Samuel to Henrietta (28 April 1872) in Barnett (1918a), p.46.
75. Barnett, (1918a), p.8.
76. Letter from Samuel to Henrietta (1 May 1872) in Barnett (1918a), p.46.
77. Barnett, (1918a), p.41.
78. Barrett Browning, Elizabeth, *Aurora Leigh and Other Poems* (Published 1856, 1995 Penguin edn cited), p.45.
79. Barrett Browning, p.46.
80. Brontë, Charlotte, *Jane Eyre* (Published 1847, 1987 Oxford edn cited), pp.203 and 382.
81. Letter from Samuel to Henrietta (15 April 1872) in Barnett (1918a), pp.41-2.
82. Ruskin, John, 'Of Queens' Gardens' in *Sesame and Lilies* (1865).

Chapter Four
1. Paterson, Marion, Unpublished biography of Henrietta Barnett (Undated, *c.*1936), p.17.
2. Letter from Samuel to Henrietta (2 June 1872) in Barnett, Henrietta, *Canon Barnett: His Life, Work and Friends*, Vol. 1 (1918a), p.51.
3. Barnett (1918a), p.50.
4. Paterson, p.17.
5. Barnett (1918a), p.50.
6. Barnett (1918a), p.7.
7. Barnett (1918a), pp.7-8.
8. Barnett (1918a), p.8.
9. Barnett (1918a), p.52.
10. Letter from Samuel to Henrietta (2 June 1872) in Barnett (1918a), p.50.
11. Barnett, (1918a), p.52.

12. Letter from Samuel to Henrietta (8 June 1872) in Barnett (1918a), p.53.
13. Barnett (1918a), p.53.
14. Paterson, p.17.
15. Barnett, (1918a), p.41.
16. Light, Alison, *Forever England: Literature and Conservatism Between the Wars* (1991), p.122; Creedon, Alison, 'Representations of Suburban Culture, 1890-1914' (2001), p.197. Unpublished PhD thesis, University of Leeds, 2001.
17. Harrison, J.F.C., *Late-Victorian Britain, 1875-1901* (1991), p.180.
18. Webb, Beatrice, *My Apprenticeship* (1926), p.223.
19. Lorraine Blair provides an insightful study into the dynamics of the Barnetts' marriage partnership in her PhD thesis, 'Comrade Wives: Different Marriages Under the Shadow of Toynbee Hall in Late-Victorian and Edwardian England' (University of Portsmouth, 1998).
20. Peterson, M. Jeanne, *Family, Love and Work in the Lives of Victorian Gentlewomen* (1989), pp.166-7.
21. Webb, p.223.
22. Barnett, (1918a), p.32.
23. Letter from Octavia Hill to Samuel Barnett (25 June 1872) in Barnett (1918a), p.61.
24. Darley, Gillian, *Octavia Hill: A Life* (1990), pp.188-9.
25. Beatrice Webb in Darley, p.190.
26. Webb, pp.219-21.
27. Webb, pp.221-2.
28. Mill, John Stuart, 'On the Subjection of Women' in Mill, Harriet Taylor, *Enfranchisement of Women* (Published 1869, 1983 Virago edn cited).
29. Hammerton, A. James, *Cruelty and Companionship: Conflict in Nineteenth-Century Married Life* (1992), pp.71-82.
30. Hammerton, p.81.
31. Barnett (1918a), p.14.
32. Paterson, p.17.
33. Barnett (1918a), p.55.
34. Barnett (1918a), p.53.
35. Barnett (1918a), p.54.
36. Letters from Samuel to Henrietta (June-July 1872) in Barnett (1918a), p.55.
37. Letter from Samuel to Henrietta (4 July 1872) in Barnett (1918a), p.56.
38. Barnett (1918a), p.60.
39. Barnett (1918a), p.62.
40. Barnett (1918a), p.65.
41. Darley, p.137.
42. Letter from Octavia Hill to Samuel Barnett in Barnett (1918a), p.67.
43. Barnett (1918a), p.67.
44. Barnett (1918a), p.68.
45. Barnett (1918a), p.54.
46. Letter from Dr Jackson, Bishop of London to Samuel Barnett quoted in Barnett (1918a), p.68.
47. Barnett (1918a), pp.73-4.
48. Paterson, p.20.
49. Barnett (1918a), p.69.
50. Barnett (1918a), pp.69-70.
51. Barnett (1918a), p.4.
52. Barnett (1918a), p.14.
53. Barnett (1918a), p.16 (author's italics).
54. Paterson, p.18.
55. Brontë, *Jane Eyre* (Published 1847, 1987 Oxford edn cited), p.271.
56. Creedon, Alison, 'A Benevolent Tyrant? The Principles and Practices of Henrietta Barnett' in *Women's History Review*, Volume 11, No.2 (2002), p.237.
57. Barnett (1918a), p.71.
58. Barnett (1918a), pp.71-2.
59. Paterson, p.20.
60. Barnett (1918a), p.72.
61. Barnett (1918a), pp.70-2.
62. Barnett (1918a), pp.71-2.

Chapter Five
1. Barnett, Henrietta, *Canon Barnett: His Life, Work and Friends*, Vol. 1 (1918a), p.73.
2. Mayhew, Henry, *London Labour and the London Poor (IV): Those That Will Not Work* (Published 1861-2, 1967 Frank Cass edn cited), p.227.
3. Barnett (1918a), p.73.
4. Frank Brien in Stedman Jones, Gareth, *Outcast London: A Study in the Relationships between Classes in Victorian Society* (1971), p.110.
5. Barnett, Henrietta, *Canon Barnett: His Life, Work and Friends*, Vol. 2 (1918b), pp.65 and 101.
6. Fishman, William J., *East End, 1888: A Year in a London Borough among the Labouring Poor* (1988), p.133.
7. Barnett (1918b), p.65.
8. Dickens, Charles, *Oliver Twist* (1837).
9. McClintock, Anne, *Imperial Leather: Race, Gender and Sexuality in the Colonial Context* (1995), pp.53 and 247. For extensive research into the experiences of newly arrived Jewish immigrants in Victorian England see Fishman, Chapter 6.
10. Stedman Jones, Gareth, p.110.
11. Kapp, Yvonne, *Eleanor Marx: Family Life 1855-1883* (1979), p.174.
12. Stedman Jones, pp.22 and 109.
13. Lees, Lynn, *The Solidarities of Strangers: The English Poor Laws and the People, 1700-1948* (1998), p.217.
14. Stedman Jones, p.189.
15. Dr Guy, quoted in Stedman Jones, Gareth, p.243.
16. Stedman Jones, p.13.
17. Barnett (1918a), p.74.
18. Fishman, p.304.
19. William Booth and Charles Booth, cited in Fishman, p.303.
20. Fishman, pp.16-17.
21. Barnett (1918a), pp.73-4.
22. Ross, Ellen, *Love and Toil: Motherhood in Outcast London, 1870-1918* (1993), p.99.
23. Barnett (1918a), p.84.
24. Barnett (1918b), pp.305-6.
25. Fishman, p.23.
26. Jordan, Thomas E., *Victorian Childhood: Themes and Variations* (1987), p.259.
27. Fishman, p.6.
28. Barnett (1918a), p.195.
29. Creedon, Alison, 'A Benevolent Tyrant? The Principles and Practices of Henrietta Barnett' in *Women's History Review*, Vol. 11, No.2 (2002), p.240.
30. Samuel Barnett (c.1877) in Barnett, (1918a), pp.75-6.
31. Barnett (1918a), p.79.
32. Barnett (1918a), pp.77-9.
33. Barnett (1918a), p.102.
34. Barnett (1918a), p.82.
35. Barnett (1918a), pp.86-8.
36. Barnett (1918a), pp.84-5.
37. Barnett (1918a), p.83.
38. Barnett (1918a), p.84.
39. Barnett (1918a), pp.82-4.
40. Stedman Jones, p.3.
41. Stedman Jones, p.11.
42. Barnett (1918a), p.100.

43. Barnett (1918a), pp.101-2.
44. Barnett, *The Making of the Home* (1875), pp.48 and 67.
45. Barnett (1918a), p.102.
46. Barnett (1875), pp.139-49.
47. Barnett, Henrietta, *Matters that Matter* (1930), p.216.
48. Barnett (1918a), p.89.
49. Barnett (1918a), p.90.
50. Barnett (1918a), pp.92-3.

Chapter Six
1. Barnett, Henrietta, *Canon Barnett: His Life, Work and Friends* Vol.1 (1918a), p.209.
2. Barnett (1918a), p.208.
3. Prochaska, F.K., *Women and Philanthropy in 19th Century England* (1980), p.222.
4. Walkowitz, Judith, *City of Dreadful Delights: Narratives of Sexual Danger in Late-Victorian England* (1994), p.52.
5. Fisher, Trevor, *Prostitutes and the Victorians* (1997), p.xi.
6. www.victoriantimes.org.lse, (accessed 19 August 2003).
7. www.victoriantimes.org.lse, (accessed 19 August 2003).
8. Nead, Lynda, *Myths of Sexuality: Representations of Women in Victorian Britain* (1988), p.6.
9. Henry Maudsley (1873) in Skultans, Vieda, *Madness and Morals: Ideas on Insanity in the Nineteenth Century* (1975).
10. Fisher, p.xii.
11. Webster, Augusta, 'A Castaway' (1870) in Armstrong, Isobel, *Nineteenth-Century Women Poets: An Oxford Anthology* (1996).
12. Barnett (1918a), p.211.
13. Nead, p.1.
14. Dickens, Charles, *Dombey and Son* (1848).
15. For insightful analysis of the symbolism in Victorian art, see Nead, *Myths of Sexuality*.
16. Showalter, Elaine, *Sexual Anarchy: Gender and Culture at the Fin de Siecle* (1991), p.193.
17. Barnett (1918a), p.209.
18. Christina Pankhurst quoted in Fisher p.xii.
19. Barnett (1918a), p.210.
20. Barnett (1918a), pp.210-11.
21. Barnett (1918a), pp.209-12.
22. Barnett (1918a), p.212.
23. Barnett (1918a), pp.210 and 212.
24. Barnett (1918a), p.102.
25. Barnett 1918a), p.116.
26. Fishman, William J., *East End, 1888: A Year in a London Borough among the Labouring Poor* (1988), p.115.
27. Barnett, Henrietta, *The Making of the Home* (1875), p.190.
28. Barnett (1918a), pp.116-18 and 121.
29. Barnett (1918a), p.118.
30. Barnett, Henrietta, 'Lady Visitors and Girls' (1890) in Canon Barnett and Mrs S.A. Barnett, *Towards Social Reform* (1909), pp.37-41 and 46-8.
31. Barnett (1890), pp.48-9.
32. Barnett (1890), p.51.
33. Barnett (1918a), pp.118-21.
34. Barnett (1918a), pp.123 and 125.
35. Barnett (1918a), p.125.
36. Barnett (1918a), pp.126-8.
37. Barnett (1918a), p.122.
38. Barnett (1918a), p.103.
39. Barnett (1918a), p.132.
40. Henry Mayhew in Quennell, Peter (ed.) *Henry Mayhew: London's Underworld* (1983), p.33.
41. Quennell (ed.), pp.33-4.
42. For first hand accounts of the experiences of London prostitutes, see Mayhew in Quennell, (ed.) pp.31-93.
43. Fisher, p.xi.
44. Fisher, pp.x-xi.
45. *Illustrated Police News*, (August-October 1888).
46. Palmer, Alan, *The East End: Four Centuries of London Life* (1989), p.94.
47. Barnett (1918a), p.306.
48. Walkowitz, p.222.
49. Palmer, p.94.
50. Fisher, p.xii.
51. Tebbutt, Melanie, *Women's Talk? A Social History of Gossip in Working-Class Neighbourhoods, 1880-1960* (1995), p.33.

Chapter Seven
1. Barnett, Henrietta, *Canon Barnett: His Life, Work and Friends* Vol. 1 (1918a), p.129.
2. Barnett (1918a), p.129-30.
3. Palmer, Alan, *The East End: Four Centuries of London Life* (1989), p.81.
4. Palmer, Alan, p.82.
5. Darley, Gillian, *Octavia Hill: A Life* (1990), p.130.
6. Barnett (1918a), p.131.
7. Darley, p.152.
8. Octavia Hill (July 1874) in Darley, p.151.
9. Darley, pp.132-3.
10. Darley, pp.133-4.
11. Darley, p.136.
12. Darley, pp.132-43.
13. Darley, pp.137-40.
14. Barnett (1918a), p.131.
15. A.G. Crowder in Barnett (1918a), p.132.
16. Darley, pp.159-61.
17. Princess Alice (November 1876) in Darley, p.162.
18. Darley, p.163.
19. Barnett (1918a) p.136.
20. Barnett (1918a), p.132.
21. Barnett, (1918a), p.133.
22. Darley, pp.154-5.
23. Darley, p.142.
24. For accounts of the Potter sisters' lives and work, see Harris, Jose, *Beatrice Webb: The Ambivalent Feminist* (1984) and Carole Seymour-Jones, *Beatrice Webb: Woman of Conflict* (1992).
25. Barnett (1918a), p.107.
26. Barnett (1918a), p.104.
27. Marion Paterson (2 June 1876) in Barnett (1918a), p.105.
28. Barnett (1918a), p.104.
29. Barnett (1918a), p.116.
30. Barnett (1918a), pp.106 and 120.
31. Barnett (1918a), p.107.
32. Samuel Barnett (1881) in Barnett (1918a), p.134.
33. Barnett (1918a), p.135.
34. Barnett (1918a), pp.137-8.
35. Barnett (1918a), p.138.
36. Barnett (1918a), p.139.
37. Samuel Smiles (1812-1904) was an Edinburgh-born surgeon, journalist and social reformer based in Leeds, West Yorkshire. He is best known for his *Self-Help* (1859), a self-improvement guide which proved highly influential throughout the remainder of the 19th century.
38. Stedman Jones, Gareth, *Outcast London: A Study in the Relationships between Classes in Victorian Society* (1971), p.302.

39. Crowder (1883) in Stedman Jones, p.195.
40. Barnett (1918a), p.140.
41. Fishman, William J., *East End, 1888: A Year in a London Borough among the Labouring Poor* (1988), p.19.
42. Fried, Albert and Elman, Richard (eds), *Charles Booth's London* (1971), pp.86-7.
43. Barnett, Henrietta, *Canon Barnett: His Life, Work and Friends* Vol. 2, (1918b), p.52.
44. Barnett (1918a), p.141.
45. Barnett (1918a), pp.141-2.
46. Besant, Walter, 'From Thirteen to Seventeen' in *Contemporary Review*, 49, pp.413-25.
47. Barnett (1918a), p.142.
48. Barnett (1918a), p.143.
49. Barnett (1918a), p.156.
50. Barnett (1918a), p.152.
51. Barnett (1918a), p.152.
52. Barnett (1918a), p.153.
53. Barnett (1918a), pp.153-4.
54. Barnett (1918a), p.157.
55. Barnett (1918a), p.153.

Chapter Eight
1. Arnold Toynbee (1883) in Stedman Jones, Gareth, *Outcast London: A Study in the Relations between Classes in Victorian Society* (1971), p.8.
2. Samuel Barnett in Weinreb, Ben and Hibbert, Christopher, *The London Encyclopaedia* (1992), p.904.
3. Barnett, Henrietta, *Canon Barnett: His Life, Work and Friends* Vol.2 (1918b), p.305.
4. Barnett, Henrietta, *Canon Barnett: His Life, Work and Friends* Vol.1 (1918a), pp.330-1.
5. For a comprehensive history of Toynbee Hall, see Asa Briggs and Ann Macartney, *Toynbee Hall: The First Hundred Years* (1984).
6. www.toynbeehall.org, accessed 11 December 2003.
7. Stedman Jones, p.259.
8. Steedman, Carolyn, *Childhood Culture and Class in Britain: Margaret McMillan 1860-1931* (1990), p.180.
9. Tebbutt, Melanie, *Women's Talk? A Social History of Gossip in Working-Class Neighbourhoods, 1880-1960* (1995), p.35.
10. Sindall, Rob, *Street Violence in the Nineteenth Century: Media Panic or Moral Danger?* (1990), pp.3-4.
11. Barnett (1918a), p.327.
12. Barnett (1918a), p.326.
13. Barnett (1918a), p.328.
14. Barnett (1918b), p.40.
15. Walkowitz, Judith, *City of Dreadful Delights: Narratives of Sexual Danger in Late-Victorian London* (1992), p.59.
16. Barnett (1918b), p.41.
17. Tosh, John, *A Man's Place: Masculinity and the Middle-Class Home in England* (1999), p.46.
18. Barnett (1918b), p.41; Barnett (1918a), p.328.
19. Barnett (1918b), p.41.
20. Tosh, p.125.
21. Barnett (1918b), pp.42-3.
22. In her 2002 novel, *Fingersmith*, Sarah Waters based the sadistic and sinister Mr Lilley on Henry Ashbee.
23. Hammerton, A. James, *Cruelty and Companionship: Conflict in Nineteenth-Century Married Life* (1992), pp.55, 144-6 and 156.
24. John Stuart Mill (20 May 1867) quoted in Tosh, p.53.
25. Unnamed Toynbee Hall resident quoted in Barnett (1918b), p.43.
26. Koven, Seth, 'Henrietta Barnett (1851-1936): the auto/biography of a late-Victorian marriage' in

Susan Pederson and Peter Mandler (eds), *After the Victorians: Private Conscience and Public Duty* (1994), pp.42-3.
27. Poovey, Mary, *Uneven Developments: The Ideological Work of Gender in Mid-Victorian Britain* (1989), p.23.
28. Henrietta Barnett (*c*.1885) quoted in Paterson, Marion, Unpublished biography of Henrietta Barnett, (Undated, *c*.1936), p.43.
29. Darley, Gillian, *Octavia Hill: A Life* (1990), p.236.
30. Martin, Jane, *Women and the Politics of Schooling in Victorian & Edwardian England* (1998) p.1.
31. Barnett (1918a), p.43.
32. Jane Nassau Senior in Barnett (1918b), pp.288-9.
33. Barnett (1918b), p.290.
34. Barnett (1918b), p.290.
35. Barnett (1918b), p.291.
36. Barnett, Henrietta, 'Verdict on Barrack Schools' (1897) in Barnett, Canon and Mrs S.A., *Towards Social Reform* (1909), p.128.
37. Barnett (1918b), p.291.
38. Barnett (1918b), p.292.
39. Samuel Barnett (29 February 1896) in Barnett (1918b), p.294.
40. Barnett (1918b), p.294.
41. Barnett (1918b), p.295.
42. Barnett (1918b), p.300.
43. Sir James Kay in Hurt, J.S., 'Drill, discipline and the elementary school ethos' in McCann, Phillip (ed.), *Popular Education and Socialisation in the Nineteenth Century* (1977), p.169.
44. Hurt, p.170.
45. Prince, J.J., *School Management and Methods* (1896) quoted in Hurt, (1977), p.181.
46. Barnett (1918a), p.298.
47. Barnett (1918a), pp.298-9.
48. Horn, Pamela, *The Victorian and Edwardian Schoolchild* (1989), p.5.
49. Rose, Jonathan, *The Intellectual Lives of the British Working Classes* (2002), p.146.
50. Barnett (1918a), p.177.
51. Barnett (1918a), pp.177-8.
52. Barnett (1918a), pp.178-9.
53. Vicinus, Martha, *Independent Women: Work and Community for Single Women, 1850-1920* (1985), p.236.
54. Barnett (1918a), p.180; Horn, p.138.
55. Barnett (1918a), p.190.
56. Barnett (1918a), pp.191-2.
57. Barnett (1918a), p.191.
58. Mrs Burrows (*c*.1930) 'Work in the Fields, 1850-60' in Clayre, Alasdair (ed.), *Nature and Industrialisation* (1985).

Chapter Nine
1. Barnett, Henrietta, *Canon Barnett: His Life, Work and Friends* Vol.1 (1918a), p.225.
2. Sir Herbert Spencer (1820-1903) coined the phrase 'the survival of the fittest' and adapted Darwin's theory of evolution into a justification of existing social hierarchies. He was deeply sceptical about contemporary efforts at social reform, arguing that 'if the inferior are helped to increase, by shielding them from that mortality which their inferiority would naturally entail, the effect is to produce, generation after generation, a greater inferiority'. (Spencer, circa 1874, cited in Alex Callinicos, *Social Theory: A Historical Introduction* (1999) p.111.
3. Barnett (1918a), pp.230-1.
4. Barnett (1918a), p.230.
5. Barnett (1918a), p.232.
6. Barnett (1918a), p.238.

7. Barnett (1918a), pp.240-1.
8. Barnett (1918a), p.242.
9. Barnett (1918a), p.247.
10. Barnett (1918a), p.248.
11. Barnett (1918a), pp.249-51.
12. Barnett (1918a), p.255.
13. Barnett (1918a), p.252.
14. Thompson, F.M.L., *The Rise of Respectable Society: A Social History of Victorian Britain* (1988), p.263.
15. Barnett (1918a), p.255.
16. Barnett (1918a), p.254.
17. Thompson, pp.262-3.
18. Thompson, p.264.
19. Barnett, Henrietta, *Canon Barnett: His Life, Work and Friends*, Vol.2 (1918b), p.152.
20. Barnett (1918b), pp.174-5.
21. Barnett (1918b), p.171.
22. Harrison, J.F.C., *Late-Victorian Britain* (1991), pp.74-5.
23. For example, see the discussion of 'cultural capital' in Pierre Bourdieu, *Distinction* (1984).
24. Barnett (1918a), pp.257-60.
25. Barnett (1918a), p.17.
26. George Goode in Paterson, Marion, Unpublished biography of Henrietta Barnett (Undated, *c*.1936), p.44.
27. Barnett (1918a), p.268; Paterson, p.211.
28. For a comprehensive introduction to Freudian psychoanalysis, see J. Neu, (ed.), *The Cambridge Companion to Freud* (1992).
29. Barnett, Henrietta, *The Making of the Home* (1875), pp.147-9 and 193.
30. Barnett (1918b), p.31.
31. Paterson, p.46.
32. Paterson, p.46-8.
33. Barnett (1918b), pp.130-1.
34. Paterson, p.47.
35. Grafton Green, Brigid, 'Hampstead Garden Suburb: Visions and Reality' (1972) Unpublished MA dissertation in London Metropolitan Archives. Brigid Grafton Green was the Hampstead Garden Suburb Archives for many years and collected a plethora of memorabilia relating to the Suburb history. She would have been Henrietta's first biographer but she died before completing her book. Brigid is remembered with much affection by the residents of Hampstead Garden Suburb.
36. Barnett (1918b), pp.131-2.
37. Paterson, pp.131-2.
38. Grafton Green, 'Hampstead Garden Suburb: Visions and Reality'.
39. Said, Edward, *Culture and Imperialism* (1993), p.177.
40. Said, p.178.
41. Grafton Green, 'Hampstead Garden Suburb: Visions and Reality'.
42. Paterson, p.49.
43. Paterson, p.50.
44. Paterson, p.51.
45. Paterson, p.52.
46. Barnett (1918b), p.132.
47. Paterson, pp.52-3.
48. Barnett (1918b), pp.132-3.
49. Barnett (1918b), p.133.
50. Paterson, p.51.
51. Barnett (1918b), p.133.
52. Grafton Green, 'Hampstead Garden Suburb: Visions and Reality'.
53. Blair, Lorraine, 'Dame Henrietta Barnett: Choosing to Settle, Daring to Dream' (2003), Unpublished, Hampstead Garden Suburb Archives pp.62-5.
54. Barnett (1918b), p.133.
55. Barnett (1918b), p.31.
56. *New York Herald*, 22 May 1935.
57. Paterson, pp.60-1.
58. Barnett (1918b), p.134.
59. Barnett, Samuel and Henrietta, 'Our Diary' (1890), p.137.
60. Barnett (1918b), p.134.
61. Mort, Frank, *Dangerous Sexualities: Medico-Moral Politics in England since 1830* (2000), p.93; Creedon, Alison, 'Representations of Suburban Culture, 1890-1914' (2001), p.232 .
62. Olsen, Donald, *The Growth of Victorian London* (1976), pp.93-8 and 102.
63. Grossmith, George and Weedon, *The Diary of a Nobody* (1965), p.62.
64. Joseph, Tony, *George Grossmith: Biography of a Savoyard* (1982), p.158.
65. Osborn, F.J. (1945) in preface to Ebenezer Howard, *Garden Cities of Tomorrow* (1965), pp.18-19 and 30.
66. Barnett (1918b), pp.314-15.
67. Barnett (1918b), p.135.

Chapter Ten

1. Barnett, Henrietta, *Canon Barnett: His Life, Work and Friends*, Vol.2 (1918b), pp.198-9.
2. Barnett (1918b), p.204.
3. Barnett (1918b), pp.210-11.
4. Barnett (1918b), p.142.
5. Barnett (1918b), pp.142-3.
6. Steedman, Carolyn, *Childhood, Class and Culture in Britain: Margaret McMillan 1860-1931* (1990), pp.1-3.
7. Steedman, p.82.
8. Barnett (1918b), p.142.
9. Samuel Barnett in Barnett, Henrietta, *Canon Barnett: His Life, Work and Friends*, Vol.1 (1918a), p.391.
10. Barnett (1918b), p.145.
11. Barnett (1918b), p.144.
12. Barnett (1918b), p.145.
13. Letter from Samuel Barnett to Frank Barnett (July 1896) in Barnett (1918b), pp.116-7.
14. Barnett (1918b), p.226.
15. Barnett (1918b), p.228.
16. Barnett (1918b), pp.228-9.
17. Barnett 1918b), p.121.
18. Thompson, F.M.L., *The Rise of Respectable Society: A Social History of Victorian Britain, 1830-1900* (1988), p.165.
19. Barnett (1918b), p.212.
20. Akroyd (1861) in Burnett, John, *A Social History of Housing, 1815-1970* (1978), p.177.
21. George Cadbury in Barnett, Henrietta, 'A Garden Suburb at Hampstead' in *Contemporary Review* LXXXVIII (1905), p.233.
22. Rules for living in Saltaire Village (1853-76) leaflet in Saltaire Historical Society archives, Saltaire Historical Society, 1988.
23. George Cadbury in Barnett (1905), p.233.
24. Stedman Jones, Gareth, (1974)'Working-class culture and Working-Class Politics in London, 1870-1900: Notes on the re-making of a working-class' in Bernard Waites, Tony Bennett and Graham Martin (eds), *Popular Culture: Past and Present* (1989), pp.99-100.
25. Thomas, Donald, *The Victorian Underworld* (1998), p.170.
26. Thomas, pp.184 and 200.
27. Charles Booth in Albert Fried and Richard M. Elman (eds), *Charles Booth's Life and Labour of the People in London: Selections* (1971), p.262.

28. Fried and Elman, p.263.
29. Barnett, Henrietta 'Principles of Recreation' in Canon Barnett and Mrs S.A. Barnett, *Towards Social Reform* (1908), p.292.
30. Charles Booth in Thomas, p.203.
31. Thomas, p.179.
32. Barnett, Henrietta, *The Making of the Home* (1875), p.32.
33. Barnett (1875), p.177.
34. Stedman Jones, p.108.
35. Dentith, Simon, *Society and Cultural Forms in Nineteenth-Century England* (1998), p.22.
36. Walkowitz, Judith, *City of Dreadful Delights: Narratives of Sexual Danger in Late-Victorian England* (1992), p.45.
37. Stedman Jones, p.108.
38. Marie Lloyd in Stedman Jones, p.108.
39. Dentith, p.177.
40. Sindall, Rob, *Street Violence in the Nineteenth Century: Media Panic or Real Danger?*(1990), pp.92-3.
41. Cohen, Stan, *Folk Devils and Moral Panics: The Creation of the Mods and Rockers* (1972).
42. Springhall, John, 'Building character in the British boy: the attempt to extend Christian manliness to working-class adolescents' in J.A. Mangan and James Walvin (eds), *Manliness and Morality: Middle-Class Masculinity in Britain and America, 1800-1940* (1987), p.53.
43. Barnett (1918b), p.71.
44. Springhall, p.53.
45. Springhall, pp.55-6.
46. Springhall, p.60.
47. Springhall, p.70.
48. Robert Blatchford (1899) in Pearson, Geoffrey, *Hooligan: A History of Respectable Fears* (1983), p.257.
49. Pearson, pp.74-5 and 255.
50. Pearson, p.77.
51. Pearson, p.85.
52. Pearson, p.80.
53. Pearson, p.79.
54. Creedon, Alison, 'Representations of Suburban Culture' (2001), p.83 Unpublished PhD thesis University of Leeds 2001.
55. Pearson, pp.93-4.
56. Barnett (1918b), p.72.
57. Barnett (1918b), p.71.
58. Barnett (1918b), p.73.
59. Barnett (1918b), pp.71-2.
60. Springhall, p.54.
61. Creedon, p.240.
62. Barnett (1918b), p.143.
63. Barnett (1918b), pp.147-9.
64. Barnett (1918b), pp.129 and 143-5.
65. Barnett (1918b), p.145.
66. Barnett (1918b), p.182.
67. Samuel Barnett to LouLou Barnett (25 January 1902) in Barnett (1918b), p.184.
68. Barnett (1918b), p.313.
69. Miller, Mervyn and Gray, A. Stuart, *Hampstead Garden Suburb* (1992), pp.38 and 14.
70. Barnett (1918a), p.314.

Chapter Eleven

1. Barnett, Henrietta, *Canon Barnett: His Life, Work and Friends*, Vol.2 (1918b), p.312.
2. Creedon, Alison, 'Representations of Suburban Culture, 1890-1914' (2001), p.ii.
3. Eden, W.A., 'Hampstead Garden Suburb, 1907-1957' in *Journal of the Royal Institute of British Architects* (October 1957), p.489.
4. Ikin, C.W., *Hampstead Garden Suburb Trust: Dreams and Realities* (1990), p.9.
5. Barnett (1918b), pp.312-3; Creedon, p.204.
6. Barnett (1918b), p.324.
7. Giles, Judy, *Women, Identity and Private Life in Britain, 1900-1950* (1995), p.67.
8. Howard, Ebenezer, *Garden Cities of Tomorrow* (1902), p.55.
9. Barnett, Henrietta, 'A Garden Suburb at Hampstead' in *Contemporary Review*, 88 (1905), p.231.
10. Barnett (1905), pp.231-2.
11. Crosland, T.W.H., *The Suburbans* (1905), p.199.
12. Barnett (1918b), p.314.
13. Barnett (1918b), pp.313-4.
14. Paterson, Marion, Unpublished biography of Henrietta Barnett (Undated, *c*.1936), p.27.
15. Webb, Beatrice, *My Apprenticeship* (1926), pp.222-3.
16. Fishman, Robert, *Urban Utopias in the Twentieth Century: Ebenezer Howard, Frank Lloyd and Le Courbusier* (1977), p.67.
17. Fishman, p.69.
18. Fishman, pp.69-70.
19. Raymond Unwin in Barry Parker and Raymond Unwin, *The Art of Building a Home* (1901), p.84.
20. Parker and Unwin, p.20.
21. Miller, Mervyn and Gray, A. Stuart, *Hampstead Garden Suburb* (1992), p.45.
22. Miller and Gray, p.40.
23. Barnett (1918b), p.316.
24. Barnett, Henrietta, 'The Hampstead Garden Suburb' in *Garden Suburb and Town Planning*, 26 (1908), pp.21-2; Unwin, Raymond, 'Proposed Garden Suburb at Hampstead' (1905). The original of this is held in the London Metropolitan Archives.
25. Slack, Kathleen, *Henrietta's Dream: A Chronicle of Hampstead Garden Suburb: Varieties and Virtues* (1997), p.15; Creedon, p.212.
26. Parker and Unwin, p.84.
27. Unwin, Raymond, *Cottage Plans and Common Sense* (1902), p.2.
28. Barnett (1905), p.235.
29. Henrietta Barnett (1903) in Barnett (1918b), p.314.
30. Creedon, p.132.
31. Barnett (1905), p.235.
32. Slack, pp.121-3.
33. Barnett (1905), p.236.
34. Barnett (1918b), p.235.
35. Howard, p.52.
36. Slack, p.132.
37. Barnett (1918b), p.303.
38. Barnett (1905), p.236.
39. Barnett, Henrietta (1906), 'Principles of Recreation' in Canon Barnett and Mrs S.A. Barnett, *Towards Social Reform* (1908), p.291; Barnett (1918b), p.256.
40. Barnett, 'The Hampstead Garden Suburb' in *Garden Suburb and Town Planning*, 26 (1908), p.22.
41. Barnett (1918b), p.315.
42. Eden, pp.491-2.
43. Paterson, p.83.
44. Barnett (1905), p.231; Barnett, 'Principles of Recreation' (1906), p.293; Barnett, 'The Hampstead Garden Suburb' in *Garden Suburb and Town Planning*, 26 (1908), pp.13 and 49 .
45. Fishman, p.69.
46. Parker and Unwin, p.30.
47. Creese, Walter L., *The Search for Environment: The Garden City Before and After* (1966), p.287.
48. Ledwith, Sean, 'Better is the Enemy of Good: An Anatomy of the Ideology of the Green

Movement' (1989) Unpublished MA thesis, University of Kent, p.33.

49. Osborn, F.J. 'Preface' (1945) to Howard, p.29.
50. Slack, p.43.
51. Barnett, Henrietta (1906), 'Principles of Recreation' in Canon Barnett and Mrs S.A. Barnett, *Towards Social Reform* (1908), p.291.
52. Samuel Barnett to Francis Barnett (7 April 1906) in Barnett (1918b), p.319.
53. Barnett (1918b), p.320.
54. Barnett (1905), p.232.
55. Barnett (1918b), p.316.
56. Paterson, p.75.
57. Barnett (1905), p.233.
58. Barnett (1905), p.232-4.
59. Barnett, 'The Hampstead Garden Suburb' in *Garden Suburb and Town Planning*, 26 (1908), p.22.
60. Barnett (*c.*1909) in Slack, p.93.
61. Creese, p.232; Miller and Gray, p.80.
62. Raymond Unwin (1936) in Paterson, p.80.
63. Edwin Lutyens in Clayre Percy and Jane Ridley (eds), *The Letters of Edwin Lutyens to his Wife, Emily* (1985), p.148.
64. Crosland, p.150.
65. Gertrude Jekyll (1989) in Kellaway, Deborah (ed.) *The Virago Book of Women Gardeners* (1996), p.26.
66. Barnett, Henrietta (1906), 'Principles of Recreation' in Canon Barnett and Mrs S.A. Barnett, *Towards Social Reform* (1908), p.292.
67. Barnett, Henrietta (1906), 'Principles of Recreation' in Canon Barnett and Mrs S.A. Barnett, *Towards Social Reform* (1908), pp.294 and 296.
68. Barnett (1918b), p.297.
69. Creese, p.227.
70. Garden Suburb Trust (GST) minutes (30 July 1907 and 13 August, 1907); Barnett, 'The Hampstead Garden Suburb' (1908), p.23.
71. GST minutes (24 November 1908).
72. Barnett (1918b), pp.316 and 320.
73. Masterman, Lucy, *C.F.G. Masterman: A Biography* (1939), p.127.
74. Paterson, p.77.
75. Mrs Paul Jewitt quoted in Paterson, p.79.
76. Barnett (1918b), p.320.
77. Barnett, (1918b), pp.320 and 323.
78. Slack; Miller and Gray; Ikin; Grafton Greene, Brigid, *Hampstead Garden Suburb 1907-1977: A History* (1977).
79. GST minutes (6 October 1908).
80. Barnett (1918b), p.324.
81. Barnett (1918b), pp.323-4.

Chapter Twelve
1. Barnett, Henrietta, 'A Garden Suburb at Hampstead' in *Contemporary Review*, 87 (1905), p.235.
2. *Town Crier* (June 1911), p.11.
3. Miller, Mervyn and Gray, A. Stuart, *Hampstead Garden Suburb* (1992), p.128. The copper pot in question currently resides in the home of Chris and Julia Kellerman in Hampstead Garden Suburb.
4. *Town Crier* (June 1911), p.35.
5. Miller and Gray, pp.127-8.
6. Henrietta Barnett in Slack, Kathleen, *Henrietta's Dream: A Chronicle of Hampstead Garden Suburb* (1997), p.93.
7. Hampstead Garden Suburb Trust Sub-Committee [TISC] minutes (29 January 1912).
8. Barnett (1905), p.235.
9. Slack, pp.144-5; GST minutes (5 October 1909).

10. Elias, Eileen, *On Sundays We Wore White* (1978), p.84.
11. Slack, p.42.
12. Barnett, 'Principles of Recreation' (1906) in Canon Barnett and Mrs S.A. Barnett, *Towards Social Reform* (1908), p.291.
13. Slack, pp.93-4.
14. Barnett, Henrietta, *Canon Barnett: His Life, Work and Friends*, Vol. 2 (1918b), p.71.
15. Lord Baden Powell (1906) in Buford, Bill, *Among the Thugs* (1992), p.12.
16. GST minutes (30 July 1907).
17. *Alliance News and Temperance Reform* (26 January 1911) in Slack, p.97.
18. GST minutes (30 July 1907).
19. TISC minutes (27 March 1911).
20. TISC minutes (25 March 1912).
21. Barnett, Henrietta (1906), 'Principles of Recreation' in Canon Barnett and Mrs S.A. Barnett, *Towards Social Reform* (1908), p.292.
22. TISC minutes (24 July 1911).
23. Loeb, Lori Anne, *Consuming Angels: Advertising and Victorian Women* (1994), p.114.
24. TISC minutes (25 March 1912).
25. McClintock, Anne, *Imperial Leather: Race, Gender and Sexuality in the Colonial Context* (1995), p.99; Church, Richard, *Over the Bridge* (1955), p.75; Elias, p.30; Loeb, p.107.
26. Slack, p.33.
27. TISC minutes (25 March 1912).
28. Carey, John, *The Intellectuals and The Masses: Pride and Prejudice among the Literary Intelligentsia, 1880-1939* (1992), pp.156-8.
29. TISC minutes (25 March 1912).
30. *Hendon and Finchley Times* (3 January 1913, p.6; 24 April 1913, p.8).
31. Mort, Frank, *Dangerous Sexualities: Medico-Moral Politics in England since 1830* (2000), p.93.
32. Barnett (1918b), p.43.
33. Slack, p.30; *Town Crier* (June 1911), p.35.
34. Summerfield, Penny, 'The Women's Movement in Britain from the 1860s to the 1980s' in Tess Cosslett, Alison Easton and Penny Summerfield (eds), *Women, Power and Resistance: An Introduction to Women's Studies* (1996), p.230.
35. Letter to the *Daily Telegraph* (20 August 1898) in Hammerton, A. James, 'Pooterism or Partnership: Marriage and Masculine Identity in the Lower-Middle-Class, 1870-1920' in *Journal of British Studies*, 38/3 (1999), p.270.
36. Edwin Lutyens (7 April 1909) in Clayre Percy and Jane Ridley (eds), *The Letters of Edwin Lutyens to his Wife, Emily* (1985), p.184.
37. Barnett (1918b), p.317.
38. Barnett, Henrietta, *The Story of the Growth of Hampstead Garden Suburb, 1907-1928* (1928), p.47.
39. Percy and Ridley (eds), p.168.
40. Ikin, Christopher, *Hampstead Garden Suburb Trust: Dreams and Realities* (1990), p.71.
41. Slack, p.25.
42. Henrietta Barnett quoted in Ikin, p.72.
43. Muthesius, Stefan, *The English Terraced House* (1982), p.44; Crow, Duncan, *The Edwardian Woman* (1978), p.148.
44. Slack, p.32.
45. Creese, Walter L., *The Search for Environment: The Garden City Before and After*, (1966), p.294; Sketch of 'An Artizan's Living Room' in Barry Parker and Raymond Unwin, *The Art of Building a Home* (1901).
46. Parker and Unwin, p.6.

47. Crosland, T.W.H., *The Suburbans* (1905), p.141.
48. Slack, p.25.
49. McCrum, Mark and Sturgis, *1900 House* (1999), p.6.
50. Slack, p.32.
51. Unwin, Raymond, *Cottage Homes and Common Sense* (1902), pp.12-13.
52. Unwin, p.15.
53. Barry Parker (1940) in Creese, p.166.
54. Raymond Unwin (1904) in Creese, p.288.
55. Parker and Unwin, pp.30 and 59.
56. Fishman, Robert, *Urban Utopias in the Twentieth Century: Ebenezer Howard, Frank Lloyd and Le Courbusier* (1977), p.74.
57. Raymond Unwin (1936) quoted in Paterson, p.80.
58. Slack, p.32.
59. White, Robert, 'Wanted: A Rowton House for Clerks' in *Nineteenth Century Review* (October 1897), p.596.
60. White, pp.596-601.
61. Grafton Green, Brigid, 'Hampstead Garden Suburb: Vision and Reality' (1972), p.72. Unpublished MA dissertation University of London, 1972.
62. Barnett (1905), p.236.
63. Slack, p.133.
64. Slack, pp.129-30.
65. Jean Moffat papers, Hampstead Garden Suburb Archives.
66. Showalter, Elaine, *Sexual Anarchy: Gender and Culture at the Fin de Siecle* (1991), p.38.
67. Alice Haw papers, Hampstead Garden Suburb Archives.
68. Muthesius, p.44; Crow, p.147.
69. Creedon, p.254.
70. Unwin, p.4; Barnett, Henrietta, *Canon Barnett: His Life, Work and Friends*, Vol. 1 (1918a), pp.73-4; Barnett (1918b), pp.305-6.
71. Creedon, p.255.
72. Slack, p.34; TISC minutes (25 March 1912).
73. Eden, W.A., 'Hampstead Garden Suburb, 1907-1957' in *Journal of the Royal Institute of British Architects* (October 1957), p.492; Creese, p.234; Slack, p.36;.
74. The *Record* (October 1912), p.4; *Town Crier* (December 1913), pp.1-3.

Chapter Thirteen
1. Barnett, Henrietta, *Canon Barnett: His Life, Work and Friends*, Vol. 2 (1918b), p.343.
2. Barnett (1918b), p.344.
3. Barnett (1918b), pp.353-4.
4. Barnett (1918b), p.355.
5. Barnett (1918b), p.357.
6. Barnett (1918b), p.327.
7. Barnett (1918b), pp.327-8.
8. Barnett, Henrietta, *Matters that Matter* (1930), p.10.
9. Barnett (1918b), p.331.
10. Barnett (1918b), p.366.
11. Barnett (1918b), pp.369-72.
12. Barnett (1918b), p.373.
13. Barnett (1918b), p.372.
14. Barnett (1918b), pp.372-3.
15. Barnett (1918b), p.218.
16. Barnett (1918b), p.367.
17. Barnett (1918b), p.367.

18. Barnett (1918b), p.375.
19. Barnett (1918b), pp.377-9.
20. Barnett (1918b), pp.377-8.
21. Barnett (1918b), p.380.
22. Barnett (1918b), p.382.
23. Memorial leaflet, London Metropolitan Archives, ACC/3816/02/01/003.
24. Barnett (1918b), p.340.
25. Barnett (1918b), pp.390-3.
26. Slack, Kathleen, *Henrietta's Dream: A Chronicle of Hampstead Garden Suburb: Varieties and Virtues* (1997), p.8.
27. Slack, p.36.
28. Slack, p.35.
29. Slack, pp.35-6.
30. Slack, p.37.
31. Alice Haws papers, Hampstead Garden Suburb Archives.
32. Slack, pp.32-3.
33. Quoted in Barnett (1930), p.110.
34. Barnett, Henrietta, 'The Ethics of Housing' in *Cornhill* (December 1925).
35. Barnett (1930), p.22.
36. Barnett (1930), p.121.
37. Barnett (1930), pp.26 and 112.
38. Henrietta Barnett (*c.*1920) in Grafton Green, Brigid, 'Hampstead Garden Suburb: Vision and Reality' (1972). Unpublished MA dissertation, p.91.
39. Barnett (1930), pp.29-30 and 87.
40. Barnett (1930), p.87.
41. Barnett (1930), p.83.
42. Barnett (1930), p.89.
43. Wilson, P.W., 'Buying up Slums: An Interview with Mrs Barnett' in the *Outlook* (26 January 1923).
44. Wilson, P.W. (26 January 1923).
45. Barnett (1930), pp.130 and 151.
46. Barnett (1930), pp.164-8.
47. Barnett (1930), p.4.
48. Barnett (1930), pp.218-22.
49. Barnett (1930), p.225.
50. Barnett (1930), pp.10 and 222.
51. Barnett, draft of response to interview questions, London Metropolitan Archives, ACC/3816/02/01/001-9.
52. Henrietta Barnett in the *Nursing Times* (9 August 1930).
53. Henrietta Barnett in the *Edinburgh Evening News* (16 August 1930).
54. Slack, p.80.
55. Author's interviews with Ruth Cass, Judy Charlton, Jean Dyson and Mollie Tripp (January 2003).
56. Barnett (1930), p.viii.
57. John Northcote in Barnett (1930), p.1.
58. John Northcote in Barnett (1930), p.4.
59. Barnett papers, London Metropolitan Archives, ACC/3816/02/01/001-9.
60. Slack, Kathleen, (ed.), Marion Paterson papers, London Metropolitan Archives, ACC/3816/02/02/01.
61. Lang (1936) in Beauman, Katherine Bentley, *Women and the Settlement Movement* (1996), pp.26-7.
62. Briggs, Asa and Macartney, Ann, *Toynbee Hall: The First Hundred Years*, (1984), p.27.
63. Paterson, Marion, Unpublished biography of Henrietta Barnett (Undated, *c.*1936), pp.77-80.
64. Henrietta Barnett in Darley, Gillian, *Octavia Hill: A Life* (1990), p.332

Bibliography

Ackroyd, Peter, *London: A Biography* (London: Vintage, 2001)

Aldrich, Richard, *School and Society in Victorian Britain: Joseph Payne and the New World of Education* (New York and London: Garland, 1995)

Armstrong, Isobel, *Nineteenth-Century Women Poets: An Oxford Anthology* (Oxford: Oxford University Press, 1996)

Ashton, Rosemary, *George Eliot: A Life* (London: Hamish Hamilton, 1996)

Auerbach, Jeffrey A., *The Great Exhibition of 1851: A Nation on Display* (London: Yale University Press, 1999)

Barker, Juliet (1994), *The Brontës* (London: Phoenix, 1995)

Barnett, Mrs S.A., *The Making of the Home: A Reading Book of Domestic Economy for Home and School Use* (London: Cassell, 1875)

Barnett, Henrietta Octavia (1890), 'Lady Visitors and Girls' in Canon Barnett and Mrs S.A. Barnett, *Towards Social Reform* (London: Fisher Unwin, 1909)

Barnett, Henrietta Octavia (1897), 'Verdict on Barrack Schools' in Canon Barnett and Mrs S.A. Barnett, *Towards Social Reform* (London: Fisher Unwin, 1909)

Barnett, Mrs S.A., *The Making of the Body: A Children's Book on Physiology and Anatomy* (London: Longmans, Green and Co., 1901)

Barnett, Henrietta Octavia, 'A Garden Suburb at Hampstead', *Contemporary Review*, 88 (1905), pp.231-7

Barnett, Henrietta Octavia (1906), 'Principles of Recreation' in Canon Barnett and Mrs S.A. Barnett, *Towards Social Reform* (London: Fisher Unwin, 1909)

Barnett, Henrietta Octavia, 'The Hampstead Garden Suburb', *Garden Suburb and Town Planning*, 26 (1908) pp.21-2

Barnett, Henrietta Octavia, *Canon Barnett: His Life, Work, Friends, Vol. 1* (London: John Murray, 1918a)

Barnett, Henrietta Octavia, *Canon Barnett: His Life, Work, Friends, Vol. 2* (London: John Murray, 1918b)

Barnett, H.O.W., *The Story of the Growth of Hampstead Garden Suburb, 1907-1928* (London: John Long, 1928)

Barnett, Dame Henrietta, *Matters that Matter* (London: John Murray, 1930)

Barrett Browning, Elizabeth (1857), *Aurora Leigh and Other Poems* (Harmondsworth: Penguin, 1995)

Beauman, Katherine Bentley, *Women and the Settlement Movement* (London and New York: Radcliffe Press, 1996)

Behlmer, George, *Friends of the Family: The English Home and its Guardians, 1850-1940* (Stanford, California: Stanford University Press, 1998)

Besant, Walter, 'From Thirteen to Seventeen', *Contemporary Review*, 49 (1881)

Blair, Lorraine, 'Comrade wives: different marriages under the shadow of Toynbee Hall in late Victorian and Edwardian England' (University of Portsmouth, unpublished PhD thesis, 1998)

Blair, Lorraine, 'Dame Henrietta Barnett: Choosing to Settle, Daring to Dream' (Hampstead Garden Suburb Archives: Unpublished MSS, 2003)

Booth, Charles, *Life and Labour of the People in London: 3rd series Religious Influences* (London: Macmillan, 1902)

Bourdieu, Pierre, *Distinction* (London: Routledge and Kegan Paul, 1984)

Briggs, Asa and Macartney, Ann, *Toynbee Hall: The First Hundred Years* (London: Routledge and Kegan Paul, 1984)

Briggs, Asa, *Victorian Things* (Harmondsworth: Penguin, 1990)

Brontë, Charlotte (1847), *Jane Eyre* (Oxford: Oxford University Press, 1987)

Brontë, Charlotte (1852), *Shirley* (Harmondsworth: Penguin, 1989)

Buford, Bill, *Among the Thugs* (London: Mandarin, 1992)

Burnett, John, *A Social History of Housing, 1815-1970* (Cambridge: Cambridge University Press, 1978)

Callinicos, Alex, *Social Theory: A Historical Introduction* (Cambridge: Polity Press, 1999)

Carey, John, *The Intellectuals and the Masses: Pride and Prejudice among the Literary Intelligentsia, 1880-1939* (London: Faber and Faber, 1992)

Carey, John, 'Hungry for Learning', *Sunday Times*, Culture supplement (1 July 2001), pp.35-6

Church, Richard, *Over the Bridge* (London: Heinemann, 1955)

Cohen, Stan, *Folk Devils and Moral Panics: The Creation of the Mods and Rockers* (London: MacGibbon and Kees, 1972)

Collins, Philip, *Dickens and Education* (London: Macmillan, 1963)

Coulter, John, *Lewisham and Deptford in Old Photographs* (Stroud: Alan Sutton, 1990)

Coulter, John, *Lewisham History and Guide* (Stroud: Alan Sutton, 1994)

Coulter, John, *Sydenham and Forest Hill Past* (London: Historical Publications, 1999)

Cox, Jane, *London's East End: Life and Traditions* (London: Weidenfeld and Nicolson, 1994)

Creedon, Alison, 'Representations of Suburban Culture, 1890-1914', (University of Leeds, PhD thesis, 2001)

Creedon, Alison, 'A Benevolent Tyrant? The Principles and Practices of Henrietta Barnett', *Women's History Review*, Vol. 11, No.2 (2002)

Creedon, Alison, 'Subversion in the Suburbs', *English Review* (April 2003)

Creese, Walter L., *The Search for Environment: The Garden City Before and After* (Newhaven and London: 1966)

Crosland, T.W.H., *The Suburbans* (London: John Long, 1905)

Crossick, Geoffrey, 'The Emergence of the Lower Middle Class in Britain' in Geoffrey Crossick (ed.), *The Lower Middle Class in Britain* (London: Croom Helm, 1977)

Crow, Duncan, *The Edwardian Woman* (London: Cox and Wyman, 1978)

Darley, Gillian, *Octavia Hill: A Life* (London: Constable, 1990)

Dentith, Simon, *Society and Cultural Forms in Nineteenth-Century England* (Basingstoke: Macmillan, 1998)

Denzin, N. and Lincoln, Y. (eds), *Handbook of Qualitative Research* (Thousand Oaks, California: Sage, 1994)

Dickens, Charles (1836), *Pickwick Papers* (Harmondsworth, Penguin, 1985)

Dickens, Charles (1838), *Oliver Twist* (Harmondsworth: Penguin, 1985)

Dickens, Charles (1848), *Dombey and Son* (Harmondsworth: Penguin, 1992)

Dickens, Charles (1854), *Hard Times* (Harmondsworth, Penguin, 1988)

Disraeli, Benjamin (1845), *Sybil: or The Two Nations* (Oxford: Oxford University Press, 1980)

Duncan, L.L. (1908), *History of the Borough of Lewisham with Supplement: Odds and Ends of Lewisham History* (London: Lewisham Borough Council, 1965)

Dyos, H.J., *Victorian Suburb: A Study of the Growth of Camberwell* (Leicester: Leicester University Press, 1961)

Eden, W.A., 'Hampstead Garden Suburb, 1907-1957', *Journal of the Royal Institute of British*

Architects (October, 1957), pp.489-95

Edmund, Rob, *Affairs of the Hearth: Victorian Poetry and Domestic Narrative* (London: Routledge, 1988)

Ehrenrich, Barbara and English, Deirdre, *For Her Own Good: 150 Years of the Experts' Advice to Women* (London: Pluto, 1979)

Elias, Eileen (1978), *On Sundays We Wore White* (Milton Keynes: Robin Clark, 1980)

Eliot, George (1872), *Middlemarch* (Harmondsworth: Penguin, 1994)

Fisher, Trevor, *Prostitutes and the Victorians* (New York: St Martin's Press, 1997)

Fishman, Robert, *Urban Utopias in the Twentieth Century: Ebenezer Howard, Frank Lloyd and Le Corbusier* (New York: Basic Books, 1977)

Fishman, William J., *East End, 1888: A Year in a London Borough among the Labouring Poor* (London: Duckworth, 1988)

Fried, Albert and Elman, Richard (eds), *Charles Booth's London* (Harmondsworth: Penguin, 1971)

Gissing, George (1893), *The Odd Women* (Oxford: Oxford Classics, 1996)

Gloag, John, *An Englishman's Castle* (London: Eyre and Spottiswoode, 1949)

Grafton Green, Brigid, 'Hampstead Garden Suburb: Vision and Reality' (University of London, unpublished thesis submitted for a diploma in History, 1972)

Grafton Green, Brigid, *Hampstead Garden Suburb 1907-1977: A History* (London: Hampstead Garden Suburb Residents' Association, 1977)

Grossmith, George and Weedon (1892) *Diary of a Nobody* (Harmondsworth: Penguin, 1965)

Gunn, Simon, *The Public Culture of the Victorian Middle Class: Ritual, Authority and the English Industrial City, 1840-1914* (Manchester: Manchester University Press, 2000)

Hammerton, A. James, *Cruelty and Companionship: Conflict in Nineteenth Century Married Life* (London: Routledge, 1992)

Hammerton, A. James, 'Pooterism or Partnership: Marriage and Masculinity in the Lower Middle Class, 1870-1920', *Journal of British Studies*, 38/3 (1999), 291-321

Hampstead Garden Suburb Trust, Minutes of Committee Meetings, 12 March 1906 – 21 March 1911 (London Metropolitan Archives, uncatalogued)

Hampstead Garden Suburb Trust, Minutes of Committee Meetings, 27 March 1911 – 28 July 1918 (London Metropolitan Archives, uncatalogued)

Hark, Ina Rae, 'The Jew as Victorian Cultural Signifier: Illustrated by Edward Lear' in Patrick Scott and Pauline Fletcher (eds), *Culture and Education in Victorian England* (London and Toronto: Associated University Presses, 1990)

Harris, Jose, *Beatrice Webb: The Ambivalent Feminist* (London: London School of Economics and Political Science Press, 1984)

Harris, Jose, *Private Lives: Public Spirit: Britain 1870-1914* (Harmondsworth: Penguin, 1994)

Harrison, J.F.C., *Late-Victorian Britain, 1875-1901* (London: Routledge, 1991)

Heilbrun, C.G., *Writing a Woman's Life* (New York: Norton, 1988)

Horn, Pamela, *The Victorian and Edwardian Schoolchild* (Gloucester: Alan Sutton, 1989)

Horn, Pamela, *Pleasures and Pastimes in Victorian Britain* (Stroud: Alan Sutton, 1999)

Horton, Thomas B., 'A search for prose that recreates the past' in Craig Kridel (ed.), *Writing Educational Biography: Explorations in Qualitative Research* (New York: Garland, 1998)

Howard, Ebenezer (1898), *Garden Cities of Tomorrow* (London, Faber and Faber, 1965)

Humphrey, Mrs, *Manners for Men* (London: John Long, 1897)

Hurt, J.S, 'Drill, discipline and the elementary school ethos' in Phillip McCann (ed.), *Popular Education and Socialization in the Nineteenth Century* (London: Methuen, 1977)

Ikin, C.W., *Hampstead Garden Suburb Trust: Dreams and Realities* (London: New Hampstead Garden Suburb Trust, 1990)

Jones, Kathleen, *The Making of Social Policy in Britain: From the Poor Law to New Labour* (London and New Brunswick, NJ: Athlone, 2000)

Jordan, Thomas E., *Victorian Childhood: Themes and Variations* (New York: State University of New York Press, 1987)

Joseph, Tony, *George Grossmith: Biography of a Savoyard* (Bristol: Tony Joseph, 1982)

Kapp, Yvonne (1972) *Eleanor Marx: Family Life 1855-1883* (Volume 1) (London: Virago, 1979)

Kellaway, Deborah, (ed.), *The Virago Book of Women Gardeners* (London: Virago, 1996)

Koven, Seth, 'Henrietta Barnett (1851-1936): the autobiography of a late-Victorian marriage' in Susan Pederson and Peter Mandler (eds), *After the Victorians: Private Conscience and Public Duty in Modern Britain* (London: Routledge, 1994)

Koven, Seth, *Slumming: Sexual and Social Politics in Victorian London* (Oxford: Princeton University Press, 2004)

Langland, Elizabeth, *Nobody's Angels: Middle-Class Women and Domestic Ideology in Victorian Culture* (Ithaca: Cornell University Press, 1995)

Ledwith, Sean, 'Better is the Enemy of Good: An Anatomy of the Ideology of the Green Movement' (University of Kent: MA thesis, 1989)

Lees, Lynn, *The Solidarities of Strangers: The English Poor Laws and the People, 1700-1948* (Cambridge: Cambridge University Press, 1998)

Light, Alison, *Forever England: Femininity, Literature and Conservatism Between the Wars* (London: Routledge, 1991)

Loeb, Lori Anne, *Consuming Angels: Advertising and Victorian Women* (Oxford: Oxford University Press, 1994)

Lowndes, Frederick W., *Lock Hospitals and Lock Wards in General Hospitals* (London: 1882)

Luckin, Bill, 'Evaluating the Sanitary Revolution: Typhus and Typhoid in London, 1851-1900' in Robert Woods and John Woodward (eds), *Urban Disease and Mortality in Nineteenth-Century London* (London: Batsford, 1984)

Lutyens, Mary, *Edwin Lutyens* (London: John Murray, 1980)

McCann, Phillip (ed.), *Popular Education and Socialization in the Nineteenth Century* (London: Methuen, 1977)

McClintock, Anne, *Imperial Leather: Race, Gender and Sexuality in the Colonial Context* (London: Routledge, 1995)

McLeod, John, *Beginning Postcolonialism* (Manchester: Manchester University Press, 2000)

Malchow, H.L., *Gentlemen Capitalists* (Basingstoke: Macmillan, 1991)

Mallan, Kathleen, 'Destitute, neglected and delinquent children' in Mrs S.A. Barnett (ed.), *Pan-Anglican Papers* (London: SPCK, 1908)

Mangan, J.A. and Walvin, James (eds), *Manliness and Morality: Middle-Class Masculinity in Britain and America, 1800-1940* (Manchester: Manchester University Press, 1987)

Martin, Jane, *Women and the Politics of Schooling in Victorian & Edwardian England* (London: Leicester University Press, 1998)

Masterman, C.F.G. (1909), *The Condition of England* (London: Methuen, 1960)

Masterman, Lucy, *C.F.G. Masterman: A Biography* (London: Nicholson and Watson, 1939)

Mayhew, Henry (1861-2), *London Labour and the London Poor (IV): Those That Will Not Work* (London: Frank Cass, 1967)

Meacham, Standish, *Toynbee Hall & Social Reform, 1880-1914: The Search for Community* (Newhaven and London: Yale University Press, 1987)

Mill, Harriet Taylor, *Enfranchisement of Women* (London: Virago, 1983)

Miller, Mervyn and Gray, A. Stuart, *Hampstead Garden Suburb* (Chichester: Phillimore, 1992)

Miller, Mervyn, *Raymond Unwin: Garden Cities and Town Planning* (Leicester: Leicester University Press, 1992)

Moffat, Jean Franklin (*c.*1990), Unpublished memoirs (Hampstead Garden Suburb Archives)

Mort, Frank, *Dangerous Sexualities: Medico-Moral Politics in England since 1830* (London: Routledge, 2000)

Mumford, Lewis, *The City in History* (London: Secker and Warburg, 1940)

Muthesius, Stefan, *The English Terraced House* (Newhaven: Yale University Press, 1982)

Nead, Lynda, *Myths of Sexuality: Representations of Women in Victorian Britain* (Oxford: Blackwell, 1988)

Neu, J. (ed.), *The Cambridge Companion to Freud* (Cambridge: Cambridge University Press, 1992)

Northcote, John, *'Introduction', Henrietta Barnett, Matters That Matter* (London, John Murray, 1930)

Olsen, Donald J., *The Growth of Victorian London* (London: Batsford, 1976)

Osborn, F.J., (1945), Preface to Ebenezer Howard (1898), *Garden Cities of Tomorrow* (London: Faber and Faber, 1965)

Palmer, Alan, *The East End: Four Centuries of London Life* (London: John Murray, 1989)

Parker, Barry and Unwin, Raymond, *The Art of Building a Home* (London: Longman and Green, 1901)

Paterson, Marion (Undated, *c*.1936), Draft of Henrietta Barnett's biography (London Metropolitan Archives: catalogue ref: LMA/4063/006)

Pearson, Geoffrey, *Hooligan: A History of Respectable Fears* (Basingstoke: Macmillan, 1983)

Pederson, Susan and Mandler, Peter (eds), *After the Victorians: Private Conscience and Public Duty in Modern Britain* (London: Routledge, 1994)

Percy, Clayre and Ridley, Jane (eds), *The Letters of Edwin Lutyens to his Wife, Emily* (London: Collins, 1985)

Perkins, Joan, *Victorian Women* (London: John Murray, 1993)

Peterson, M. Jeanne, *Family, Love and Work in the Lives of Victorian Gentlewomen* (Bloomington and Indianapolis: Indiana University Press, 1989)

Phillips, Jane and Peter, *Victorians Home and Away* (London: Croom Helm, 1978)

Pinar, William F. and Pautz, Anne E., 'Construction scars: autobiographical voices in biography' in N. Denzin and Y. Lincoln (eds), *Handbook of Qualitative Research* (Thousand Oaks, California: Sage, 1994)

Poovey, Mary, *Uneven Developments: The Ideological Work of Gender in Mid-Victorian Britain* (London: Virago, 1989)

Prochaska, F.K., *Women and Philanthropy in 19th-Century England* (Oxford: Oxford University Press, 1980)

Purvis, June, 'Social class, education and ideals of femininity' in Madeleine Arnot and Gaby Weiner (eds), *Gender and the Politics of Schooling* (London: Unwin Hyman, 1987)

Reed, John R., 'Learning to Punish: Victorian Children in Literature' in Patrick Scott and Pauline Fletcher (eds), *Culture and Education in Victorian England* (London and Toronto: Associated University Presses, 1990)

Richards, Jeffrey, 'Passing the love of women: manly love and Victorian society' in J.A. Mangan and James Walvin (eds), *Manliness and Morality: Middle-Class Masculinity in Britain and America, 1800-1940* (Manchester: Manchester University Press, 1987)

Roper, Michael and Tosh, John (eds), *Manful Assertions: Masculinities in Britain since 1800* (London: Routledge, 1991)

Rose, Jonathan, *The Intellectual Lives of the British Working Classes* (Newhaven and London, Yale University Press, 2002)

Ross, Ellen, *Love and Toil: Motherhood in Outcast London, 1870-1918* (Oxford: Oxford University Press, 1993)

Rover, Constance, *Love, Morals and the Feminists* (London: Routledge and Kegan Paul, 1970)

Ruskin, John (1865), *Sesame and Lilies* (London: G. Routledge, 1907)

Said, Edward, *Culture and Imperialism* (London: Vintage, 1994)

Scott, Patrick and Fletcher, Pauline (eds), *Culture and Education in Victorian England* (London and Toronto: Associated University Presses, 1990)

Seymour Jones, Carole, *Beatrice Webb: Woman of Conflict* (London: Allison and Busby, 1992)

Shonfield, Zuzanna, *The Precariously Privileged: A Professional Family in Victorian London* (Oxford: Oxford University Press, 1987)

Showalter, Elaine, *Sexual Anarchy: Gender and Culture at the Fin de Siecle* (London: Bloomsbury, 1991)

Sindall, Rob, *Street Violence in the Nineteenth Century: Media Panic or Real Danger?* (Leicester: Leicester University Press, 1990)

Skultans, Vieda, *Madness and Morals: Ideas on Insanity in the Nineteenth Century* (London: Routledge and Kegan Paul, 1975)

Slack, Kathleen (ed.), 'The Youth of Miss Marion Paterson' (London Metropolitan Archives, ACC/3816/02/01/010)

Slack, Kathleen, *Henrietta's Dream: A Chronicle of Hampstead Garden Suburb – Varieties and Virtues* (London: Hampstead Garden Suburb Trust, 1997)

Smiles, Samuel (1859), *Self-Help with Illustrations of Conduct and Perseverance* (London: IEA Health and Welfare Unit, 1997)

Springhall, John, 'Building character in the British boy: the attempt to extend Christian manliness to working-class adolescents' in J.A. Mangan and James Walvin (eds), *Manliness and Morality: Middle-Class Masculinity in Britain and America, 1800-1940* (Manchester: Manchester University Press, 1987)

Stedman Jones, Gareth, *Outcast London: A Study in the Relationship between Classes in Victorian Society* (London: Oxford University Press, 1971)

Stedman Jones, Gareth, 'Working-class culture and Working-Class Politics in London, 1870-1900: Notes on the re-making of a working-class' in Bernard Waites, Tony Bennett and Graham Martin (eds), *Popular Culture: Past and Present* (London: Routledge, 1989)

Steedman, Carolyn, *Childhood, Culture and Class in Britain: Margaret McMillan 1860-1931* (London: Virago, 1990)

Steedman, Carolyn, *Strange Dislocations: Childhood and the Idea of Human Interiority, 1780-1930* (London: Virago, 1995)

Summerfield, Penny, 'The Women's Movement in Britain from the 1860s to the 1980s' in Tess Cosslett, Alison Easton and Penny Summerfield (eds), *Women, Power and Resistance: An Introduction to Women's Studies* (Buckingham: Open University Press, 1996)

Sweet, Matthew, *Inventing the Victorians* (London: Faber and Faber, 2001)

Tebbutt, Melanie, *Women's Talk? A Social History of 'Gossip' in Working-Class Neighbourhoods, 1880-1960* (Aldershot: Scolar, 1995)

Tennyson, Alfred Lord, 'The Princess' (1847) in *The Works of Alfred Lord Tennyson* (London: Wordsworth Classics, 1994)

Thomas, Donald, *The Victorian Underworld* (London: John Murray, 1998)

Thompson, F.M.L., *The Rise of Respectable Society: A Social History of Victorian Britain, 1830-1900* (Fontana, 1988)

Timko, Michael, 'Thomas Carlyle and Victorian Culture' in Patrick Scott and Pauline Fletcher (eds), *Culture and Education in Victorian England* (London and Toronto: Associated University Presses, 1990)

Tosh, John, 'Domesticity and manliness in the Victorian middle class' in Michael Roper and John Tosh, (eds), *Manful Assertions: Masculinities in Britain since 1800* (London: Routledge, 1991)

Tosh, John, *A Man's Place: Masculinity and the Middle-Class Home in Victorian England* (London: Yale University Press, 1999)

Unwin, Raymond, *Cottage Plans and Common Sense* (London: Fabian Tract No.109, 1902)

Unwin, Raymond, *Town Planning in Practice* (London: Fisher Unwin, 1909)

Unwin, Raymond, *Nothing Gained by Overcrowding* (London: P.S. King, 1912)

Ussher, Jane, *Women's Madness: Misogyny or Mental Illness?* (Hemel Hempstead: Harvester Wheatsheaf, 1991)

Vicinus, Martha, *Independent Women: Work and Community for Single Women, 1850-1920* (London: Virago, 1985)

Wagner Martin, Linda C., 'The issue of gender: continuing problems in biography' in Craig Kridel (ed.), *Writing Educational Biography: Explorations in Qualitative Research* (New York: Garland, 1998)

Walkowitz, Judith (1992), *City of Dreadful Delights: Narratives of Sexual Danger in Late-Victorian London* (London: Virago, 1994)

Walton, James (1975), 'Residential amenity, respectable morality and the rise of the entertainment industry' in Bernard Waites, Tony Bennett and Graham Martin (eds), *Popular Culture: Past and Present* (London: Routledge, 1989)

Walvin, James, *A Child's World: A Social History of English Childhood, 1800-1914* (Harmondsworth: Penguin, 1982)

Watkins, Micky, 'Henrietta Barnett before the Suburb', *Hampstead Garden Suburb News*, May 2001

Watkins, Micky, *Henrietta Barnett in Whitechapel: Her First Fifty Years* (London: Micky Watkins/ Hampstead Garden Suburb Trust, 2005)

Webb, Beatrice (1926), *My Apprenticeship* (Harmondsworth: Penguin, 1972)

Webster, Augusta (1870), 'A Castaway' in Isobel Armstrong (ed.), *Nineteenth-Century Women Poets: An Oxford Anthology* (Oxford: Oxford University Press, 1996)

Weinreb, Ben and Hibbert, Christopher, *The London Encyclopaedia* (London: Macmillan, 1992)

White, Robert, 'Wanted: A Rowton House for Clerks', *Nineteenth Century Review* (October 1897), 594-601

Winter, James, *London's Teeming Streets, 1830-1914* (London: Routledge, 1993)

Yeo, Eileen Janes (ed.), *Radical Femininity: Women's Self-Representation in the Public Sphere* (Manchester: Manchester University Press)

Archives

Samuel and Henrietta Barnett, 'Our Travel Diary', London Metropolitan Archives, LMA ACC/3816/02/02/01

Barnett papers, London Metropolitan Archives, LMA ACC/3816/02/01/D01-009

Henrietta and Samuel Barnett, correspondence, LMA ACC/3816/02/01/001

Hampstead Garden Suburb Trust, Minutes of Committee Meetings, 12 March 1906 – 21 March 1911 (London Metropolitan Archives)

Hampstead Garden Suburb Trust, Minutes of Committee Meetings, 27 March 1911 – 28 July 1918 (London Metropolitan Archives)

Hampstead Garden Suburb Trust Institute Sub-Committee, Minutes of Committee Meetings, 1912 (London Metropolitan Archives)

Paterson, Marion (Undated, *c.*1936) Draft of Henrietta Barnett's biography (London Metropolitan Archives: catalogue ref: LMA/4063/006)

Slack, Kathleen, (ed.) 'The Youth of Miss Marion Paterson' (London Metropolitan Archives, ACC/3816/02/01/010)

Reviews of Henrietta Barnett, *Matters that Matter* (1930) LMA ACC/02/04

Papers of Alice Haws (Hampstead Garden Suburb Archives)

Memoirs of Jean Moffatt (Hampstead Garden Suburb Archives)

Websites

www.dovermuseum.org.uk
www.victoriantimes.org.lse
www.toynbeehall.org.uk

Index